ALDUS MANUTIUS

☞ Books in the RENAISSANCE LIVES series explore and illustrate the life histories and achievements of significant artists, rulers, intellectuals and scientists in the early modern world. They delve into literature, philosophy, the history of art, science and natural history and cover narratives of exploration, statecraft and technology.

Series Editor: François Quiviger

ALDUS MANUTIUS

The Invention of the Publisher

OREN MARGOLIS

REAKTION BOOKS

Excudent alii spirantia mollius aera,
credo equidem, vivos ducent de marmore voltus
VIRGIL, *Aeneid*

Published by Reaktion Books Ltd
Unit 32, Waterside
44–48 Wharf Road
London N1 7UX, UK
www.reaktionbooks.co.uk

First published 2023

Printed and bound in India by Replika Press Pvt. Ltd

A catalogue record for this book is available from the British Library

ISBN 978 1 78914 779 7

COVER: Printer's mark of Aldus Manutius, title page
of Erasmus of Rotterdam, *Adagia* (Venice, 1508).
Photo Universitätsbibliothek Basel (UBH DB III 7).

CONTENTS

NOTE ON NAMES AND TRANSLATIONS

With the exception of popes and monarchs, for whom I use the English form, for each person discussed in this book I have used either the Latin or the vernacular form by which they are most commonly known: hence Aldus Manutius, but Paolo Manuzio. I sometimes refer to the *Hypnerotomachia Poliphili* by the title *Polifilo*, as it is regularly called in Italian scholarship, but the protagonist is Poliphilo, as in Francesco Colonna's text.

Unless noted, all translations into English in the book are my own.

Luciani Erasmo interprete

Dialogi & alia emuncta. Quorum quædam recentius/quędam
annos abhinc octo sunt versa: sed nuper recognita: vt indice ad
finem apponendo declarabimus.

Quædam etiam a Thoma Moro latina facta: &
Quædam ab eodem concinnata.

Prelo Ascensiano

Venundantur in ędibus Ascensianis.

Introduction

here is a problem with this picture (illus. 1). The mark of Parisian printer Josse Bade (1462–1535) depicts three men gathered around a printing press. One, the *compositor* on the right, reads from an open book – perhaps a manuscript – as he picks the type and places it in the composing stick. Of the two on the left, the one known as the *beater* holds a pair of leather ink balls, for inking the type, while the *puller* cranks the wheel to roll the *bed* bearing paper and type under the *platen* and pulls the *bar* that turns the screw to bring the weight of the press down upon it. It was about them that the Italian polymath Leon Battista Alberti (1404–1472) wrote when he praised 'the German inventor who lately made it possible with certain impressions of characters for in a hundred days more than two hundred volumes copied through the labours of no more than three men to be produced from a given original'.[1] Technically speaking, from the nebulous mid-fifteenth-century origins in the Rhineland of printing with the hand press and moveable type until the Industrial Revolution and the rise of steam, these three – compositor, beater and puller – and the machine were, if served with paper, ink, type and texts, entirely sufficient for the printing of books. Pulling, especially, was hard work, a job which one conceivably might not do by choice: in François Rabelais' novel *Gargantua* (1534), a work of imagination to be sure, it would be the task set for the defeated followers and *fouace* bakers of the enemy King Picrochole,

1 Printer's mark of Josse Bade, title page of Lucian of Samosata, trans. Erasmus of Rotterdam and Thomas More, *Dialogi et alia emuncta* (1514).

who were made to toil in the eponymous and victorious giant's new printing house.[2]

Josse Bade does not appear in his own printer's mark. Instead, blackletter characters identify the press as the *Prelum Ascensianum*, literally the 'press of Josse Bade', who is indicated by his Latin sobriquet, Ascensius, which he took from his home town of Assche (Asse) in Brabant.[3] Bade was himself a scholar and a minor author; he had worked as an editor, and now he was the leading printer of classical and humanist texts in Paris. Although much of his enterprise was still relatively new, *prelum*, to which he attached his name, was a good classical word attested in ancient sources for a wine press, an oil press, even a laundry press. But no one looking at this mark could mistake that at the heart of this enterprise was a machine, and that Josse Bade's business was the physical task of putting books into print: manual labour and mechanical art.

Looking at three more printers' marks, however, we start to see something very different. These are the marks of Johannes Froben (*c.* 1460–1527), Robert Estienne (1503–1559) and Christophe Plantin (1520–1589), leading exemplars of the European scholarly press in three successive generations. This image (illus. 2) of Froben's is a painted version by Hans Holbein the Younger (*c.* 1497–1543) of the *impresa* that the artist had designed for the Basel printer. A semantically rich image, the caduceus (wand entwined by two serpents) clutched by two hands and surmounted by a dove triggers a series of connections: to the commercial success and power of eloquence associated with the god Mercury, whose attribute the caduceus was; to the biblical injunction to 'be wise as serpents and harmless as doves' (Matthew 10:16); and, as glossed by Froben's most prolific author, Erasmus of Rotterdam (1466–1536), to 'the closest and most indissoluble friendship', signified by the entwined serpents, male and female, who 'come together for a kiss'.[4] Estienne's olive tree (illus. 3), its falling branch

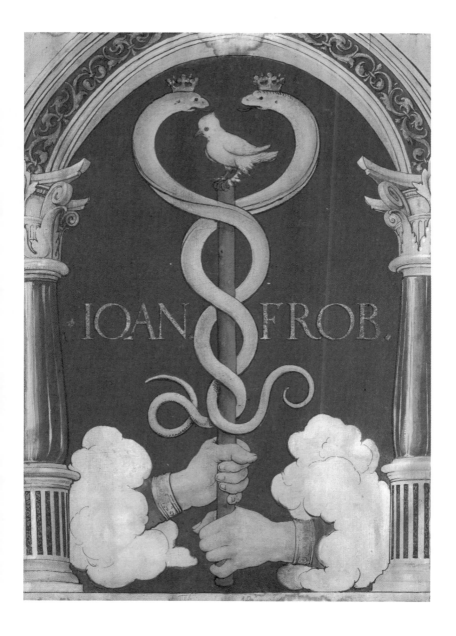

2 Hans Holbein the Younger, *Impresa of Johannes Froben*, c. 1523, tempera on canvas.

Oliua Roberti Stephani.
M. D. LIII.

ANTVERPIAE,
Ex officina Chriſtophori Plantini,
Architypographi Regii.
M. D. LXXVI.

representing the knowledge allowed by Athena to fall to earth for the benefit of mankind, stood in the first place for the mission of Bade's son-in-law, France's Royal Printer; the injunction borrowed from St Paul (Romans 11:20), *Noli altum sapere, sed time* ('Be not proud, but fear'), for intellectual humility and likely too for the Protestant sympathies that eventually forced him from Paris to Geneva.[5] From there the *oliva Stephanorum* continued to stand for the press itself, as well as for the shelter it provided to Greek scholarship and Calvinist theology, much as the plane tree sheltered Socrates and Phaedrus in Plato's dialogue. The printer's mark of Plantin, publisher of the Antwerp Polyglot Bible (1568–1573) and arch-typographer to King Philip II of Spain, meanwhile illustrates the motto *Labore et constantia* ('Through labour and constancy') with the moving and fixed legs respectively of a pair of compasses (illus. 4) – a device that bears no relation to the printing process. As a class, then, these marks are allegorical or emblematic. Though perhaps inferior to most members of the Estienne dynasty, Josse

3 Printer's mark of Robert Estienne, from title page of John Calvin, *Institutio Christianae religionis* (1553).
4 Printer's mark of Christophe Plantin, from title page of Augustine of Hippo, *Opera*, vol. I (1576).

Bade was certainly the intellectual superior of Froben and probably also of Plantin. Yet, if the evidence of the marks is anything to go by, Bade understood and presented his contribution to the enterprise in a less intellectual key. From Bade to Plantin, what we are witnessing is an effacement of manual labour and an intellectualization of print.

'All workers are engaged in low-status activity,' wrote Cicero, 'and a workshop cannot have anything liberal about it.'[6] Effacement or demotion of manual labour has a long pedigree within the Western tradition. As an idea, it stretches back at least to Plato and Aristotle, to whom manual labourers were quite literally living tools, controlled like machines by their natural masters; it lingers to this day in perceived hierarchies between 'blue-' and 'white-collar' work, workers and cultures.[7] For those of us who study the Renaissance, it is something we are used to seeing in discourses around the arts, especially in relation to the so-called *paragone*. An Italian word meaning 'comparison', *paragone* is the historian's term for the ongoing debate (often an intellectual game) joined by artists and literary men about the relative supremacy of either painting or sculpture.[8] Over its long history, the debate broke down along various lines, including over such questions as which art was the better imitator of nature or indeed which could best imitate the other (a contest painting invariably won). One of most familiar arguments, however, put forward by painters and their advocates, was that painting was superior because it was the work of the mind, for which the hand that held the brush was little more than an extension, whereas sculpture was the work of physical labour, technical skill, sweat, toil and dust. The effect of these arguments was to reconceive painting – 'which today', in the words of Castiglione's Count Ludovico, rising to its defence, 'perhaps appears mechanical and little suited to a *gentilomo*' – as a liberal art, fit for a gentleman, much like poetry, to which it was often compared.[9] The impact in Italy was remarkable to those who encountered it:

'In Venice I have become a *gentiluomo!*' proclaimed a visitor from Germany, the artist Albrecht Dürer (1471–1528).[10] To Leonardo da Vinci (1452–1519), painting was rather like writing: 'You call [painting] mechanical because it is in the first place manual, in that the hands depict what they find in the imagination – you writers, drawing manually with the pen what is found in your mind.'[11] Sculpture, meanwhile, was 'not a science but a very mechanical art': 'the sculptor executes his works with greater bodily exertion than the painter, and the painter executes his works with greater mental exertion.' Even more conciliatory voices in the *paragone* debate shared Leonardo's anti-mechanical bias. Giorgio Vasari (1511–1574), who advocated the essential equality and sisterhood of the arts, asserted that these lay in the common paternity of *disegno* (design, drawing, draughtsmanship), 'their foundation and in fact the very soul that conceives and nourishes within itself all parts of our intellects'.[12]

So much for painters. Printers, on the other hand, did not shy away from the manual skill and technical expertise that distinguished their art. They celebrated it – and why not? Their art evoked wonder. For no less than that wide-eyed emotion was behind Alberti's praise of the unnamed 'German inventor'. The humanist Aeneas Sylvius Piccolomini, later to become Pope Pius II (b. 1405, r. 1458–64), reported in a 1455 letter that this *vir mirabilis*, this 'marvellous man', had appeared in Frankfurt, and that he himself had seen a number of quires of the 42-line Bible.[13] Presumably that man was Johannes Gutenberg (*c.* 1400–1468), or perhaps one of his business partners, Johann Fust (*c.* 1400–1466) or Peter Schöffer (*c.* 1425–*c.* 1503). The first printers in Venice were German, and they wanted to be marvelled at as well. The brothers Johann (d. 1470) and Wendelin of Speyer (d. 1477?) had their prowess in the new art declared in verse, in the colophons of their very earliest publications. Johann was 'first in the Adriatic city' to put books in print: 'you see, reader,' he announced in his

1469 edition of Cicero's *Letters to Friends*, 'how much hope there is to be had when this first fruit of my labour has surpassed the art of the pen.'[14] 'Four hundred printed volumes of Sallust, O reader, Wendelin of Speyer now gives to the Venetians,' proclaimed his brother the following year: 'and yet you dare look upon books marked up with pen when lettering formed from bronze is more beautiful?'[15] It was in the copper matrices themselves, rather than with the lead-tin-antimony type, that he expressed his mastery. To the humanist Raffaele Zovenzoni (1431–c. 1485), an early collaborator, Wendelin was like Daedalus, the mythical craftsman and inventor.[16] Germans, as Italians conceded, were talented with their fingers.[17] But the moniker 'another Daedalus' was most closely associated with the Frenchman Nicolas Jenson (c. 1420–1480), the greatest printer of the 1470s, who beautified the roman type and did more than anyone to turn Venice into the pre-eminent printing centre of Europe. His colophons resound with praise for his own ingenuity, his technical knowledge and aptitude, and even the 'Daedalean hand' with which 'he delivered this gift to the world'.[18]

Thus we see how printers, more than painters or sculptors ever did, first embraced the mechanical nature of their art, the technical skill on which it depended, and the manual labour through which they brought forth the wonder of the book. And then something changed. While painters were still playing with their *paragone*, Europe's leading printers had seemingly already decided that their work primarily lay elsewhere. Not all printers, of course. 'Estienne corrects copy and Colines fashions type; with well-taught hand and mind Sebastian Gryphius does both': the battle between learning and skill, science and craft, was not decided once and for all around the year 1500 and then set in stone.[19] But the change, the arrival of a new discourse, was real nonetheless. How do we get from a place where a master printer bestrides the world of craft like a new Daedalus to one where craft and handiwork are at least diminished and just as often effaced? They are effaced by the intellectualism of the Estiennes and Plantin; diminished, as in Bade's unfortunate mark, by the association of printing with humble presswork – a task so little esteemed that it was fit for Gargantua's prisoners of war. It is not the contention of this book that this is merely a consequence of some inevitability, like the novelty of printing wearing off. And while it might only have been possible, at least in the form it took, in the intellectual climate of the turn of the century, it is insufficient to attribute it to some vague 'spirit of the age'. Rather, it was in large part the doing of the most unlikely and most important figure in the history of the Renaissance book: a printer who was not a printer at all.

WHEN SPEAKING OF THE ACHIEVEMENT of Aldus Manutius (*c.* 1450–1515), it is natural to begin with the formal innovations. These include the invention of the italic type; the perfection of the roman; and the distillation of the small, octavo volume into the *enchiridion* or *libellus portatilis*, the portable, satchel-sized book of literature. On account of this, Aldus is often hailed as the father of the paperback. The mysterious *Hypnerotomachia Poliphili*, published in 1499 and supposedly more admired than read ever since, is probably the most beautiful printed book of the Renaissance, a tour de force of elegant typography and exquisite woodcuts. Yet the scholarly achievements were at the heart of his contemporary reputation and, even if seemingly less visionary, also of his vision. In a second career that unfolded in Venice, lasting approximately twenty years (*c.* 1495–1515) and including a number of inter-ruptions, Aldus issued more *editiones principes* (first editions) of classical texts than any publisher before or since. These comprise those by almost all the Greek authors – Plato and Aristotle, Sophocles and Euripides, Herodotus and Thucydides, Hesiod,

ERASMI ROTERODAMI ADAGIORVM CHILIADES TRES, AC CENTV-RIAE FERE TOTIDEM.

ALD·STVDIOSIS·S·

Quia nihil aliud cupio,q̃ prodesse uobis Studiosi.Cum uenisset in manus meas Erasmi Roterodami,hominis undecunq̃ doctiss·hoc adagiorũ opus eruditum.uarium. plenũ bonæ frugis,
& quod possit uel cum ipsa antiquitate certare,intermissis antiquis autorib· quos pa-
raueram excudendos, illud curauimus imprimendum,rati profuturum uobis
& multitudine ipsa adagiorũ,quæ ex plurimis autorib.tam latinis , quàm
græcis studiose collegit summis certe laborib.summis uigiliis ,&
multis locis apud utriusq̃ linguæ autores obiter uel correctis
acute, uel expositis erudite·Docet præterea quot modis
ex hisce adagiis capere utilitatem liceat,puta quẽ
admodum ad uarios usus accõmodari pos-
sint.Adde,qd̃ circiter decẽ millia uer-
suum ex Homero·Euripide,&cæ
teris Græcis eodẽ metro in
hoc opere fideliter,&
docte tralata ha
bétur,præ
ter plu
rima
ex Pla-
tone,De-
mosthene,& id
genus ali
is·An
autem uerus sim,
ἰδοὺ ῥόδος,ἰδοὺ καὶ τὸ πήδημα.
Nam,quod dicitur, αὐτὸς αὐτὸν αὐλεῖ·

AL   DVS

Præponitur hisce adagiis duplex index·Alter secundum litteras
alphabeti nostri·nam quæ græca sunt, latina quoq̃
habentur,Alter per capita rerum.

Liber Ensie S͞n leonardi in basilea Ordinis Canonicorũ Regularium

5 Printer's mark of Aldus Manutius, title page of Erasmus of Rotterdam,
Adagia (1508).

Aristophanes, Plutarch, Pindar and more – who make up the
canon today. 'Increaser of Latin books', he was, as a friend said,
'restorer of Greek literature'.[20] His volumes of the fourteenth-
century poets Petrarch (1501) and Dante (1502), edited by the
Venetian humanist, poet and future cardinal Pietro Bembo
(1470–1547), remain monuments in the history of European
literature, bringing ideas of fixity and authority imported from
classical philology to the new classics of a modern language and
shaping in a very real way the future of the literary vernacular.
He printed works by Bembo himself and also by Erasmus, who
worked for him for a time, and, through a large, learned network
and dedicatory prefaces addressed to princes, scholars and

6 Jean Clouet, *L'Homme au Pétrarque*, c. 1530–35, oil on panel.

'students' across Europe, he positioned himself at the centre of
the Renaissance republic of letters, its benefactor and its servant.
His own printer's mark, the famous dolphin and anchor (illus. 5),
was promoted as a personal guarantee of quality. The emergence
in the early sixteenth century of the portrait genre of a man or
a woman holding a small volume of literature – often a *Petrarchino*
(illus. 6 and 7), a copy of that poet's vernacular 'fragments' in
the format Aldus was first to put in print – is witness to how he
unchained literature from desks and remade reading as a pastime.[21] His editions spread so widely that, within a year of his
death, they had already (according to Thomas More) reached
Utopia.[22] And yet these achievements belonged to someone

7 Andrea del Sarto, *Dama col Petrarchino*, *c.* 1528, oil on panel.

who had no training in the art of printing and no technical skills whatsoever.

Aldus did not identify as a printer: he used the word *impressor* to refer to other master printers – nominally his peers – and his own employees alike, eliding the complexity of printing-house practice with a word.[23] Nor did he identify with Daedalus: he would save the association with the craftsman for the hands of his punchcutter. He was not an impresario like William Caxton (c. 1415/24–1492), creating and feeding a market where the consequences of his editorship were slight.[24] Aldus instead was a humanist who saw in the press the opportunity to achieve humanistic goals, above all that of promoting the learning of Greek and the study of ancient Greek texts, especially in philosophy. To realize this vision, he had to redefine the role of the technology and the identity of its true protagonist, previously understood as the skilled practitioner of a mechanical art. How he did this is the subject of this book. It would be the great intellectual project of Aldus' Renaissance life, and its consequence was an innovation to rival any of his other formal and scholarly achievements: the invention of the publisher.

If this were a traditional history of the book, or an economic history of early printing, this last claim of mine would be distinctly bizarre. In a material sense, a publisher is simply the one who puts up the money for a book to be produced and issued. Much of the other work can be contracted to a printer. These identities, then as now, are not fixed. A printer by trade may be a publisher by occasion, authors may publish their own work, printers and publishers may be regular collaborators or a particular printer may be engaged for a particular job. Such arrangements, long-term or ad hoc, were not at all unusual in the early decades of print: along with that between Gutenberg, Fust and Schöffer from which printing with moveable type emerged in Europe, the Parisian collaboration between Josse Bade and Jean Petit (*fl.* 1496–1530) is a notable example. By contrast, Jenson in Venice represents an early example of the printer-publisher, raising and providing the capital for the books that his firm then put into print; the Aldine Press, which was a legal partnership, represents another.[25] But it is not the publisher in a material sense that I am claiming Aldus invented. This 'invention' – and here I mean a *process* more than an outcome – unfolded in the realm of ideas. These ideas then produced a new reality. For the special charisma of the Aldine Press, its basis not in typographical art and technical expertise but in a specific publishing programme identified with one member of the partnership – *this* was new. An Aldine book was not just a deposit of material relationships: it stood for some-thing; it stood for what Aldus stood for. Buying one was to buy into an ideology. Aldus' prefaces resound with such themes as an ironclad commitment to excellence and accuracy, an indefatiga-ble zeal for improvement, the selfless exertions expended and the despair when these scholarly labours were in any way compro-mised, interrupted or delayed. Here, form served function, skill served ethos, and *in this way alone* the instrument that allowed him to bring forth the editions to which he attached his name served the highest aims of Renaissance humanism: the reform of society and the eradication of barbarism through the revival of eloquence and the recovery, promotion and proliferation of true learning and good literature. Aldus never let his readers forget who he was or what mattered to people like him.

Intellectualization of work is not the same as effacing work altogether. It was just that, here, work was what happened in rela-tion less to the book than to the text: tracking down manuscripts, then editing, correcting, proofreading, publishing. Anything that was properly the purview of the printer, that belonged to the illiberal workshop, was a potential obstacle, containing the possibility of corruption. As a result, Aldus became a powerful promoter of a scholarly work ethic. This was not entirely his own invention, but the way he articulated it would be especially influential for how subsequent generations, often taking their cue from Erasmus, would characterize their own tireless efforts as labourers in the garden of the humanities.[26] *Interim studeo* – 'In the meantime I study,' he supposedly told his Dutch friend, when asked why he put in the extra hours and effort to read proofs himself.[27] Yet Aldus could sometimes sound a seemingly divergent note: this apostle of scholarly labour would become, almost despite himself, an evangelist for gentlemanly lettered ease. There are more surprises. A foreign resident in a lagoon city, Aldus was a rural landowner. Many humanists entertained relations with princes, and greater ones, but few were as involved over so many years, at proximity and at distance, as he was with the house of Pio. Thus, for reasons quite particular to Aldus, the invention of the publisher was implicated not only in distinctions of learning and skill, but also in those of class and politics. The impact of these particularities – on Aldus, certainly, but for his contemporaries and successors as well – was not insignificant. It is in part because of them that I can write this book with its focus on one man's life and career. This is an exploration of how and why printing – from its origins recognized as a mechanical skill – was reconceptualized around the turn of the century as a liberal art; but it treats – and treats as determinative – the evolving practice and ideology of its most important exponent.

As this is not a typical biography, chronicling a life recorded in archival or personal documents from beginning to end, our story will primarily be set in Venice – though in a Venice in conversation with a world of books and letters that reached from Messina to Milan, from the Danube to the Thames. But Venice was only the setting for the last 25 years (or so) of Aldus' life: even if their subsequent stories would have been very different without him, he was not a product of the Venetian book trade and Venetian Renaissance culture alone. Born in Bassiano, a small town perched

in the Monti Lepini of Lazio around 65 kilometres (40 mi.) south
of Rome, he would generally identify as Roman. And after Bassiano,
then Rome and Ferrara, and yet still before Venice, was Carpi.
The town on the Po Plain, little more than a fortress of the house
of Pio at first, would exercise an outsized impact on the career
that Aldus, who came there as preceptor to the young princes
Alberto and Leonello in the early 1480s, went on to have. In the
first chapter, we shall follow Aldus from Carpi to Venice and from
teaching to printing, taking note of the personal attachments and
intellectual preoccupations he brought with him. Chief among
these was his commitment to editing and publishing Greek philosophical and scientific literature, the main focus of the press's
early years and the rationale for its existence. It was in those years
that Aldus printed the first edition in Greek of the works of
Aristotle. But this moment would not last. As we shall see, the year
1499 represented a crisis in Aldus' business model, putting his
project in doubt. The Aldine Press after 1499 was a changed entity
with a changed publishing programme, one that gave greater
prominence to Latin and the vernacular. In other words, it was
more like everyone else. For a press that was defined not by technical skill but by a scholarly agenda, on which it – and, just as
pertinently, its founder – relied for status and prestige, this mattered. It was in this context that most of the major ideological
work – the invention of the publisher of which I have spoken – was
undertaken. How this was done, and with what results, will be
the subject of the subsequent chapters.

    The evidence, to a great extent, is in the works. Aldine publica-
tions from the years around 1500 include some of the strangest
but also the most innovative of their maker's entire career. A history
of classical philology can overlook the *Hypnerotomachia Poliphili* and
the *Epistole*, or Letters, of St Catherine of Siena (1500); this book
will not. Indeed, it is a premise of this study that it is in what most
challenges a conventional notion of Aldus as publisher or what

seems 'least important' to his purportedly core business – in other words, in what appears least straightforwardly explicable – that we really come to know him. A history of the book will usually focus on inventories and ledgers, not paintings, medals and coins. Yet in all of these – woodcuts and other visual images; prefaces, colophons and even sometimes the texts themselves – are conscious traces of and responses to the publisher in the making. This is the case because, although Aldus was a visionary and a creative mind, he was not really an original thinker: necessarily, he was a man of his time, and he only ever used, while repurposing, ideas that were already in the air and at his disposal. Ultimately, Aldus' refashioning of printing as a humanistic discipline paved the way for a European republic of letters based on a new form of community and mobility – the scholarly press; but it was in con-temporary art theory, discourses around language, gender and religion, and changing political contexts that the resources for inventing the publisher were found.

As one of the finest historians of the Renaissance wrote, 'the final goal of all history [is] not knowledge but . . . understanding.'[28] We probably know more about Aldus than about any other printer of his day; but it is fair to say that I am taking a different approach to him and indeed to the Renaissance book than most of those who have come before me. This is an argument, based on the read-ing and interpretation – I hope a convincing one – of the sources. It is not a summary of the bibliographic scholarship, on which I rely, that has built on centuries of collectors' interest to make Aldines the most extensively documented and catalogued of all early books; nor of the philological research that has shed so much light on Aldus' editorial and publishing work and on his place in the classical textual tradition. Only in limited ways is it about the so-called 'Printing Revolution', or the impact of print-ing on the Renaissance; much more is it about the impact of the Renaissance on printing. For the history of Aldus as a printer and the Aldine Press under his stewardship as a printing house, the reader can often still turn profitably to Martin Lowry's *The World of Aldus Manutius: Business and Scholarship in Renaissance Venice* (1979). Because of Lowry, we first learned that, despite the testimony of Erasmus and the self-promotion further amplified by others, the foundations of the Aldine Press were actually rather precarious. To a great extent, Lowry exposed how 'Aldus', the preternaturally selfless and successful scholar-printer, was a myth. His dogged pursuit of every relevant manuscript (instead of relying on learned interpolations) and perhaps especially his uncanny ability to make scholarly printing lucrative (instead of the close-run thing it often was) were also myths. And yet these were myths created by Aldus and fed by men like Erasmus and Bembo. Lowry showed us behind the myths; here I want instead to understand them.

The world of this book is not that of Aldus Manutius alone. At the heart of my approach is an understanding of Aldus and his books as artefacts, inhabiting a world and obtaining their meaning alongside other books, texts, images, people and ideas. While still the forebear of Froben, Estienne and Plantin, the Aldus who emerges from these pages is, with respect to his intellectual and cultural attachments and preoccupations, in every way a contemporary of Pietro Bembo and Erasmus, Leonardo da Vinci and Albrecht Dürer. It is their world, the world of the High Renaissance, that we aim to illuminate too.

ONE

Carpi and Venice

n the princely chapel of the castle at Carpi, on the right-hand wall of the presbytery and interposed among frescoes illustrating the life of the Virgin, there is a depiction of the man who caused both this chapel and the building works that, at the time of its consecration, still surrounded it to be (illus. 8). Immediately above, a monumental inscription – gold lettering on blue frieze – tells us his name: CONSECRAVIT D. ALBERTVS PIVS. Alberto III Pio di Savoia, prince of Carpi (1475–1531), stands before us, his arms folded into the weighty sleeves of a fur-lined cloak. Behind him is a temple, perhaps an evocation of a centrally planned church in the style of Bramante (1444–1514), then ascendant in Rome – a foretaste of the future architectural desires and diplomatic (mis-)adventures of this ambitious prince.[1] The composition recalls that of the 'Meeting Scene' in the famous *Camera picta* (1465–74) of Andrea Mantegna (*c.* 1431–1506) for the ducal palace of Mantua. The artistic execution here, by the court painter Bernardino Loschi of Parma (*c.* 1460–1540), is not of that aspirational standard. Everywhere Carpi shows the strain inherent to the position of the man who tried to build it in his image. But the name of Alberto Pio was known throughout Renaissance Europe, and it was not because of fresco cycles or building works. Through his diplomatic service, he was known at courts; throughout the republic of letters, he was known from books. And the key to this second,

8 Bernardino Loschi, *Alberto III Pio and Companions*, 1504–11, fresco, Cappella di Palazzo dei Pio, Carpi.

more lasting fame is likely staring out at us from Loschi's fresco.

The fresco depicts five men in the foreground. Alberto appears between those who reinforce his identity as Renaissance scholar and hereditary prince.[2] Behind him stands his brother Leonello II (1477–1535), and partially obscured by a fluted column is a figure likely representing Leonello I (*c.* 1440–1477), the father they would not have remembered. *Here* is a dynasty – an image of patrilineal descent and inheritance that elided the realities of Pio power. The man in the long black robes who approaches Alberto from the left looks to be a university scholar, perhaps even the controversial Aristotelian philosopher Pietro Pomponazzi (1462–1525), with whom the prince of Carpi had studied at Ferrara during a period of exile. Another, older man is positioned between them but with the aristocratic group, like Leonello arresting us with his gaze. He too is clad in black, but his garment is shorter, falling just below the knee. Neither flatteringly aristocratic nor capaciously clerical, nor the garb of a university man, there is something about this dress and its more practical cut that is even bourgeois – something smacking of business and of trade. The ancient Romans might have called him *tunicatus*, 'tunic-wearing' – a word that was not a compliment.

No scholar was closer to the house of Pio than Aldus Manutius, and no prince was as reliant on his former tutor for his reputation than this. Nevertheless this image – if indeed it is of Aldus – speaks further to his singularity in the intellectual landscape of Renaissance Europe. By the time it was painted (1504–11), Aldus was already the renowned printer of Venice: the editor of Aristotle and the Greeks and of the portable Latin classics. *Venetiis, apud Aldum* – a place and name associated with each other wherever his books were read. Yet he had also been granted the Pio family name. He held rural estates; he fantasized about receiving castles and shared these fantasies with his book buyers; his profits from this landlocked statelet supported him in the lagoon city; he was even, sometimes, his patron's man in Venice. It was in Carpi that he longed to be buried – but he was not from Carpi either: both his roots and his intellectual exemplars were elsewhere. Between them, however, Carpi and Venice shaped his mature career. To the end, they represented two spheres, to neither of which he entirely belonged.

TODAY CARPI BELONGS to the province of Modena in Emilia-Romagna. A *comune* of slightly more than 70,000 people, it is situated on the road and rail routes that link Modena with Mantua, on the other side of the river Po in the modern-day region of Lombardy. Any visitor to the town will be struck by the enormous piazza, now Piazza dei Martiri, long (276 metres/ 905 ft) and narrow, seemingly outsized for its location but for the large castle, a partially harmonized complex of palace buildings and towers that once projected into a now-filled moat and which runs along the piazza's entire east side.[3] Additionally, there is the 52-bayed portico flanking the west side of the square. This would have surveyed the length of the castle from across the moat and served as frontage for the Borgogioioso, the neighbourhood laid out regularly behind it at the beginning of the sixteenth century. The medieval church known as the Sagra, properly Santa Maria in Castello, belonged to the castle complex and housed the seign-eurial tombs. It was truncated in 1514 when the palace was ex-panded, leaving only the apse, though the important Romanesque portal with lunette of the Crucifixion was maintained in the Bramantesque facade designed by the Sienese architect Baldassare Peruzzi (1481–1536).[4] It was not a cathedral (Carpi would not have a bishop until 1779), but had once been a collegiate church and *nullius dioecesis*, subject to the Holy See alone. In 1458–9, the college of Augustinian canons was suppressed by order of Pope

Pius II, who awarded its benefices in perpetual commendation to the Pio. A new Collegiata of Santa Maria Assunta, projected by Peruzzi, was established at Alberto's instigation and stands at the north end of the square. Beyond this castle-centred cluster, there are a few churches belonging to the mendicant orders, with attendant *borghi*, or districts, around them. By 1515, the year Aldus Manutius died in Venice, this was Carpi (illus. 9). When Aldus resided there in the 1480s, it was not even this. Though in principle it was a *condominium*, or jointly held lordship, of the two or three branches of the Pio family, the branches were often in conflict and regularly one or the other was in effect in exile. It was only the death of their cousin Giberto II in 1500 that allowed Alberto and his brother to consolidate power in their own hands. A *catasto* (tax survey) of 1472 suggests that the town's population was around 3,500, while, at its greatest territorial extent, the entire *signoria*, or state, of Carpi was little over a third of the size of the Isle of Wight.

Certainly there is more than one way to tell the story of Carpi. In matters of style, Alberto Pio would eventually look to Urbino and Rome, though an apt comparison has been made to Vigevano, near Milan, where a castle city replete with dramatic square, covered galleries and entranceway fit for horses was fashioned by Milan's de facto duke Ludovico Sforza (1452–1508) around the residence in which he was born.[5] In political terms, however, the comparison is inexact, and furthermore highlights a key difference between Carpi and most of the other princely states of the Renaissance in Lombardy and the Po Plain: while they were city-states that in large part emerged from medieval bishoprics and communes (as indeed had Milan), Carpi was fundamentally a rural lordship that emerged, and quite late, from a *castrum* or fortress that belonged to a family of military nobility. The neighbouring *signorie* of Correggio and Mirandola were similar. The tag 'di Savoia' added to the Pio name was a sign of favour from

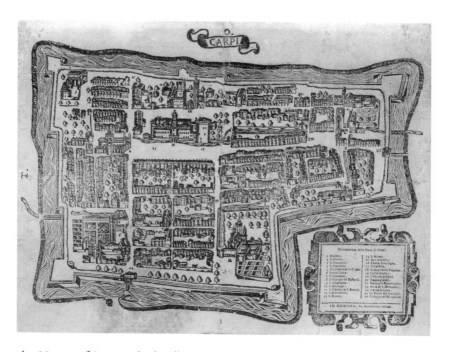

9 Luca Nasi, *Carpi*, *c.* 1677, woodcut, east orientation, with castle in upper centre-left portion.

the House of Savoy, which Alberto's grandfather had served as a military captain, but also of the fact that, on the peninsular scene, they were smaller fish, often dependent on more powerful others. Meanwhile the Gonzaga court of Mantua, to the north, was at the vanguard of the quattrocento, boasting Andrea Mantegna as court artist and new churches designed by Leon Battista Alberti. Modena, to the south, was the second city of the domains of the Este, who ruled mainly from Ferrara, and who were distinguished by the antiquity of their lineage, the splendour of their chivalric and courtly festivities, and their long-standing patronage of literati and of humane learning, especially in Greek. Along with the students produced by the schools established there by Vittorino da Feltre and Guarino da Verona respectively – a distinguished crop of alumni who hailed from many European nations and included Gonzaga and Este princes themselves – in the person of Isabella d'Este (1474–1539), betrothed to Francesco II Gonzaga in 1480 and married to the marquess in 1490, Mantua and Ferrara produced one of the pre-eminent patrons and tastemakers of the High Renaissance in northern Italy. While these states were neither notably large nor notably powerful by fifteenth-century Italian standards – neither, for example, was signatory to the Italian League of 1454, which provided a general structure, if not perfect peace, to peninsular politics for the next forty years – in political, diplomatic and (perhaps especially) cultural spheres they punched above their weight. Compared to these, Carpi was provincial, but it was not remote or isolated from the major trends or trend centres of Italy in the last quarter of the quattrocento. After her first husband's death, Alberto Pio's mother Caterina (1454–1501) married Rodolfo Gonzaga (1452–1495), an uncle of Francesco II of Mantua, in 1484. Alberto himself spent much of the 1490s in Ferrara: in 1497–9, an enforced permanence coincided with his receipt from Aldus of the dedication of the works of Aristotle. In 1527 Carpi was acquired by the Este; apart from during the Napoleonic period, it remained in their hands and the hands of their Habsburg–Este heirs as part of the duchy of Modena until it was subsumed in 1859 into what became the unified Italian state.

Glimpses of the Carpi that Aldus would have known exist inside the palace complex, above all in the Gothic wall paintings – heraldic and chivalric murals, episodes from Petrarch's *Trionfi* – that look towards the decoration of Ferrara's Palazzo Schifanoia for inspiration and capture the military ethos that would have permeated this fortified place. But more important to the story of Aldus is what lies approximately 15 kilometres (9 mi.) to the north around the small town of Novi, and then further to the east, on the banks of the river Secchia at Sant'Antonio in Mercadello. If printing, as he claimed, became his *provincia* (his province, meaning his business), nonetheless these, in the word-playing comparison made in his dedicatory preface to Alberto Pio of the second volume of Aristotle (1497), were his *agri* (fields, lands, territories). 'You have stated openly that you will give me very fertile and expansive estates too'; and it was there that these were received.[6] They amounted to 100 *biolche carpigiane*, or around 28 hectares (70 ac) – an amount which, at a time when even 6 hectares (15 ac) could support in a modicum of comfort a small peasant family that actually worked and lived off the land, would have made him not truly wealthy but very comfortable indeed.[7] Perhaps Aldus expected even more than this:

> Indeed you promise me that one of your agreeable towns will be mine, so that there I can command like you. This you do so that there I may more conveniently and easily furnish everyone with an ample supply of good books in both Latin and Greek and an academy may also be created, where, with barbarism discarded, one may devote oneself to good literature and the liberal arts, and at last men who have fed on acorns for six hundred years and more may nourish themselves with the fruits of the earth.

A letter to Aldus from Leonello Pio, who tended to base himself at Novi, gives us the details of the grant and reports the affection with which Alberto spoke of his former tutor: 'there is no one who can desire more than me that Aldus establish himself [there] . . . I shall make such a show that he will know that I love him, perhaps more than he would ever believe.'[8] Indeed it seems at one point that Alberto did envision Aldus setting up shop in some form at Novi. 'For my part, I shall willingly come whenever you call,' Aldus had written, 'and, with you, whom I have educated and instructed "since", as they say, "your fingernails were soft", devote myself to the study of wisdom, which with a Greek word we call "philosophy".[9] Whether the summons came or not – by 1505, Alberto was insisting that Aldus visit rather than relocate – this never happened.[10] From Leonello's subsequent correspondence, however, we know that this prince oversaw the estates and their harvest on Aldus' behalf.[11] By noble standards this was no vast holding; but, as the chapel fresco makes clear, Aldus was no noble. And it produced an income – an income not derived from selling books.

I dwell on these details because they are easy to overlook in a study of the Aldine Press. Venice is where it happened; Carpi's limitations are too apparent. Even Alberto Pio acknowledged this: for the altarpiece of his planned funeral chapel, a *Lamentation* for which he devised a theologically complex iconography, he turned to Cima da Conegliano (*c.* 1459–*c.* 1517) – a commission which still made him much this Venetian painter's most socially distinguished patron.[12] Beneath its warmth and good humour, a playful letter to Aldus on the occasion of the latter's marriage – the former student playing the role of the provincial, unsure of a gift for a bride who might have to content herself with something *ala forestiera* (in foreign, or outsider's, fashion) instead of *ala Venetiana* – also reveals his awareness of the cultural gulf.[13] If, meanwhile, we look at the Aldine Press as a business, like any other printing business, then its economic basis is certainly in the partnership Aldus formed in Venice, and in the vagaries of that industry. I am not interested just in that, however. For Aldus the man, the land grants would not have been negligible. His sisters, with whom he apparently remained close for his entire life, followed him from Bassiano to Carpi and married locally. It is not enough, then, to say that his move to Venice and demurral (if that is what it was) from settling on his Novi estates represents his keeping 'his old pupil politely at arm's length', when Carpi was in effect now his family home and continued to represent a source of both freedom and imposition in his life.[14] Some

impositions seem slight, like finding a teacher for Leonello's son
Rodolfo (1500–1564): 'Above all I want him to be a man of honest
background, well brought up, and of pleasing appearance – I ask
of you nothing else'; others are more sensitive, like a request that
Aldus pursue a *condotta* (captaincy contract) for Leonello in the
Venetian army.[15] The diarist Marin Sanudo (1466–1536), Venetian
patrician humanist and friend of Aldus, records one of those heraldic murals that, already in 1494, surmounted the entryway to
Alberto and Leonello Pio's family palace in the Carpi castle com-
pound: the coat of arms of King Charles VIII of France (r. 1483–
98), with an inscription in Latin that read, 'I shall live, I shall
conquer, I shall reign.'[16] Such a display would have been raised
to mark the French monarch's Italian invasion of that year, when,
with great reverberations felt by all Italian powers, he marched
through the peninsula to make himself king of Naples – a dramatic prologue to the Italian wars that would commence in earnest
with the campaign of Charles' successor Louis XII (r. 1498–1515)
in 1499. Around 1506, a portrait bust of Louis was painted in the
so-called Sala dei Mori, the palace's grand reception room.[17] Being
Alberto and Leonello Pio's man in Venice – as one who held
lands of them, and certainly one who sought out military contracts
for them, would have been – could also mean exposure to the
consequences of their diplomacy and politics. When political realities finally did intrude and Aldus sought to make himself scarce,
Leonello Pio could write to his former tutor with princely blunt-
ness: 'elsewhere you would be under obligation; here you would
be *padrone*.'[18] The estates were thus a form of safety, too, from the
risks that pertained to what holding them implied. Aldus seems
to have sourced his domestic servants from there as well; at least
that's where they ran away to.[19]

   With that safety came a kind of freedom. Often discussion
of Carpi and Aldus' relations with the Pio focuses on the question
of intellectual impact, of how much the interests of the students

and their immediate and family circles influenced the editorial programme of the printer; of how and why a 'second-rank man of letters' with no obvious aptitude for business or previous reputation for Greek philology would take on a change of career and residence in middle age, and set about publishing the masterworks of Greek philosophy and literature.[20] These are important questions; but to ask them without first thinking more seriously about Carpi is to ignore the material circumstances in which decisions like these are made. The ability to formulate and act upon a vision is a privilege. With the support of his patrons, eventually converted into real estate, no failure of the Aldine Press would have jeopardized Aldus' material comfort: there was always, in the background, a plan B. Exceptional cases, so regularly valorized, are misleading; for most, the freedom to take risks and create begins with a freedom from want.

OUR FIRST RECORDS OF Aldus Manutius come from the end of 1483, in the correspondence of two friends. Giambattista Scita of Feltre writes to Aldus from Pavia, with an update on the progress of 'our prince' in his study of philosophical disputation and a request for news of and recommendation to Alberto and Leonello Pio and their mother Caterina in Carpi. 'Our prince' is Giovanni Pico della Mirandola (1463–1494), uncle to the Pio, their mother's brother. The Cretan Manuel Adramyttenus (d. 1484) writes, meanwhile, from Mirandola itself, congratulating his much-missed friend on having deservedly secured, from what he hears, the favour of Lady Caterina.[21] These letters and names offer an intimate glimpse into Aldus' world. The most interesting name, however, is that of the recipient: the man we know as Aldus Manutius is addressed by Scita as *Altus Cato* – simply as *Cato* in the letter itself. Adramyttenus' letter is in Greek, but the name is the same: Κάτων.

It was not uncommon for humanists to experiment with sobriquets. *Altus* (meaning high, lofty or noble in Latin), as either sobriquet or possible variant spelling, is both respectful and tame. No less a luminary than Angelo Poliziano (1454–1494) would use it for him too; as, later, would a down-on-his-luck acquaintance who claimed that he once knew Aldus in Rome.[22] But what of *Cato*? The name evokes two of the most renowned statesmen of Roman antiquity, both named Marcus Porcius Cato: Cato the Censor, the Elder (234–149 BCE), a stern upholder of traditional Roman values; and his great-grandson Cato of Utica, the Younger (95–45 BCE), a no less inflexible foe of political corruption and immorality. As standard-bearers of *Romanitas*, as good as anyone could find, perhaps their name suited the outsider and self-styled Roman come to dwell in these more northern lands. It certainly implies, perhaps ever so slightly teasingly, a consciously adopted attitude of moral uprightness uncontradicted by any of Aldus' written output. Yet these letters are also reminders of the obscurity that still attaches to the early professional years of Aldus Manutius. For, if this is in part a reference to Cato the Elder, then what we have here is an instance where Aldus – editor of the Greek canon, who, twelve years on from this letter, would print the *editio princeps* of Aristotle – is likened to Rome's most famous opponent of the influence of Hellenism and of the philosophy and science of the Greeks.

There is no indication that Aldus owed this name to such a stance. The historical Cato's supposed opposition to Hellenism had not, anyway, extended to the Greek language, which he knew: according to Cicero, he even studied Greek literature in old age.[23] Aldus would cite this example favourably in his preface to the first volume of Aristotle (1495) – though he misinterpreted it somewhat, his conflation of language learning with literary study saying more about Renaissance practice than anything else. 'In our day, in fact,' he continued, 'one can see many *Catones*, that is, old men learning Greek in old age,' while 'the number of teenagers and young people going in for Greek literature is now almost as great as that of those for Latin.'[24] Like many other humanists (including Erasmus), Aldus did not look back on his own early education with much fondness. As the preface to his Latin grammar of 1501 reveals, he remained unimpressed with the made-up mnemonic devices and eminently forgettable rote learning to which he had been subjected and which he continued to associate with school.[25] He says nothing about having studied Greek then, so presumably, unlike the fortunate youth of the last years of the century, he was a Cato in the sense of being a somewhat later learner too. These letters can still be reconciled with a relatively new-found zeal for Greek learning in a broader sense developing in the 1480s. By the mid-1490s, however, such a sobriquet would have been entirely incongruous.

The period before Aldus Manutius' arrival in Carpi has been characterized by a recent scholar as the 'dark years'.[26] Except for what we can glean from later evidence, often in references and recollections from his dedicatory prefaces, details of his life before his early thirties are sparse. The mountains from which he emerged belonged to the great Roman barons, who from their castles overlooked the Pontine Marshes and the main road to Naples; Bassiano was a fief of the Caetani. Aldus seems to have left it and its educational disappointments and gone to study in Rome in 1467–75, where he was taught by Domizio Calderini (1446–1478) and Gaspare da Verona (d. 1474); then he went to Ferrara and the celebrated school that Battista Guarini (1434–1503) had inherited from his father Guarino.[27] A few years later, he had his first teaching job that we know of: Ercole Strozzi (1473–1506), son of Tito Vespasiano Strozzi (c. 1423/5–1505), later to become a poet like his father, was in his class.[28]

Ferrara was both a centre of Greek studies and, as we have heard, a political and cultural pole for the smaller states of the

Po Plain. There at the same time to study at the university was
the precocious philosopher-prince Giovanni Pico della Mirandola,
a younger son of the ruling house of Carpi's neighbouring prin-
cipality. His eldest sister Caterina had married Leonello I Pio, and
was, since 1477, a widow with two small children. Her brother-in-
law Marco II Pio (r. 1463–94), nominally co-ruler with the minor
Alberto, was regent, but in this uneasy arrangement she had over-
sight of her boys' education. Perhaps a recommendation from
Tito Vespasiano Strozzi – who would hail Caterina, herself distinguished in 'the studies of the Cecropian goddess [Athena] and
the Muses', for her care in these matters in a poem he wrote for
Pico, part of a collection Aldus later published – led the young
prince to recommend in turn the man more than ten years his
senior as tutor to his nephews.[29] Perhaps – thinking of the Cato
appellation – he was simply looking for similar qualities to those
Leonello II would later seek in a tutor for his own son: upright
character, unimpeachable background and fine appearance, combined with the proven ability to give solid instruction in grammar.
The importance of upright instructors for princes (and the dire
consequences for society if these were not found) was a view that
Aldus shared, or at least later promoted in his own educational
writings.[30] Pico was on a meteoric rise to European renown. A
daring reconciler of Neoplatonic, Aristotelian and Averroist phi-
losophies, he was, alternately, an ornament of Lorenzo de' Medici's
Florence; a pioneering Hebraist, Hermeticist and Kabbalist; a
controversial theologian; and an influential critic of what he saw
as the primacy afforded by his society to grammar and rhetoric
over ideas, of superficial style over the pursuit of those truths that
belonged to philosophy alone.[31] For tutor to the children of
Caterina Pico, he found someone who was none of these things:
the raising of noble youths was evidently a different business.

    Exactly when Aldus first came to Carpi on this mission is
unknown. Until recently he was understood to have possessed

both citizenship and a house in the Borgo di Sant'Antonio, just
north of the castle complex, already in 1480, but the authenticity
and even the existence of the documents purporting to show
this – and which gave a more prominent role to Marco Pio in
securing Aldus' services than the literary evidence reflects – have
now been contested by Stefano Pagliaroli.[32] It seems instead that
he settled in Carpi full-time in 1483, and at any rate after 1482,
when a Venetian military campaign against Ferrara encouraged
him to retreat from that city. His first stop on that occasion was
Mirandola, Pico's family seat, where he presumably met Scita,
Adramyttenus and, for the first time, Gianfrancesco Pico (1470–
1533), son and heir of the ruling prince Galeotto. Like his uncle
Giovanni, Gianfrancesco would become an important scholar
and philosopher – an author Aldus would put in print. But some
association with the Pio (and not just the Pico) may still date
from earlier, as Pagliaroli has proposed elsewhere and as Aldus'
own claim to have known Alberto since his fingernails were soft
suggests.[33]

It was through Giovanni Pico that Aldus also began to make
his first connections with the intellectual world of Florence. A
1484 exchange of letters with Angelo Poliziano – humanist and
poet, the leading philologist of his day – lays bare the power
relations that nevertheless then pertained. Aldus initiates it with
a letter that advertises all that links them, and showers praise on
the man he has never met. He recalls his visit to Mirandola in
1482, where Adramyttenus read him one of Poliziano's Greek
letters – a demonstration of such style that it seemed to belong
more to an Athenian than to a Roman. He tells him of Pico's
subsequent visit to Carpi, where he brought with him a copy of
Poliziano's Latin poem *Rusticus*, which left Aldus once again in
awe of the other man's literature and learning. Finally, he asks
for his friendship, urging Poliziano to treat him as freely as he
would his domestic servants. In contrast to that of the earnest

Aldus, Poliziano's letter is playful, ironic, humorous: a difference in character, but also in power. He accepts Aldus' request on the grounds that anyone recommended by Pico must be a worthy friend.[34]

When Aldus and Poliziano finally met, it was 1491 and it was in Venice, where Poliziano had come with Pico to search for manuscripts for Lorenzo de' Medici ('the Magnificent', 1449–1492), and where Aldus was laying the groundwork for his new venture. The prize encounter, however, was with a now-famous fifth-century manuscript of the ancient playwright Terence, written in rustic capitals and kept in the library of the Venetian patrician Bernardo Bembo (1433–1519), a former ambassador to Florence. Poliziano's notes, made in the manuscript itself and in a printed copy of Terence with which he collated it, speak of his delight and of the help he received from Bernardo's son Pietro.[35] In the margins of his notebook from the journey, in a list of the scholars and notables he encountered in Venice, we find the name of the man whose friendship he had accepted almost seven years before (illus. 10).[36] Many on the list are patricians of an intellectual bent; among those who aren't is Antonio Vinciguerra (1468–1502), secretary of the Venetian Republic, who some years before had hosted Pico at a banquet where, on the basis of Kabbalah, a Jew named Dactylus sensationally confessed the Christian doctrine of the Trinity.[37] This may tell us something of the society in which Aldus moved in this period, or of yet more doors that the presence of Pico opened up for him. It is a sign of the lasting esteem and authority attached to Poliziano's name that Aldus allowed that earlier, obsequious correspondence to appear in his edition of the Tuscan's works, which he would print in 1498, four years after the author himself had died. Among the differences between this edition and the surviving manuscripts of the letters, however, is that the name of Poliziano's correspondent has changed from *Altus Manuccius* to *Aldus Manutius*

10 Page from the notebook of Angelo Poliziano, 1491; in left margin, line 7: *Alto Ma(n)nuccio*.

bis(ita me deus amet)&eleganter, Nec quaſi diuerteris in hæc ſtudia,
Sed quaſi migraueris· Vale·

Aldus Manutius Romanus Angelo Politiano· S· D·

Nnum ab hinc tertium,quo Veneti Ferrariā oppugnabāt,
a me,ut uel dei(ut aiunt)ne dū hoīum bellum fugerē,ex urbe
Ferraria Mirandulā contuli ad Ioannem Picū Principem
ætatis noſtræ doctiſſimum, quod et amaret literatos uiros,& faueret
ingeniis·Ibi Emanuel Adramyttenus, familiariſſimus meus,tuā mi
hi græcam,quam ad ſe dederas oſtendit epiſtolā,ornate qdem,& docte
atq; copioſe ſcriptam,quæ non à Romano uiro,ſed à mero attico,qui
Athenis ſemp fuiſſet,e lucubarata uidebatur ·Quāobrē cœpi mi An
gele amare te uehementer,doctrinam tuam,atq; ingenium non me
diocriter admiratus·Deinde Emanuel ſuo cum Principe Ticinum
profectus eſt,ubi paucis ante mēſibus,q̄ ad te ſcriberem,exceſſit e ui
ta·Cuius interitu,ita quidem moueor,ut multis annis grauius nihil,
& moleſtius tulerim·Erat enim homo,& moribus ap prime ornatus,
& græcis literis ſane q̄ doctus, meſq; amantiſſimus·Non poſſum igiē
non tuerere,tali amico orbatus,q̄q̄ meo magis ipſius incōmodo,quā
illius·Nam illi ad ſuperos facillimum fuiſſe curſum,quoniam & be
ne,& beate ſemper uixit,nō ſum neſcius·Qua propter malū fis q̄d acci
dit,meū e iuit inq̄ ille Ticinū,Ego uero Mirādula Carpū perrexi,quo
cū aliquot poſt menſibus ueniſſet & Picus noſter,Ruſticū mihi oſtē
dit tuā,quæ mi Angele mirifice auxit amorē,erga te meū· Ibi enim p
ſpici facile poteſt,quantum abundes ingenio,quanti homo fis ſtudii,
quāta tibi bonarū literaʒ ſit copia.Nec uereor tibi me adulari ducas,
ἐ παν∂υ γυώσκεις· Scis eni q̄ ipſe ſcripſerim eſſe impendio plura.Ta
ceo autē,& quæ de te mihi dixit is ipſe Picus,& dicit quoties in tui ici
dimus ſermonē(nactus es eni dignum præconē laudū tuarū)& quæ
retulit mihi Alexander Sarcius Bononienſis homo uerus,ac integer
uitæ,ſceleriſq; purus,nec non quantū ex ipſius ſermone colligere po
tui,tui ſtudioſiſſimus·Quid plura?Hiſce tuis ipulſus laudibus,nō po
tui ad te non aliquid literaʒ dare,ut facerē te certiorē,me ita eſſe tuī,
ut poſſes omnia de me tibi conſtantiſſime polliceri·Incredibilis enim
erga doctiſſimū quenq; meus eſt amor, qui me ēt coegit, ut ad te ſcri
berem,pereremq;,ut me pro tua erga ſtudioſos uiros humanitate, iter
tuos mi Angele connumerares,quod ut facias,te, quantum poſſum

i ii

11 Letter of Aldus Manutius to Angelo Poliziano, printed in Poliziano,
Opera omnia (1498).

Romanus – the name by which the printer was by this point widely known (illus. 11).[38]

Poliziano's reputation was undimmed by death, and the same was the case for Pico, who followed his friend to the grave in similarly (possibly) mysterious circumstances less than two months later. Indeed, from the evidence of Aldus' early prefaces, it seems that the importance of the late philosopher-prince only increased. The end of a cultural moment in Florence – the deaths of Lorenzo de' Medici, Poliziano and Pico in rapid succession, and the transformation of the city into a 'New Jerusalem' inspired by the millenarian friar Girolamo Savonarola (1452–1498) – left space for Aldus, launching his Venetian press around the same time, to present himself and his enterprise as its inheritor. Pico's reputation, his learning, the loss that his death represented to letters and philosophy, and the closeness of Aldus to him and his family are regular refrains – especially in the many dedications to (and even a publication by) his nephews, Alberto Pio and Gianfrancesco Pico.[39] A famous epistolary dispute from 1485 between Pico and the Venetian humanist Ermolao Barbaro (1454–1493) on rhetoric and philosophy was included among the letters in Aldus' Poliziano edition (this is how Erasmus came to know it).[40] Meanwhile, from Sicily, where he had gone to study Greek with Constantine Lascaris, Pietro Bembo, who only a few years earlier had collated his father's Terence with Poliziano, brought to Venice an authorially corrected copy of his teacher's *Erotemata*, a Greek grammar; in March 1495, this popular work was Aldus' first publication.[41] Bembo himself became Aldus' first published original author with the *De Aetna* (Etna) – inspired by that Sicilian experience and his ascent of the famous mountain – early the following year. In 1497 Aldus published the Latin translations of Iamblichus and other Neoplatonist writers by Marsilio Ficino (1433–1499), the older eminence of Florence and leader of the city's so-called Platonic Academy. The worlds of Florence and Venice had hardly been walled off from each other, but the intimate and very real connections between Aldus and the family of Pico made the claim to this inheritance more plausible. Overall, they go a long way to explaining how Aldus went from relative obscurity as a pedagogue to European fame as a printer in such short order.[42] As for his vocation as a Greek printer, Pico may even have had a hand in providing some inspiration: in 1490, he sent him from Florence a copy of the first printed edition of Homer.[43]

It would nevertheless be wrong to attribute all of Aldus' development in these early years to the influence of Florentine humanism, his contacts with Poliziano and his networking in Pico's intellectual world. Aspects of Aldus were numbingly consistent. A lengthy letter to Caterina Pico, datable to early 1484, sets out clear views (with reference to all the usual ancient authorities and examples) about the importance of the study of Greek and is prefaced by a description of lack of leisure and overwhelming workload stemming from complete dedication to his job that would seem at home in any of his printed prefaces even thirty years later.[44] Around 1489, newly arrived in Venice and without (yet) a press of his own, Aldus had the letter printed in a single-quire pamphlet alongside some Latin poems he had written at a similar date. These included *Musarum panagyris*, or 'The Celebration of the Muses', who one after the other offer Alberto praise and prophecy – lurid punishments for his enemies – in elegiacs stuffed with dense allusions to Greek mythology.[45] In both letter and poems Aldus acknowledges his authorship of other grammatical works: one – the Latin grammar – which was revised and published, and the rest, which do not survive. Among these was a short treatise on Latin and Greek accents, which Aldus presented to Alberto as a New Year's present on 1 January 1484 amidst the court's 'Saturnalian' (his word) festivities.

The printed pamphlet as a whole was surely Aldus' attempt to establish himself in people's minds in connection both with the Pio–Pico family and with Greek learning. He gets his names and number of the Muses from a passage of Hesiod's *Theogony* (77–9), which is provided in both the original Greek (albeit with a misplaced τ where a π should be in Melpomene) and a Latin translation immediately before the letter to Caterina. The notion that they regard princes with special favour owes to this text as well.[46] But despite an accompanying exhortation to read Greek as well as Latin authors and the references to works for the teaching of both languages, the Hellenism of the *Musarum panagyris* itself exists mainly as a patina. For all the mythological allusions, not one of them is reliant on a Greek literary source, with content and language drawn mainly from the classical Roman writers Ovid and Virgil. The rare intrusions of Greek are instructive: *Cerberon* (instead of *Cerberum*) *trifaucem* for the three-throated infernal guard dog in the accusative case; the phrase *minoae machina Pasiphaae* ('contraption of Minoan Pasiphaë'), borrowed from the late antique Latin poet Ausonius, given the Greek genitive ending *Pasiphaes* instead.[47] In other words, they are limited to points of basic grammar, useful less for learning Greek than for recognizing the Greek forms that not infrequently occur in Latin literature. The original intention behind the *Panagyris* therefore must have been to familiarize Aldus' still very young charge with the usages of the Latin poets and to help him digest the tales of gods and mortals of which their works were full. This would have served the purpose for which Aldus had been hired: making fluent and ultimately eloquent an educated prince in a language in which he could be expected to perform.

Meanwhile, a surprising reminiscence comes to us from the renowned physician Jacopo Berengario da Carpi (*c.* 1460–*c.* 1530). In his 1522 dedication to Alberto Pio of the *Isagoge breves*, the first fully illustrated anatomical treatise, Berengario, by now professor of surgery and anatomy at the University of Bologna, recalled a close connection with the prince from his early years, and particularly the fact that they were instructed together 'in the first principles of the gentler muses' by Aldus Manutius.[48] Alongside such tuition, they apparently dissected a pig. This indeed would have been an unusual form of princely education from a teacher such as Aldus, whose writings on the subject invariably advise letters, morals and possibly military arts, and who, as we shall explore further, would endeavour to keep himself far removed (ideologically at least) from *chirurgia* (surgery), literally 'hand-work'. Given Berengario's background (his father was a barber-surgeon) and the fifteen-year age difference with Alberto, most likely it was *he* who gave anatomy lessons to the curious young man, directing a dissection with Aldus' blessing and receiving grammatical instruction for himself; that is certainly one way this remembrance can be read.

Yet, taken together, Berengario's reminiscences and Aldus' poems shed light both on the intellectual scene of the city Aldus left behind and on the original conception of the Aldine publishing programme. They show us Aldus the grammarian in practice, and they perhaps explain, but just as probably reveal, Alberto's interest in philosophy and science, which he would nurture his entire life.[49] Many of the works published in the early years of the Aldine Press were indeed philosophical and scientific, and these, throughout Aldus' career, were almost invariably dedicated to Alberto Pio. We will surely never have a complete picture of Aldus Manutius' Carpi years, but hardly less significant than the material impact that Carpi exercised on his career in Venice may have been that which it had on the fashioning and conceiving of the most characteristic aspects of his press's intellectual agenda.

IN CONTRAST TO THE INTIMATE sphere of the Carpi court, Venice – imperial and republican, basking in the moment of its greatest pomp – must indeed have seemed, in Aldus' words, 'another world more than a city' (illus. 12). But by 1498, when he lauded it as such in his dedication of Poliziano's works to Marin Sanudo, he had, by his own testimony, already been in the lagoon city for nine years.[50] Although he did not yet hold the estates at Novi, the patronage of Alberto Pio would have been essential, allowing him to support himself through the years of preparation and presumably freeing him from the need to take much money out of the firm he founded. It is possible that Alberto

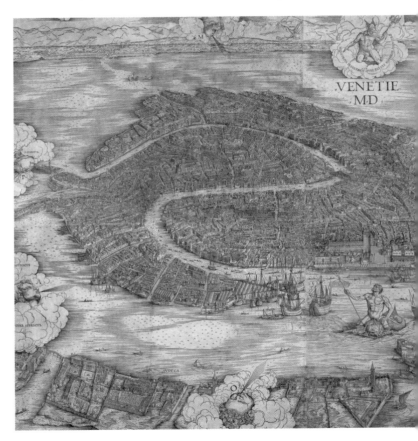

also provided subventions for the Aristotle edition, a work of enormous scale, special difficulty and particular interest to him.[51] When it came to the actual business, however, the prince of Carpi had no share. Operating out of premises in Campo Sant'Agostin, the Aldine Press was a partnership between the vision, reputation, editorial agenda and humanist charisma of Aldus Manutius; the printing know-how and business nous of Andrea Torresani (1451–1529), called Andrea d'Asola after his home town in the

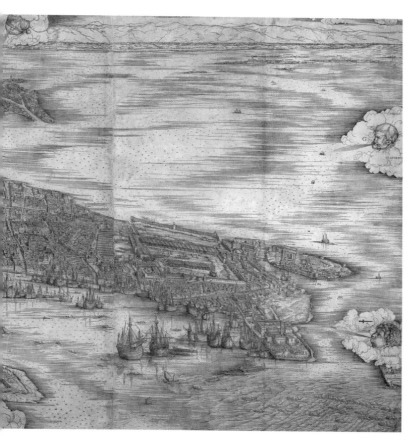

12 Jacopo de' Barbari, *View of Venice*, 1500, woodcut.

Venetian mainland territory west of Mantua, an established printer who had worked with Nicolas Jenson and then purchased his types; and the deep pockets and unmatchable links to Venetian high society of a silent partner, Pierfrancesco Barbarigo – son of the late doge Marco (r. 1485–6) and nephew of Agostino Barbarigo, the current doge (r. 1486–1501). Notarial documents pertaining to its dissolution in 1542 and a surviving account book reveal a company split in half between Barbarigo and Torresani shares, with Aldus' indeterminate but evidently much smaller part associated with Torresani's.[52] These documents prove three things: the impressive financial, moral and political backing for the Aldine Press at the very beginning and the confidence that Aldus must have inspired, but, beyond that, the very limited power that, if push ever came to shove, he would actually have in the press that always bore his name.

A few colophons from that initial year of 1495 do find Aldus sounding slightly like Jenson or the brothers from Speyer, lauding his own 'dexterity'.[53] But this celebration of craftsmanship soon fell from his lexicon. Rather, the technical virtuoso in this period – undoubtedly the most important individual for the story and legacy of the Aldine Press apart from its namesake – was the punchcutter Francesco Griffo of Bologna (c. 1450–1518?). Basing his work in part on contemporary Greek and Italian humanistic book hands, including the handwriting of Aldus himself, the talented Griffo developed the Greek, roman and eventually italic types that, especially in the case of the roman, have in aesthetic terms perhaps never been bettered.[54]

Printing Greek was a special challenge, as an object of more limited demand that nevertheless – with its accents, breathings and complex ligatures – required a much wider range of sorts. It involved 'extraordinary labours and costs on our part', as Aldus admitted in the preface to Lascaris' *Erotemata*, his 'preparation' for the bigger works to come.[55] Aldus, however, was clearly already becoming uncomfortable with the implications of manual craft. In the colophon to the second volume of Aristotle (February 1497), the printing press was characterized almost as if it were an autonomous actor for which he provided a home: 'Copy made in Venice by the metallic hand in the house of Aldus Manutius, Roman and scholar of the Greeks'.[56] Instead, for all the visual appeal of the types – to which Aldus was not insensitive and which was not immaterial to his success – it was Greek scholarship and the promotion of Greek language and studies more broadly on which the identity of the Aldine Press was founded. Its circle of collaborators and contributors included a number of Greek émigrés from the Venetian and former Byzantine (now Ottoman) empires.[57] Alongside the Aristotelian corpus and other philosophical and scientific texts, and some important writers like Theocritus and Aristophanes, the remaining output was largely in Greek grammatical and lexicographical works. Indeed, despite the purported dream of establishing a scholarly press in both languages in Carpi, in the real world there was to be no publication dedicated entirely to an ancient Latin text until 1500 – a fact which is significant and will be explored further.[58] Although even by the philological standards of the time his editions were by no means flawless – a criticism he acknowledged and a fact he lamented – Aldus spoke to scholars as *one of them*.[59] 'It is a tough business indeed', he wrote, 'to print Latin books correctly'; 'Printing Greek ones accurately is tougher, and toughest is printing either without errors in tough times. In which language I put books in print and in what times, you see for yourself.'[60]

In 1497, therefore, Aldus could rightly say to his readers: 'for you the tools for attaining liberal knowledge are everywhere at hand,' and 'already from us you possess a great number of Greek volumes, both in dialectics and in philosophy.'[61] When, in these years, the Bolognese humanist and professor Antonio Urceo Codro (1446–1500) chose in an inaugural lecture to name Aldus among the few printers who were actually of service to letters, it was specifically as a printer of Greek.[62]

Aldus often liked to present his publications in the Greek language (especially the grammatical publications) as his response to a furious pent-up demand. Yet their impact could be made to appear almost cosmic. In launching his first publication, Aldus was motivated not just by an eager market, but, he said, by the

> state and circumstances in which we live, the monstrous wars which infest all of Italy and which, with God angry at our offences, look like they will soon stir or rather shake the entire world to its foundations on account of the crimes committed by men everywhere, which are much greater in number and magnitude than those for which an angry God drowned and destroyed the entire human race.[63]

What is not said – that is, how studying Greek language and grammar will alleviate these disasters and save mankind – is the essential mystery at the heart of the humanist faith that Aldus and his peers, from Petrarch onwards, shared: the belief that the eradication of barbarism and the restoration of ancient language(s) and eloquence was necessary for a broader moral and political recovery.[64] Its logic (to our eyes) notwithstanding, there is no doubting the sincerity of this belief or the strength with which it was held. And it was a belief that did not preclude the possibility of fun. When, in 1502, Aldus and his friends Scipione Fortiguerra (1466–1515) and John Gregoropoulos ('the Cretan', c. 1475–after 1508) drew up the statues of a *Neakademia* (New Academy), proscribing conversation in any language other than Greek on penalty of a small fine (or, for the non-payer, expulsion 'from the community of the Grecians'), the aim was not only to improve their spoken language and pronunciation but also to contribute to camaraderie and general merriment:

If there is enough for the cost and outlay of a party, it shall
be handed to Aldus as master, and from it he shall enter-
tain us handsomely, not in the style for the typesetters
but for men who are already quite properly dreaming of
the New Academy and have all but established it after
the fashion of Plato.'[65]

A mock-serious mission statement for a bunch of socially symposi-
astic colleagues and philhellenes, the statutes nevertheless evince
the prejudice in favour of intellectual pursuits that would lead to
that reformed and restored society and against the manual work
and workers that enabled them. In this environment, with these
cultural values, the printing press *could* appear merely instrumental to a greater mission. That was at least how Aldus, benefactor
of letters, chose to present it.

Except, in reality, it was not merely instrumental. The Aldine
Press was a business that had costs to cover and a product to sell.
Greek was its *raison d'être*, but, while grammars had a ready market
of young (or not-so-young) language learners, the compendious
Greek editions it produced were capital-intensive and slower to
turn over. The amount of moral support Aldus received from
Pierfrancesco Barbarigo must have been significant, on the evidence of the changes that took place from 1499, the year of his
death. The ownership structure of the firm did not yet change,
and Barbarigo's share was inherited by two nephews, but they
would not have had the same interest or commitment as the co-
founder. The subsequent death in 1501 of Doge Agostino
Barbarigo, generally held to have governed the crowned republic
with an overmighty hand, led to the family's political eclipse. At
any rate, it seems that a greater sway in business affairs was from
this point on exercised by Andrea Torresani.

Perhaps this is only to say that business imperatives came to
play a more obvious role in the press's publishing decisions than

they had previously done. Aldus, as we know, had by this time received his estates, so from a personal standpoint he was in a position of greater financial security than ever before. It would, therefore, not have been a sudden need on his part that led to the change. Nor would it be fair to lay the blame – as some humanists apparently did – on Andrea, who was an expert in the printing trade but had no publishing agenda of his own. The result, however, was a dramatic shift towards printing the Latin literary classics in portable editions. Today, this is viewed as Aldus' greatest innovation; it was not seen that way by his humanist peers. In 1501, Janus Lascaris (c. 1445–1535), the former Medici librarian in Florence who had also published the Greek Anthology and was now serving the king of France at the royal library at Blois, wrote Aldus a jovial letter nonetheless revealing of the learned chatter circulating in that period. Hearing that his friend wished to make an *enchiridion* (pocket-sized edition) of Homer just as he had done of Virgil and Horace, Lascaris expressed pleasure and approval. But others were starting to talk about what he called 'your transmigration from Greece to Italy', and, notwithstanding its 'true cause', they were saying that its motive was the quest for profits. If this was indeed necessary, then with what he earned easily in 'Italy' he ought to sustain what was more difficult in Greece, 'the head and origin of the entire enterprise'.[66] By 1505, a year in which he wed Andrea Torresani's daughter Maria, it is clear that not all humanists believed Aldus was pulling off this balancing act successfully, or even could if he wanted to. Apart from Aesop and Phornutus, said Johannes Cuno (1462/3–1513), writing from Venice to the Nuremberg patrician Willibald Pirckheimer (1470–1530), 'he hasn't printed anything in Greek this entire year,' and this despite having been offered a number of important works, including Plato and commentaries on Euripides, Sophocles and Aristotle. Instead, 'he printed [Giovanni] Pontano's works in verse, the elegies of a certain Aurelio, a little work attractively written by some Italian on the captivity and liberation of the king of the Romans in Flanders, and, on top of that,' now referring to Pietro Bembo's *Asolani*, 'some vernacular thing on the stages of love.'[67] We will consider in a later chapter what motivated Aldus to print these works in particular, but, as the purpose of this letter was to discuss plans to bring Aldus to Germany, evidently Cuno believed that Aldus shared this rather low opinion of his recent activities. 'His father-in-law Andrea d'Asola, the famous book dealer, wouldn't have accepted Greek books to print one after the other the way he used to,' he added.[68] In Rome, Scipione Fortiguerra even heard, apparently from Andrea himself, that Aldus had stopped printing Greek entirely – 'although you are to resume'.[69] The perception was worse than the reality: in no year bar 1500 had Greek been absent from the press's new releases. And yet the perception clearly was that a programme launched with enthusiasm had run aground. To cap it all off, the disintegration in 1502 of the relationship between Aldus and his punchcutter Francesco Griffo meant that the formal innovations stopped then as well: not a single new type was invented.

But between 1499, and the death of Barbarigo, and 1501, and the publication of Virgil in the *enchiridion* format that would embody the new publishing programme for an expanded market, there were still nearly two years of activity. From the point of view of the cultural historian, these are the most interesting years in the history of the press. For it was at this moment that Aldus, faced with his new circumstances, began to formulate answers to the following questions. Without his truly distinctive publishing agenda, what made the Aldine Press different? What distinguished him from those, like his partner, his punchcutter or even his own pressmen, who made their living by labour rather than by scholarship? How could a man formed and sustained by the peculiar climate of Carpi preserve a reputation and the prestige he had garnered in the face of the dispiriting impositions of running a business in Venice? The answers, as we have seen, did not please everybody, and may not even have entirely pleased Aldus either. A printer despite himself, he began working towards these solutions in his books, including in the strangest and most beautiful book he ever published.

TWO

After Daedalus

oliphilo is pursued by a dragon through a dark and mysterious labyrinth. Escaping at last, he emerges from the sinister maze to find himself in a delightful and verdant landscape. The environment is agreeable, fertile, pulsing with controlled nature, stirring with erotic potential: a veritable *locus amoenus*, that enduring literary *topos*. A chestnut grove offers welcome shade; the grass underfoot is invitingly damp. It is the perfect place for a suggestible lovestruck wanderer such as this one, whose eyes have been feasting on the strange monumental half-ruined dreamworld through which he has been meandering – driven forward by a burning desire for the beloved Polia but waylaid by an equally urgent need to look and interpret as he goes.

Passing with pleasure under the leafy canopy, eventually Poliphilo reaches an ancient, single-arched marble bridge. In the usual way in which this world, though apparently unpopulated, is yet uncannily expectant of some human presence (and likely his), the bridge is furnished beneath each parapet with seats. Though tired from his brush with death and his close escape, he decides not to tarry and rather to make progress towards his love's aim. But, not for the first time, his polyamorous (that is, *Poliphilian*) eye for antiquity arrests his journey long enough for him to take in the exotic decorations and account for their materials and meaning in the detailed, descriptive style that we, his readers, have come to know:

In the middle of those parapets, above the flat surface at the top of the keystone of the arch underneath, there rose to a certain eminence a porphyritic square-cornered slab, with an exceptional cyma of fine lineaments: one on one side, and a similar one on the other, though of serpentine. On the right-hand side of my path, I saw extremely noble Egyptian hieroglyphs of such description: an antique helmet crested with the head of a dog, the bare skull of an ox with two tree boughs of fine foliage bound to the horns, and an ancient oil lamp. Setting aside the boughs, which whether they were of fir or pine or larch or juniper or something similar I knew not, the hieroglyphs I interpreted like so:

PATIENCE IS THE ORNAMENT, SENTINEL,
AND PROTECTION OF LIFE.

On the other side, a carving of such elegance I saw: a circle, and an anchor, upon the shaft of which a dolphin was turned around on itself. And these I interpreted best like so: ΑΕΙ ΣΠΕΥΔΕ ΒΡΑΔΕΩΣ. *Semper festina tarde* [Always make haste slowly].[1]

Poliphilo's description of the hieroglyphs, or carving, called *scalptura*, reveals that these do not actually resemble Egyptian characters but rather the sort of sculpture in low relief familiar, in style as well as (in some respects) iconography, from the friezes of imperial Rome.[2] We get to see this for ourselves: the two stone panels are depicted, one above the other, in a woodcut (illus. 13).

What is the *Hypnerotomachia Poliphili*? No less than the most celebrated and strangest book of the Italian Renaissance. A hybrid between the ancient novel and the medieval romance, it is a grab bag of archaeological bric-a-brac, an audacious linguistic experiment, and a peek under the covers of the humanist movement.

Poliphilo's pursuit of the beloved Polia, which culminates in their union on the island of Cythera, unfolds amidst temples, gardens, palaces and mausoleums seemingly abandoned by a superior ancient civilization yet simultaneously inhabited by nymphs, queens, priestesses and deities celebrating a succession of elaborate banquets, triumphs and Priapic rites (illus. 14 and 15). Technical (if often impossible) descriptions and detailed measurements of buildings and sculptures give way repeatedly, fetishistically, to transports of passion and desire, making of Poliphilo's twice-somnambulant quest (the narration is of a dream within a dream, though Polia, we are made to understand, exists as the narrator's love object in reality) the pornographic Pevsner guide to the Renaissance antiquarian imaginary. The work is also shrouded in mystery, much of it evidently intentional. 'But who, I ask,

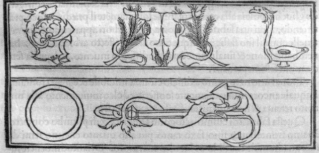

13 Woodcut from Francesco Colonna, *Hypnerotomachia Poliphili* (1499).

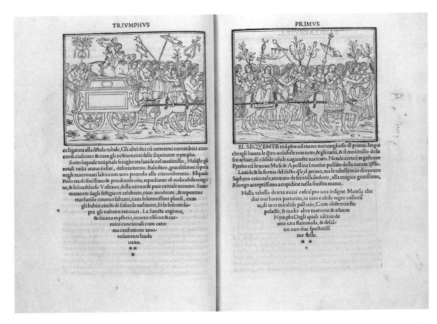

actually is it going by the name Poliphilo?' Andrea Marone da Brescia (1474/5–1528) demands of his muse in an epigram that precedes the text. 'We will not say.'[3]

The title comes from the Greek words for sleep (ὕπνος, *hýpnos*), love (ἔρως, *érōs*) and battle, struggle or fight (μάχη, *máchē*). An acrostic made from 39 woodcut initials identifies the lover of Polia as a certain Francesco Colonna, fuelling a modern cottage industry dedicated to identifying him and to attributing the real authorship to all kinds of improbable candidates. The most popular of these remains Fra Francesco Colonna (1433/4–1527), a Dominican of ss Giovanni e Paolo in Venice; while others proposed include Francesco Colonna, lord of Palestrina, Fra Eliseo da Treviso, Leon Battista Alberti and even Aldus Manutius. For reasons that will become clear, I am entirely sure that neither of the last two is 'Francesco Colonna', and I find most convincing

14 'The First Triumph', from Francesco Colonna, *Hypnerotomachia Poliphili* (1499).

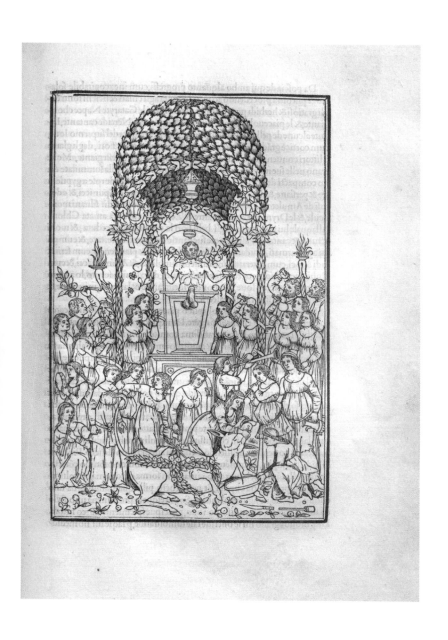

15 'Sacrifice to Priapus', woodcut from Francesco Colonna,
Hypnerotomachia Poliphili (1499).

the arguments for the Venetian-resident Dominican as author, but my use of the name is mainly a matter of convention.[4] The appearance of a surprisingly precise date and place – 1467 in Treviso – at the end of the second of the work's two books, which provides Polia's account of their real-life courtship (though still relayed within Poliphilo's overarching dream), cannot at any rate apply to the much longer first book, where almost all of the work's uniqueness lies, for abundant textual and other reasons, some of which are central to this chapter. The 172 woodcuts represent the bowsprit of graphic culture in northeastern Italy at the end of the fifteenth century and chief credit for their design is now generally attributed to Benedetto Bordone (1460–1531), an important figure in humanistic book illumination, but there is no contemporary attribution or – unless we count an initial '.b.' that appears in one of the first images – even (as for the author) a clue.

Poliphilo's Struggle of Love in a Dream thus remains deliberately opaque, occluded and obscure. Some inscriptions are translated into Hebrew, and some, even, into Arabic – the first Arabic writing ever printed.[5] The text bears the influence of writers ancient and modern, such as Vitruvius, Pliny the Elder, Apuleius, Dante, Alberti and Ficino, but is inconceivable without the images.[6] Indeed, in a remarkable feat of typographical and compositorial prowess, which keeps the text of a work never before published in manuscript or print in near-perfect alignment with its related woodcuts, the book overturns all conventions by inverting the expected relationship between image and text: rather than narration in text and illustration in image, the serene, often stately woodcuts propel the story forward, while Colonna's ekphrastic prose luxuriates in description, detail and delay.[7] The book might even with justice be itself classed as a hieroglyph – at least as a hieroglyph was understood at the time: as a complete and perfect visual encoding of profound meanings reserved solely for initiates.[8] Its hybrid, macaronic language was intended for just such a purpose according to Leonardo Crasso, the jurist from Verona who commissioned it and dedicated it to Guidobaldo da Montefeltro, Duke of Urbino (1472–1508). 'Although it speaks our native tongue,' he explained in his (Latin) dedication, meaning by this the version of the northern Italian dialect shared by most elites as well as its widespread literary alternative, 'for understanding it one needs the Greek and Roman no less than the Tuscan and vernacular':

> Indeed, the extremely wise man thought that speaking in this fashion would be the one way and manner whereby no one who would learn something could say his negligence had been indulged. Yet he also made sure that, if only the most learned could enter the holy place of his teaching, still the unlearned who approached would not fall into despair. Here are not things laid open for the masses, to be shouted out loud at the crossroads, but those distributed from the inner sanctum of philosophy: drawn up from the springs of the Muses perfected with a certain novelty of speech, they deserve the favour of all superior men.[9]

The best way, then, to understand the *Hypnerotomachia Poliphili* is as a work produced by and for the connected communities of connoisseurs and literati who generally took pleasure from archaeological fragments and so too from creating, reading and deciphering learned puzzles of their own.[10] The appropriate company for pursuing these sometimes eclectic and esoteric interests was male: Baldesar Castiglione (1478–1529) characterized as *parole di Poliphilo* ('Poliphilian words') the sort of grandiloquent pedantry that could not be better designed to bore the ladies and leave them feeling unintelligent.[11] Yet one of the very few things we are actually told about the book *from the book itself* is found in the printer's colophon, squeezed into a single line at the bottom of a full page of errata: '[Printed] at Venice, in the month of December 1499, in the house of Aldus Manutius, with the greatest accuracy' (illus. 16).[12] The evidence of blind impressions reveals that a larger, more prominent colophon, surrounded by white space and with a November publication date, was intended, only to be revised to make room for the lengthy list of corrections.[13] But surely, in the ominously *fin-de-siècle* version that ultimately emerged, the trumpeting of the famous name of Aldus, prized for his accuracy, among this catalogue of errors was one more learned joke.

Scholars of the Aldine Press have struggled to know what to make of the *Hypnerotomachia Poliphili*. Colonna's book fascinates historians of art and architecture and, of course, those of typography. It holds little for the historian of classical philology – certainly nothing pertaining to Aldus' work as editor and publisher of classical texts. Aldus, according to one of the more generous scholarly interventions, must simply have appreciated it as 'an amusing pastiche'.[14] For historians of the book, meanwhile, working within a framework where printing is business first and foremost, it is a work for hire – and, commercially speaking, perhaps not a very successful one. This, combined with its sheer unlikeness to the rest of his publishing programme, has led to a near-universal attempt to discount it: a supreme typographical achievement, to be sure, but hardly Aldus' 'titolo di gloria'; nor even, with his own involvement either strictly limited to the printing job or immediately regretted, really an Aldine publication at all.[15] An urge to do down its significance has overcome even the most important modern scholars of the Aldine Press. To Giovanni Mardersteig, a work like this 'must have given a man of such austere tastes the feeling that someone else's egg had ended up in his nest'; only with the greatest reluctance would Aldus have conceded the inclusion

Li errori del libro.facti stampando,liquali corrige cosi.

Quaderno a Charta.3.fazata pria.linea fecūda ne fa nel_fazata feconda linea.18.diffufo. fa diffifo
ch.5.f..l.26. dilectione fa delectatione, Quademo b ch.6.f.5.l.34.limata.fa liniata. Quademo c
ch.2.f..l.20.loquace.fa nó loquace.f..5.l..liberaméto,fa libraméro.l.19.præminétia fa prominetia.c.
3.f..l..laftra.fa laltro.f.5.l.5.edifinitio.fa ædificio.ch.4.f..l.20.in imo.fa i minimo.ch..r.f..l.25.nexuli
fa Nextruli.f.5.l.18.decunati.fa decimati.ch..6.f..l.14.coniecturia.fa cóiecturai.l.15.prime fa pinne.ch.
7.f..l.5.inufitata.fa inuifitata.l.10.incinnato.fa uicinato. Quaderno. d. ch..f..l.2. Et quanta.fa
Et di quanta.ch..f.5.l.9.hippotanii.fa hippopotami.ch.5.f..l.11. trepente. fa repente.l.33. uerucofto.
fa uerucofo.f.5.l..8.Solitaméte fa folicitamente.ch.4.f..l.20.afmato.fa afinato.l.27.fera.fa ferra.f.5.l.
34.mortali fa mortui.ch.5.f.f.l..forma.fa ferma.l..aderia.fa adoria.l.16. Incitamente.fa incitatamen
te.ch..6.f.5.l.25.& pofcia & quella antiqua.fa.poftica & quella antica.ch.7.f..l.14.cunto.fa cuneo.f.5.l.
21.certamente.fa certatamente.l.24. benigna patria di gente. fa benigna patria ma di gente.ch.8.f.5.
l..le cofe.fa le coxe.l.4.ftrifti petali.fa ftricti petioli.l.11.irricature. fa irriciature. Quademo e
ch.2.f..l.4.aretrorfo.fa antrorfo,ch..f.5.l.24.afede.fa affeole.ch..6.f..l.36.era.fa Hera.ch.8.f.5.l.7. aru-
rini.fa azurini. Quademo f ch..f..l..preftamente.fa preftantemente.ch.7.f..l.ultima.angufta
fa augufta.ch.8.f..l.33.politulatamente fa politulamente.f..5.l.24.fuccedeterno.fa fuccedeteno.
Quademo g ch..f..l.7.fori.fa fora.ch..6.f.5.l.10.tuti recolecti & inde afportati.manca & fa cofi tuti
recollecti & tuti gli analecti ide afportati.ch.7.f.5.l.20.Vireti.fa Vireti.ch.8.f.5.l..uifione.fa iuffione.
Quademo h. ch.3.f..l.17.βοζα.fa λοξα.l.27.conduce.fa conducono.ch.4.f..l.16.Lamulatione.fa
lamutilatione.ch..f.5.l.12.factiloquia.fa fatiloquia.ch..6.f.5.l.8. confabulamen.fa confabulamento.
l.11.micrebbe.fa rincrebbe.l.16.che e uno elephanto.fa che e uno. Quademo. i ch..f..l.18.dixe-
ne.fa.di Sene.f.5.l.9.uoluprate pro uoluptate.c.4.f.5.l.4.teffute. p texuto.ch..f.5.l..8.di feta.pro defo-
to.ch.7.f..l.7.mortali.pro mortale.f.5.l.23.fauilla.p fcintilla. Quademo K ch..4.f.5.l..carolette.
pro parolette.ch..f..l.4.uditante.p uolitante.f.5.l.,fractura.pro factura. ch.3.f..l..fa cógrumati ha-
ueano,cum exquifiti tormétuli tripharia infieme,& di uoluptica textura inodulati.Altre diffufamen
te fa inftabile .l.17.ferice.pro fericei.l.33.o ueru.pro o uero.f.5.l.3.nale fforza pro uale fe fforza.ch.6.
f..l.7.longo.pro longe. QVademo. l ch.3.f..l..di feta.p defoto.l.15.laducitate pro laducitate-
f.5.l.8.nū.pnó.l.19.eū.pro cū.ch.4.f..l.35.fi.pro.in.f.5.l.8.lune.p lume.l.17.ornata.pro ornato.ch..6.f.
5.l.3.Columna.p Coluba Quademo. m ch..f..l.12.miratione.pro ruratióe. Quademo n
ch..f..l.12.foforia adallo.pro fuforia dalo.ch..f.5.l.ultima reftitudine.pro reftitudine.ch.6, f.5.l.16.
Di quelle.pro Di que,le.l.31. inuifta.pro iuifa. Quademo o ch.4.f..l..di numere.pro di numero.
ch..f..l..nelamino.pro nelanimo. Quademo p ch.3.f..l.33.certamete.pro certatamente.ch.5
.f.5.l.4.& miarchitatrice.pro mia architatrice.ch.7 .f..l.6.triumphale.manca Tropheo Quaderno. q ch..f.5.l.15.laquale.pro leâle.ch.3.nel epitaphio.l..ella fa PVELLA.l.2.germinoe.p germi-
naua .f.5.nello epitaphio.l.5.LAGVOREM.pro languorem.l.14.tamo .pro Tano.ch.4.f..l..Dê-
drocæfo.Dêdrocyffo.f.5.l.16.laefure .p le Sure.l.19.Area.pro Arca.c.5.f.5.nel epitaphio.NEDT.p
NEPT.ch..6.f..l.7.torque.pro torque.l.19.delinfimo.pro deliffimo.l.21.unoquali fuperfiuo.ch.7.f..l.
6. riferuati.manca.uidi.ch.8,nello epitaphio.l.42.culpa pro culpâ.luftia.aethernû.p eterno. Quaderno r ch.3.f.5.l.8.o uero .pro oue.ch.5.l.16.fractici pro fracticii.ch.7.f.5.l.14.confulaméto.pro con
fabulamento.ch.8.f.5.l.22. & dapofcia.manca.La. Quademo f ch.3.f..l.ultima.tinge.pro tri-
ge.ch.7.f..l.19.& il fuo.pro & dil fuo Quademo. t ch..f.5.l.8.pullnarie.pro pullarie.ch..6.f..l.7.
limariī. pro lunarii.ch. 7. f..l.20.citrino.pro citimo.ch.8.f..l.19.cimiadeo.pro Cimiadon.
Quademo. u ch..f..l.29.pergutto.pro pergutato.charte.7.f.5.l.14.in hafta.pro in hafte.
Quademo. x. ch..f..l.37.de pilo.p depilo.ch.6.f..l.19. Tribaba .pro Tribada.ch.7.f..l.26. Cof-
modea.pro cofmoclea.ch.8.f..l.23.Syrimati.pro Syrmati. Quademo. y ch..f..l.16. dædalifa-
cti. p dædale facti.f.5.l.18.capo pro capto.ch.5.f.5.l.14.calice.pro calce.ch.6.f..l.31.ioui.pro Loui.ch.7.
f..l.5.continua.pro continuâ.f.5.l.20.Vrotiothia.pro Vranothia.ch.8.f.5.l.37.Cóexo.pro Cóuexo.
Quademo. z. ch..f.5.l.13.mufcho.pro mofco.ch.3.f..l.19. ferimo.pro firmo.f.5.l.37 .Carinatione.
.p Cariuatione.ch.5.f..l.1. Ornate.pro ornato.l..Arfacis.pro Arfacida.l.ultima.uerna.pro uernea.
f.5.l.3.excedente pro excedeuano.prope io.uacat.l.17. aptiffima.pro aptiffime.l.35.mirando .pro ua-
rio.ch.6.f..l.31.cópecto.pro comfpecto.l.ultima.diafpre.pro dediafprea.di.uacat.ch.8.f.5.l.37.fecuro
fo.p fi curiofo.l.17.picto.pro pecto.l.ultima.appropriauano.p approbauano QVademo. A ch.
.2.f.5.l.22.Melinia.pro Melmia.l.20.perimorida.pro periucunda.l.12.truncuto.pro troncato.ch.5.f.5
l..4.manca dapo.Comente gli pectinaua.Dindi acafo paffando allhora Poliphilo.ch.7.f.5.l.7. Com
moffa.p comofa.ch.7.f..l.19.difpumale.pro defpûa Lecanefcéte.l.16.petrace.p petracee. Quaderno. B ch.5.f..l.32.Saporofo.pro Soporofo,l.36.fere. pro. fere.ch.8.f.5.l.2.iftimatione. proeftimatióe
QVademo C ch.3.f..l.16.cótemto .pro cótempto.l.20.fuspicare.pro fufpicace. QVademo. D
ch.2.f.5.l.19.parare.p parlare.ch.5.f..l.5. fa parturifce.ch.6.f.5.l.16.Gratis.p Gracis. QVademo. E.
ch..4.f.5.l.ultima.feguitoe.p feguiroe.ch..6.f..l.14.feruli pro ferali. QVademo F ch.3.f.5.l.ultima
amante.pro amâtime.ch.5.f.5.l.2.Garo.pro Claro.   Nó fe numera le linee delle maiufcule.
Venetiis Mense decembri.M.JD.in ædibus Aldi Manutii accuratiffime.

16 Errata to Francesco Colonna, *Hypnerotomachia Poliphili* (1499), printed by
Aldus 'with the greatest accuracy'.

of his name in the meagre colophon (which we have since learned was supposed to be much more prominent).[16] Martin Lowry downplayed the role of the *Polifilo* in Aldus' oeuvre. Deeming his involvement in the project to be 'fairly slight', he presented it as an embarrassment, a dalliance in paganism and romance quickly to be expunged by the pious Aldus through the publication in the very next year of the letters of St Catherine of Siena.[17] The double standards are remarkable. Not only, as we shall see in the next chapter, was the Catherine edition a co-publication and not one man's act of penance, but that book was then immediately followed by the Roman poet Lucretius, an atomist who denied the immortality of the soul and whose name was a byword for atheism: hardly the author on which a printer so purportedly desperate to buck up his orthodox bona fides was likely to shed ink. What these moralizing interpretations lack is evidence, and what they fundamentally boil down to is the conviction that *Aldus didn't publish books like this*. But who did?

It is one thing to dismiss the notion that the *Hypnerotomachia Poliphili* was little more than an Aldine embarrassment. But a case for Aldus' genuine involvement and investment in the project can be proven too. In 1545, when the *Polifilo*, already a 'cult classic' of sorts, received a second edition, most of the woodblocks were reused from the 1499 original. As the blocks had remained in the possession of the Aldine Press, they would have almost certainly been commissioned by it. And though a link between Aldus and Francesco Colonna is naturally hard to prove without proving first who Colonna was, a poem in praise of the patron Leonardo Crasso included at the beginning of the book represents the only piece of writing by Giambattista Scita to survive apart from the letter of some sixteen years earlier in which he addressed Aldus as *Cato*.[18] So it is possible to place the *Polifilo* in his workshop and his network. The kind of involvement I am speaking of is more profound, however. And our first clue of this is the hieroglyph on the bridge. For it was there, in the woodcut image and Poliphilo's interpretation, that Aldus' printer's mark and motto appeared together for the first time. The mark, of course, is the dolphin and anchor, while the motto is σπεῦδε βραδέως, 'make haste slowly', rendered into Latin by Poliphilo as *festina tarde*.[19]

The story goes that the dolphin and anchor was an ancient emblem, standing for the motto; at some (indeterminate) point, Pietro Bembo gave Aldus a coin of the emperor Vespasian which bore it on the reverse (illus. 17).[20] But that story dates from as late as 1508 and its source is Erasmus, in whose celebrated collection of ancient proverbs, called the *Adagia*, the Greek motto was given the Latin translation by which it is best known: *Festina lente*. The first edition of the *Adagia* to feature this proverb was that published by Aldus when Erasmus was in Venice in 1508. According to the Dutch scholar, the adage had also been a favourite of the emperor Augustus, but its origins were in the most ancient philosophy, whereupon wise Egyptian priests encoded it in hieroglyphs with the symbol of the dolphin and anchor. The symbol had then been *decoded* in a book on hieroglyphs, since lost, written by Chaeremon of Alexandria (*fl.* first century CE), 'from whose works are excerpted, I suspect, the records of this sort of thing which I have seen lately'.[21]

The truth, however, is rather different. It is unlikely that Bembo's coin (in reality not a coin of Vespasian but of Vespasian's

17 Denarius of Titus (reverse), 80 CE, silver. Bembo's coin would have resembled this.

son Titus) appeared on the scene before 1502. Meanwhile, Aldus had used the motto already in July 1498, in the preface to the Poliziano edition addressed to Marin Sanudo. His dedicatee had apparently been urging Aldus to hurry up ever since hearing that this volume was in the works: 'yet [to this urging] you add the Greek adage, *make haste slowly*.'²² In October 1499, in the dedication to Alberto Pio of (pseudo-)Proclus with Thomas Linacre's translation, published in the collection of ancient astronomical writers, Aldus for the first time made reference to the dolphin and anchor, though without explicit connection to the motto or indeed to any pictorial illustration:

> Although I know, Alberto my protector, that many charge me with the fault of slowness [*tarditas*] because I appear to put off much of what I have many times promised to produce for scholars, still we have reckoned that these complaints of the literati ought to be borne with equanimity, both because I can yet endure greater burdens so long as I am being useful, and also because I myself am my own best witness to the fact that – as they say one ought – I always have as my companions the dolphin and the anchor. For, while going slowly, we have produced a great deal and are doing so continually.²³

Two months later, Poliphilo wandered off the presses and into his mysterious quest, where, on the bridge, motto and device for the first time aligned. The dolphin and anchor would still have to wait until the second volume of *Poetae christiani veteres* (Ancient Christian Poets) in June 1502 for their first appearance as Aldus' printer's mark, however.²⁴ Motto (in Greek) and device featured together on a portrait medal of Aldus, first cast around 1503/4 (see illus. 30 and 31). For at least the space of time in between – and, considering the medal's limited circulation, probably longer – the *Hypnerotomachia Poliphili* would have been the only means available for directly deciphering the aquatic image.[25]

The brief chronology of adoption I have sketched illuminates some key issues surrounding Colonna's work, its date and Aldus' role in it. To sum up: when Aldus first invoked the motto, citing Sanudo's counsel, he did so without the device, and by the time he publicly adopted the device in the letter to Alberto Pio, the *Hypnerotomachia Poliphili* – with the hieroglyphic woodcut and the Latin translation using *tarde/tarditas* – was already in press.[26] The *Polifilo* and not the Roman coin was the printer's mark's immediate prototype. This fact is evident even in minor details: for instance, the anchors in all versions of the printed device feature triangular flukes (the pointed projections at the end of the arms), unlike on the coin – triangular flukes were a medieval innovation unknown in antiquity – but precisely like in the *Polifilo*. By contrast, the medal, likely cast after Bembo's gift, more closely resembles the coin. Our recovered story also suggests that the text of the *Hypnerotomachia Poliphili* was open for alteration until the very last stages. Of course we cannot know when Colonna decided to include an encounter for Poliphilo with the dolphin and anchor. He may well have seen the image on a coin (they aren't rare); though, if he did, fealty was no requirement and, whether in an attempt to render a frieze or from a need to fit the available space, the artist, probably in concert with Aldus or the compositor, was also free to turn it on its side. But that he did not come at the Aldine motto independently – that is, that Colonna is not the source for both – is clear from the incongruity between Poliphilo's interpretations of the two hieroglyphic panels on the bridge: the first is an oracular saying, interpreted in the form of a Latin epigraph, totally in keeping with Colonna's usual style; the second, the Aldine motto, is a Greek adage of ancient provenance. It must therefore have been after its use by Aldus in 1498 that Colonna chose to append it to the device. To this reconstruction, Erasmus offers support. His claim to have recently seen the emblem elucidated in extracts of Chaeremon's lost work on hieroglyphs has often been understood as a cryptic, playful allusion to the *Polifilo*, to which he must have been exposed during his Venetian residence in 1508, but in fact it was an allusion to the real origins. We would do well to take more seriously the relationship between the printer and his most famous book.

There is still more. As an Aldine publication, the *Hypnerotomachia Poliphili* now appears an outlier. But, around 1499, the very idea of what an Aldine publication might be was in a state of flux. As we have seen, the Greek-dominated, Aristotle-led publication programme that had been the press's *raison d'être* was starting to falter: 1500 saw no new Greek editions. There was, as yet, no Latin programme, and, even once there was, it would be many years before that satisfied (if it ever fully did) the *padrone* and the scholarly audience with which he always identified. Aldus published very few books with illustrations, though the astronomical texts published earlier in 1499 had also been decorated with woodcuts, albeit of lower quality. Still, the stripped-back aesthetic, to which the *Polifilo* is so antithetical, was really a product of the octavo age after 1501. Aldus published no other book that gave such attention to architecture: there was no Aldine Vitruvius, for example, let alone a modern like Alberti. Yet we know, with regard to printing, how concerned he was with the distinction between the mechanical and the liberal arts, between the work of the hand and the work of the mind. With regard to architecture, these were preoccupations of the *Polifilo*'s author too. Thus, for the second part of this chapter, the hieroglyph on the bridge will be our anchor. Proof of the work's openness, can it also be so of its importance? If we explore further the relationship between Aldus and this most remarkable book, what other resonances might we find? And what might their significance be for how we understand the printer's thinking about his art amidst those of others?

THIRTEEN FOLIOS BEFORE ARRIVING on the bridge and deciphering the hieroglyph – before being chased by the dragon through the labyrinth and into the *locus amoenus* – Poliphilo emerges from a cleft in the steep wooded hills to find himself before a partly ruined but awe-inspiring structure (illus. 18). Its massive square base running six *stadía* a side is hewn from the living rock and stretches uninterrupted across the valley. The base supports an enormous pyramid culminating at the top of 1,410 steps in an obelisk surmounted by a hollow metal statue of a nymph, which rotates and resounds with the wind. There is no way past except through the single portal in the centre of the structure. Poliphilo is left 'witless with wonder' by the immense obelisk, but also by the outstanding nature 'of the subtlety of the rich and sharp intelligence and of the great care and exquisite industry' of the man identified in Greek on a bronze tablet (but also in Latin in the book) at the obelisk's base as 'Lichas the Libyan, architect'.[27] Before the structure is a large forecourt strewn with fragments of columns and sculptures. There are also two colossal monuments: a winged horse in bronze, its base clad in inscriptions and reliefs, and an elephant of black stone, hollowed out and containing two ancient tombs featuring male and female nudes and cryptic instructions written in Hebrew, Greek and Latin. After exploring and extolling these fascinating creations, Poliphilo returns to the ancient portal, 'marvellously constructed with exquisite rule and art, magnificent ornamentations of sculpture [*scalptura*], and variety of lineament', where he is 'eager and aflame with pleasure at the chance to contemplate the fertile intellect and penetrating mind of the discerning architect'.[28] He ponders the portal's admirable symmetry and begins to lament the decline of architecture in his own time. At length he lists the measurements and ratios of the extravagant construction.

Architecture and exotica like this take clear inspiration from Pliny the Elder's *Natural History*, specifically Book 36, which is

18 Portal, pyramid and obelisk, woodcut from Francesco Colonna,
Hypnerotomachia Poliphili (1499).

dedicated to stone and its uses. For instance, the pyramid-and-obelisk complex appears modelled on Pliny's accounts of the Mausoleum at Halicarnassus and, perhaps especially, of the tomb at Clusium of Etruscan king Lars Porsenna: a massive labyrinth, pyramids stacked on pyramids, a brazen globe and giant wind chimes. But these superficial resemblances reveal deeper differences. Colonna tends to praise ecstatically what Pliny deplored in equally emotional tones of moral censure. Even more significant is the very different notion of artistic responsibility. Of the Etruscan monstrosity, the Roman had declared, 'What insane folly, to have sought glory with an outlay of no benefit to anyone, to have exhausted the resources of the kingdom besides, and, after all this, that the craftsman [*artifex*] would get the greater share of the praise!'[29] Decrying in a similar vein another morally suspect building, the revolving theatres built at Rome for the games of C. Scribonius Curio, Pliny wondered out loud whether it was the patron who gave the orders or the architect who followed them who ought to be the greater object of amazement and indeed of blame for having successfully enticed the Roman people to put their lives at risk in this fantastical machine.[30] These two cases and the language used reveal how, to Pliny, architecture expressed the mind of the patron, whom he even called *inventor* or *auctor*, and not that of the architect or *artifex*.[31] As an *inventor*'s will was impressed upon his invention, so too, in Pliny's parallelism, was it upon the craftsman. The ambitious statesman sought to excite and impress through a dangerous extravagance; the Plinian architect followed orders.

The architect of the *Hypnerotomachia Poliphili* does not. Unlike Porsenna's mausoleum or Curio's theatres, whose architects go unnamed, here the only name provided is that of Lichas, and it is the architect's mind that Poliphilo seeks to know. Instead of a hierarchy between patron and artist, what we get is one between the arts. This is propounded within a lengthy discourse prompted by Poliphilo's encounter with the portal. No building can be satisfying unless it adheres to 'order and the norm' (*ordine e la norma*). Yet 'notwithstanding this, in order that the appearance will gratify the eye, the expert and assiduous architect can refine his work freely with additions and subtractions, granted that above all the solid whole is preserved and the entirety is harmonious': the fabric, says Poliphilo, 'demonstrates the superiority of his intelligence, because decorating afterwards is an easy business'.[32] The act of building itself is virtually absent from this vision, which jumps from an ideal conception in the mind to ornament on the structure's surface. The ornament, comprising what Poliphilo has called *scalptura*, is classed as decoration, subsidiary to the architect's work: 'the ordering, then, and the original invention are for rare men, and the more numerous everyday types – the regular dolts, in other words – are given the ornaments to work on.'[33] The discourse and chapter conclude with another equally pointed reiteration of these distinctions. It is 'the distribution of the solid matter and the determination of the universal fabric' that belongs to the architect, 'rather than the ornamentations, which are accessories to the chief concern': 'for the first thing, the abundant expertise of one man is alone required; but, for the second, contributions are necessary from many manual labourers or uneducated workmen (called *ergati* by the Greeks), who (as it is said) are the instruments of the architect.'[34]

Here too Colonna is not wholly an original. Beholden to Pliny for much of his most memorable edifice, he is even more indebted as a theorist to Leon Battista Alberti's treatise on architecture, *De re aedificatoria* (c. 1450, printed 1485). It was in part to Alberti that Poliphilo was referring ('as it is said') as the source for the idea that workmen are merely the architect's instruments – Alberti and also Aristotle, with whom the idea of workmen (and slaves) as tools in the hands of architects (and masters) originates.[35] He may be drawing on Plato too, and a passage in the dialogue *The*

Statesman where, in an analogy to a political ruler, an architect is
described not as a workman but as the ruler of workmen (ἐργατῶν
ἄρχων, *ergatôn árchōn*) – those *ergati* of Colonna's transliteration.[36]
Alberti had advised that a building's sculptural surface orna-
mentation be tasked to 'the many hands of average craftsmen
[*mediocrum artificum*]'.[37] The novelty of Colonna is his equation of
these craftsmen with common workmen. Colonna also drew on
Alberti's distinctive moral outlook. Compared to Pliny, bothered
by corruption of nature and materials, Alberti is more concerned
with decorum and personal morality. These are preoccupations
inherited from the Roman rhetorical tradition so familiar to this
humanist and so useful in his efforts to make the arts liberal. In
a famous passage from his architectural treatise, Alberti breaks
with the requirement of Vitruvius, his own ancient source, for
an architect to exhibit mastery over a large number of disciplines,
and instead emphasizes aptitude, character and moral qualities:

> He who dares to call himself an architect must be endowed
> with the highest natural ability, the most eager application,
> the best learning, and the greatest experience . . . For him
> levity, obstinacy, ostentation and immoderate behaviour
> are to be avoided entirely, as too is anything that may
> lessen the good favour and increase the contempt of his
> fellow citizens.[38]

Following his model, Colonna's Poliphilo enumerates qualities
in a similar way. But a comparison of the two passages reveals a
key difference: 'Beyond his learning, [the architect] should be
good, moderate in speech, kind, benevolent, mild, patient, good-
humoured, rich in ideas, a careful investigator, universal in interests, and slow [*tardo*] – slow, I say, so as not to be hasty [*festino*] in
error afterwards.'[39] The final quality, so emphatically articulated,
has no precedent or correlate in Alberti. Instead, its message is

what Poliphilo will shortly have confirmed by the hieroglyph at the bridge: *semper festina tarde*. Going beyond available architectural discourse, Poliphilo–Colonna reaches for the Aldine motto. To put it another way, what he suggests is that *an architect ought to be like Aldus*.

But this passage does still more. While instructing an architect to be like Aldus, it also implies that Aldus is like an architect – at least as that figure appears in the *Polifilo*: not a manual labourer; detached from the exercise of craftsmanship; conceiver and sole author of a project realized by human instruments. It was not the first time these thoughts had crossed someone's mind. In the Bologna university address he gave around four years previous, when he singled out Aldus Manutius for his contribution to Greek studies, Urceo Codro had classed him and Janus Lascaris (who had been an editor–publisher, never actually a printer) 'not [as] craftsmen [*artifices*] but leaders [*auctores*] of craftsmen and, as I say, learned architects and men of great honesty'.[40] This turn of phrase is actually a translation of the passage from Plato's *Statesman* from which Colonna also appears to have drawn inspiration, with what Colonna borrowed from Greek as *ergati* rendered into Latin as *artifices* instead.[41] Aldus was dedicating the second volume of Greek epistolographers to Codro in April 1499, when the *Hypnerotomachia Poliphili* was already in the printer's shop. While the lack of any surviving manuscript of Codro's text makes it impossible to tell whether Aldus had read the subsequently printed address by then (if at all), let alone whether Francesco Colonna somehow knew of it, its existence proves that this way of thinking about Aldus was possible precisely within his scholarly circles. We have already established how late the references to Aldus' motto must have entered Colonna's text and probably there been joined to the dolphin-and-anchor device: it was almost certainly in the last months before publication. To insert the motto into the most theoretical section of the work – in effect to associate Aldus with Poliphilo's ideology of architecture – ought therefore to be understood as an intentional act. Architecture, as recognized by Codro, offered a way of understanding the role of a publisher whose contributions lay in scholarship but whose works only made it into print through the craftsmanship of others. The decision to introduce the motto into the *Polifilo* when it was under Aldus' supervision suggests that Aldus recognized this too. The relationship between architect and workman could offer him and his humanist colleagues a model for thinking about publishing that prized intellectual labour over manual craft. It was a model that allowed for a humanist printer-publisher with no mechanical expertise to distinguish himself from the artful master printers who were by other standards his peers and from the *ergati* who worked in his shop alike.

Further evidence in support of this view is found in the way the terminology of the arts is shared between the *Hypnerotomachia Poliphili* and Aldus' own writing. Colonna had made the art of *scalptura* subsidiary to architecture: in his work the practitioner of this art, on whose 'ornamental' surface-works Poliphilo goes on to gaze with admittedly no less admiration and extolls in a tone of no less rapture, is referred to simply as the *artifice*, or craftsman. The architect, *contra* Pliny but as Codro too had recognized, is therefore not a craftsman but his superior. This word for craftsman – *artifex* in Latin – was the term Aldus used when treating his fellow master printers who lacked his scholarly credentials. In his preface to Niccolò Perotti's *Cornucopiae*, published less than six months before the *Polifilo* and therefore with Colonna's text in the shop, Aldus deployed it pointedly in a lament for how his peers' motivation for profit and evident lack of concern for the treasures they were ill-equipped to appreciate had corrupted the potential of 'this wonderful, this most exceedingly laborious way of writing books': 'we see in the hands of what kind of *artifices* the sacred monuments of literature have fallen!'[42] Reading this

preface in light of the other texts surrounding him in that
moment helps us see the two-pronged point Aldus is making: distinguishing himself from the others in kind (as a scholar instead
of a tradesman) but also in status (as an 'architect' instead of a
craftsman).

The word *scalptura*, meanwhile, has the most interesting res-
onance. A term associated mainly with surface work (versus the
more deeply cut or free-standing *sculptura*), along with its verbal
forms it refers in the *Polifilo*, as elsewhere, primarily to sculpture
in low relief.[43] It was used for the hieroglyph of the dolphin and
anchor, and, in one case, to characterize two words displayed in
'perfect Attic majuscules' under the upper cornice of the pedi-
ment of our portal (illus. 19).[44] But it resurfaces at the critical
juncture in Aldus' career, in what is probably one of the most
significant – and, among the significant, certainly one of the short-
est – pieces of writing in the history of print: Aldus' epigram on
his Virgil edition of April 1501. It appeared as a preface to the
volume that represented the launching of both the classical literary Latin publishing programme and the octavo volume printed
in italic type. The epigram was titled simply 'In Praise of the
Punchcutter', or *grammatoglypta*, Greek for 'sculptor of letters', and
in three Phalaecian hendecasyllables it celebrated the craftsmanship of Francesco Griffo, the man who had cut every type that
Aldus had employed (see illus. 27):

> Behold, Aldus, who gave them to the Greeks,
> now gives to the Latins letters carved [*scalpta*]
> by the Daedalean hands of Francesco of Bologna.[45]

The word choice fits the metre – *incisa*, say, would have been awk-
ward – but is notable still, given that Griffo was, of course, a
metalworker.[46] The tone is laudatory, and in fact Francesco Griffo
is the only non-scholar and non-patron that in his prefaces Aldus

19 Attic majuscules *in sculptura*, woodcut from Francesco Colonna,
Hypnerotomachia Poliphili (1499).

ever credits for anything by name. Evidently he was proud of what Griffo had accomplished for him. But this makes even more striking his deployment of the epithet 'Daedalus'. There was, as we have seen, good precedent behind this name: it was how Nicolas Jenson, Aldus' great predecessor, had referred to himself. Yet with this epigram Aldus assigned it to the hands of one of his own craftsmen. In the context of a workshop, run hierarchically, this represented a diminishment in the status of skill: its consignment to the realm of the *artifice* rather than the architect. As in the *Polifilo*, moreover, *scalptura* here is not really the craftsman's possession either. His hands are instrumental, and, despite the praise for what those hands could achieve, the letters they produce are unambiguously in Aldus' gift. Daedalus, once the master, was being demoted.

Like the moment of happiness in the middle of a Zola novel when the seeds of everyone's downfall become suddenly, horribly visible, this epigram has been read as a harbinger of the breakdown in relations between Aldus and his punchcutter, a clash between labour and capital, or a tug-of-war between two different visions of the nascent notion of intellectual property. What it has not been seen as is a clue to the place of craft in the Aldine enterprise *on an ideological level*. When read alongside the *Hypnerotomachia Poliphili*, however, and viewed in the context of the lendings and borrowings between Aldus and Colonna's book, it takes on richer colours. It seems to tap into a cluster of ideas about the arts, with words of special valence in the early history of Venetian printing or with a wider presence in Renaissance thought bearing a new notion of the kind of art that printing was understood to be. Aldus may be seen to share something else with Poliphilo: neither, after all, was insensitive to craftsmanship, as long as it knew its place.

THE *HYPNEROTOMACHIA POLIPHILI* can be an intoxicating work, one that leads us into the category errors of its protagonist: declaring Aldus the 'architect of the book' in a material sense – because we have a more material notion of the art and tend metaphorically to speak of a book as having architecture – would be one of these. Rather than influences, I have spoken mainly of shared ideas, exchanges and resonances. That it not to say that the *Polifilo* is a 'template' for understanding Aldus or his enter-prise. In its linguistic eclecticism, it can be wildly and (for us) maddeningly inconsistent. The architect with whose supreme mind Poliphilo is enraptured is also characterized as *multiscio*, or 'knowledgeable of many things' – a new coinage in the vernacular derived from the Latin of Apuleius, but which in the work of the second-century writer often had ambiguous connotations, or served as a backhanded compliment: 'handy' in the mechanical arts or knowledgeable in how to do or make many *useful* things, but lacking in the true intelligence and wisdom of a philosopher.[47] This type of encyclopedic knowledge of *artes sellulariae* or mechanical craft – which Apuleius had dramatized through the image of the sophist Hippias making his own clothes, sandals, even his own strigil, 'like a Daedalus' – is antithetical to the qualities associated with the architect by Alberti and indeed by Colonna.[48] Though Aldus himself never published Apuleius, his appreciation of the word's connotations is evident from his adaptation of it in 1501 in the preface to his Latin grammar, where he condemned those seemingly all-knowing but fundamentally corrupt people who have not learned their morals with their letters.[49] Cicero had used *inscius* for the opposite of *artifex*, which may have provided support for Renaissance writers to associate the Apuleian *multiscius* with the latter.[50] Eclectic, copious, occasionally contradictory as his vocabulary may be, however, Colonna (possibly under the influ-ence of Apuleius) never describes the architect as Daedalean. He uses this word instead to characterize the workmanship of

a marvellously fashioned fountain (illus. 20), and in relation to other creations where the wonder is not in how they were conceived but in how they are wrought.[51] In other words, it serves as a quality associated not with architecture but with sculpture. This was the primary association of Daedalean art in Greek commentary and philosophical sources, which may explain Colonna's rare exhibition of consistency.[52] But, all the same, and not for the first time, it was a point on which he and his printer would align.

By 1503, and despite the misgivings of the scholarly philhellenic community, Aldus' Latin publishing programme had been

20 Fountain, *opera daedalea*, woodcut from Francesco Colonna, *Hypnerotomachia Poliphili* (1499).

established. The format spawned imitators, and in March of that
year, dismayed by the printers of Lyon who were now pirating his
editions and counterfeiting his italic type, Aldus issued a printed
warning. The danger was that the unsuspecting would fall for
the superficial resemblance and end up with an inferior product
– to their own loss but also to Aldus', in money and reputation.
Readers were alerted to various inadequacies that they would
find in these unattributed imitations: paper with an unpleasant
odour, misshapen lettering bespeaking a certain distasteful but
unmistakable 'Frenchness', lack of ligatures between consonants
and vowels (a sign of relative lack of sorts, but also of lack of philological concern for articulating individual morphemes), smudgy
ink and, of course, errors.[53] For the benefit of scholars – and,
predictably, of the counterfeit printers themselves – Aldus provided a list of corrections to some of the major Latin authors. He
also set forth the clear signs that for prospective readers would
distinguish his works from the rest:

> In all of their books, you will find neither the name of the
> printer, nor the place of printing, nor the date of issue.
> In all of ours, however, you will find it like so: 'At Venice,
> in the house of Aldus of Rome, on this or that date.'
> Likewise, no printer's marks are to be found in those ones;
> in ours there is a dolphin wrapped around an anchor, as
> you may see below.[54]

Thus, in the woodcut at the bottom of the page, was the symbol
first encountered by Poliphilo on the bridge canonized as the
guarantee of quality and of the scholarly and aesthetic values that
the Aldine Press embodied (illus. 21). Aldus' own encounter with
that symbol and with the *Hypnerotomachia Poliphili* was more significant than we have previously supposed. And it was an encounter
that, starting in 1502 but particularly from this public warning

onward, would leave its trace. For the warning, Aldus had the device reproduced in the format he most commonly used for editions in folio or in quarto. But, just as in the slightly squatter device used for his octavo volumes (and for Erasmus' *Adagia*, see illus. 5), the dolphin was twisted around the anchor, facing to its right. Some years later, confronting other, Florentine counterfeiters, Aldus' heirs would be adamant about the direction in which it faced.[55] The dolphin in the *Hypnerotomachia Poliphili*, however, had turned counterclockwise, to its left. In the case of the Florentine counterfeiters, it is reasonable to understand their reversal of the dolphin as the result of copying the image onto a woodblock of their own from a printed prototype. But if we think of the hieroglyph carved, like Griffo's italic, in *scalptura*, we might say that the trace Colonna's marvellous book left on the Aldine Press was its own printed image.

The traces of Griffo's Daedalean hands are found throughout the *Hypnerotomachia Poliphili*. Indeed, the exquisite typography is a great part of the book's visual appeal and enduring significance. In Aldus Manutius, Griffo had found an ideal partner for realizing his talents: it was in service of his particular agenda that the Bolognese punchcutter got to develop multiple Greek types, elegant romans and an entirely novel cursive, or italic font, about which we will hear more in the next chapter. In order to evoke contemporary handwriting and isolate morphemes – both priorities for his unusual, scholarly master – he created ligatures that enhanced the beauty of his creations and remain lasting testaments to his dexterity and ingenuity.[56] Yet another testament is that Aldus never found, or found the need for, a replacement. But their collaboration had nonetheless been based on divergent understandings of craft and creation.

This divergence burst out into the open with the public break between the printer and the punchcutter. Around four months after Aldus issued his warning against the printers of Lyon, another

Cum primum cœpi suppeditare studiosis bonos libros : id solum negocii fore mihi existimabã : ut optimi quiq́ libri & Latini:& Græci exirent ex Neacademia nostra quã emendatissimi:omnes q̃ ad bonas literas:bonas q̃ artes:cura:& ope nostra excitarentur. Verum longe aliter euenit.Tantæ molis erat Romanam condere linguam. Nam præter bella:quæ nescio quo infortunio eodem tempore cœperunt:quo ego hanc duram accepi prouinciam:atq̃ in hunc usq̃ diem perseue rantatia ut literæ iam septẽnium cum armis quodammodo strenue pugnare uideant:quater iam in ædibus nostris ab ope ris : & stipendiariis in me conspiratum est : duce malorum omnium matre Auaritia : quos Deo adiuuante sic fregi:ut ual de omnes pœniteat suæ perfidiæ. Restabat:ut in Vrbe Lugduno libros nostros & mendose excuderent:& sub meo nomi ne publicarent:in quibus nec artificis nomen:nec locum,ubi nam impressi fuerint,esse uoluerunt:quo incautos emptores fallerent:ut & characterum similitudine:& enchiridii forma decepti:nostra cura Venetiis excusos putarent . Quamobrem ne ea res studiosis damno:mihi uero & damno:& dedecori foret:uolui hac mea epistola oẽs:ne decipiantur,admonere:in frascriptis uidelicet signis. Sunt iam impressi Lugduni(quod scierim)characteribus simillimis nostris:Vergilius.Horatius Iuuenalis cum Persio.Martialis.Lucanus. Catullus cum Tibullo:& Propertio.Terentius.In quibus oibus nec est impresso ãis nomen:nec locus:in quo impressi:nec tẽpus,quo absoluti fuerint. In nostris uero omnibus sic est : Venetiis in ædibus Aldi Ro. illo:uel illo tẽpore.   Item nulla in illis uisuntur insignia. In nostris uel Delphinus anchora: inuolutus:ut in fra licet uidere. Præterea deterior in illis charta:& nescio quid graue olens. Characteres uero diligentius intuenti sapius: (ut sic dixerim)gallicitatem quandam. Grandiusculæ item sunt perquãdeformes. Adde q̃ uocalibus cõsonãtes non cõ nectuntur:sed separatæ sunt. In nostris pleraq̃ omnes inuicê coinexas:manum q̃ mentientes:operæpretium est uide re. Ad hæc hisce:quæ inibi uisuntur:incorrectionibus:non esse meos,facile est cognoscere. Nam in Vergilio Lugduni impresso in fine Epistolij nostri ante Bucolicaq̃ Tityrum, perperam impressum est: optimos quosq̃ autores : pro opti mos quosq̃. Et in fine librorum Aeneidos:in prima Epistolæ nostræ semipagina ad Studiosos extremo uersu male impressum est: maria omnie circũ:pro maria omnia circum.ubi etiam nulli accentus obseruantur:cum ego eam epistolam propterea composuerim:ut ostenderem:quo nam modo apud nostros utendum sit accentunculis. In Horatio:in mea Epistola:secundo uersu sic est excusum : Imprissis uergilianis operibus : pro impressis. Et tertio sic: Flaccum aggrsŝi:pro aggrsŝi. Grandiusculæ præterea literæ ante primam Oden primo:& secundo uersu sunt impressorio atramento supra: & infra:quasi linea conclusæ ptur̃piter. In Iuuenale in mea Epistola:tertio uersu est publicamus:pro publicamus. Et de cimo uersu : Vngues quæ fuos : pro ungues q̃ suos. Item in prima semipagina : Semper & assiduo ruptæ rectore : pro lectore. In eadem. Si nacarũ& placidi rationem admittitis:eadem : pro edam. Et paulopost. Cum tenet uxorem:pro te ner. Item inibi : Eigat aprum:pro figat. In Martiale statim in principio primæ semipaginæ est impressum literis gran diusculis:sic AMPHITEATRVM:pro AMPHITHEATRVM. Et in eadem. Quæ tam se posita : pro seposita. Item in Libro secundo ad Seuerum deest græcum ιϱχτϰαλιϰϱ́. Et in Candidum:ubiq̃ deest græcum:idest κϱϱ̃ι φιλϱϲ πϱ́ϰτϱ. Et in fine : καιϱ̃ φιλϱϲ. In Lucano nulla est epistola in principio:at in meo maxime. In fine Ca tulli eam:quæ in meo est:epistolam prætermiserunt.Quæ etiam possunt esse signa Lugduni:ne:an Venetiis mea cura im pressi fuerint. Terentium etsi egô nondum curaui imprimendum:tamen Lugduni una cum cæteris sine cuiusquam no mine impressus est:Quod ideo factum est:ut emptores meum esse:& libri paruitate:& characterum similitudine:existiã in tes:deciperentur. Sciunt enim quem nos in pristinam correctionê:seruatis etiam metris:restituedum curamus:in summ᷒a esse expectatione:& propterea suum edere accelerarunt:sperãtes ante eum uenisdatumiri:q̃ emittatur meus. Sed q̃ ili᷒. emê datus exierit:uel hinc cognoci pot᷒iq̃ statim in principio fic est impressum:EPITAPHIVM TER MI᷒ pro Terentii. Item Bellica prædia sui : pro præda. Et : Hæc quinq̃ leget:pro quicunq̃. Præterea in principio secund᷒... char tæ. Acta ludis Megalensibus.M. Fuluio ædilibus.&.M.Glabrione.Q.Minutio Valerio curulibus:pro.M. Glabrione. Qu.Minutio Valerio ædilibus curulibus.Quod etiam putates esse argumentũ:impresseruñ. ARGVMENTVM. ANDRIAE. Ante etiam Sororem falso est.TERENTII ARGVMENTVM.cũ argumenta omnia Comœdiarũ Terentii : non Terêtius:sed Sulpitius Apollinaris cõposuerit.Sic enim in uetustissimis habetur codicibus.C.Sulpini Apol linaris periocha. Metra etiam confusa sunt omnia.Versus enim primæ scenæ:quæ tota trimetris constat:tã cĩ̃q̃ chaos in elementa:separati ab inuicem in suum locum sunt restituendi.

Si. Vos istæc intro auferte.abite.Sosia
   Ades dum:paucis te uolo. So. Dictum puta.
   Nempe:ut curentur recte hæc. Si. Immo aliud. So. quid est?
   Quod tibi mea ars efficere hoc possit amplius?&c.

Item secunda scena:cuius tres primi uersus sunt trimetri.Quartus tetra
meter. Quintus dimeter:& cæteri omnes quadrati : sic cĩ̃: debet.

Si. Non dubium est : quin uxorem nolit filius . ·
   Ita Dauum modo timere sensi:ubi nuptias
   Futuras esse audiuit. sed ipse exit foras.
Da.Mirabar hoc si sic abiret:& heri semper lenitas
   Verebar quorsum euaderet.
   Qui postquam audiuit non datum:iri fillio uxorem suo:
   Nunquam cuiquam nostrum uerbum fecit:neq̃ id ægre tulit.
Si. At nunc faciet:neq̃(ut opinor)sine tuo magno malo.
Da.Id uoluit:nos sic opinantes duci falso gaudio:
   Sperantes iam amoto metu:interea oscitantes obprimi:
   Ne esset spatium cogitandi ad disturbandas nuptias.
   Astute.Si.Carnifex quæ loquit̃.D Herus est:neq̃ p̃uideram &c.

Qua in re quantus sit mihi labor:cogi᷒ ut:qui intelligút . Certe pluri
mum die:noctu᷒q̃ elaboramus.

Hæc publicada iussi:mus:ut q̃ libellos enchiridia forma excusos emptu
tus est:ne decipiatur:facile·n.cognosce:Venetiis:ne in ædibus nostris
impressi fuerint:an Lugduni. Vale. Venetiis.xvi. Martii.M.D.III.

21 Aldus' warning against the printers of Lyon, 1503.

Voi, ch'ascoltate in rime sparse il suono
Di quei sospiri, ond'io nudriua il core
In sul mio primo giouenile errore,
Quand'era in parte altr'huom da quel, ch'i sono;
Del uario stile, in ch'io piango et ragiono
Fra le uane speranze e'l uan dolore;
Oue sia, chi per proua intenda amore,
Spero trouar pietà, non che perdono.
Ma ben ueggi'hor, si come al popol tutto
Fauola fui gran tempo: onde souente
Di me medesmo meco mi uergogno:
Et del mio uaneggiar uergogna e'l frutto,
E'l pentirsi, e'l conoscer chiaramente
Che quanto piace al mondo è breue sogno.

Per far una leggiadra sua uendetta,
Et punir in un di ben mille offese,
Celatamente amor l'arco riprese,
Com'huom, ch'a nocer luogo et tempo aspetta.
Era la mia uirtute al cor ristretta;
Per far iui et ne gliocchi sue difese,
Quando'l colpo mortal là giu discese,
Oue solea spuntarsi ogni saetta.
Pero turbata nel primero assalto
Non hebbe tanto ne uigor ne spatio,
Che potesse al bisogno prender l'arme;
O uero al poggio faticoso et alto
Ritrarmi accortamente da lo stratio;
Del qual hoggi uorrebbe, et non po aitarme.

ii

22 Pietro Bembo's copy of the Aldine Petrarch, with Griffo's first
italic: *Le cose volgari di Messer Francesco Petrarcha* (Venice, 1501).

SONETTO   I

    Oi;ch'ascoltate in rime sparse il sono
v   *Di quei sospiri, ond'io nodriua il core*
    in sul mio primo giouenil errore,
Quãd'era i pte altr'hom da quel, ch'io sono,
Del vario stil, in ch'io piango & ragiono
    Fra le vane speranze e'l van dolore
    Oue sia, chi per proua intenda amore,
    Spero trouar pieta, non che perdono.
Ma ben veggi'hor, si come al popul tutto
    Fauola fui gran tempo : onde souente
    Di me medesmo meco mi vergogno :
Et del mio vaneggiar vergogna è il frutto,
    E'l pentirsi, e'l cognoscer chiaramente
    Che quanto piace al mondo è breue sogno.

SONETTO   II

Per far vna leggiadra sua vendetta,
    Et punir in vn di ben mille offese,
    Celatamente amor l'arco riprese,
    Com'hom, ch'a nocer luogo & tẽpo aspetta.
Era la mia virtute al cor ristretta
    Per far iui & ne gliocchi sue difese,
    Quand' il colpo mortal la giu discese,
    Oue solea spuntarsi ogni saetta.
Pero turbata nel primero assalto
    Non hebbe tanto ne vigor, ne spatio,
    Che potesse al bisogno prender l'arme;
O vero al poggio faticoso & alto
    Ritrarme accortamente dallo stratio;

                    a   ii

23 The Soncino Petrarch, with Griffo's second italic: *Opere volgari di Messer Francesco Petrarcha* (Fano, 1503).

printer, this time operating out of Fano on the Adriatic coast, issued a new edition of the *Rime* and *Trionfi* of Petrarch in italic type. This edition could not, however, be considered a counter-feit. In the first place, it was openly acknowledged by its publisher, the Jewish printer Gershom (Girolamo) Soncino (*c.* 1460–1534). Second, its italic letters were cut by the very same hands that had produced those for Aldus (illus. 22 and 23). In his dedicatory preface, printed in those characters and addressed to Cesare Borgia (1475–1507), son of Pope Alexander VI and ruler of Fano, Soncino explained his desire to bring together in his lord's city 'not common and base punchcutters and printers, but those more excellent than all the rest':

> And at my urging, not only have there come here com-positors as notable and capable as it is possible to call upon, but furthermore a most noble sculptor of Latin, Greek and Hebrew letters named Messer Francesco da Bologna, whose talent in this field I certainly believe to be without equal. For not only does he know perfectly how to do conventional printing, but he has even devised a new type of lettering called cursive, or rather *cancelleresca*, of which the first inventor and designer was not Aldus of Rome, nor the others who have cunningly tried to adorn themselves with *penne* [pens or plumes] that don't belong to them, but this Messer Francesco. It is he who has cut all the letter types that Aldus has ever printed, as well as the present type, with as much grace and beauty as in it can easily be perceived.[57]

Soncino's preface is, of course, a piece of advertising, yet through it we can also hear the frustration of the talented craftsman deprived not only of what he deemed just remuneration for the fruits of his labours, but also of just recognition for the fruits of his ingenuity. The matter went beyond his lack of legal protection for his invention: it was also a matter of artisanal pride. Perhaps the warning against the printers of Lyon, where Aldus had the audacity to claim the technical achievement of his types as a hallmark of his enterprise, distinguishing it from all others, sent him over the edge: how much difference, after all, was there between Aldus and the *Lyonnais*? By treating Griffo's metallic plumes as feathers in his cap, he was dishonestly laying claim to inventions that were not his own. The rift between Aldus and his punchcutter thus represents a climacteric in ideas of work, the nature of which our exploration of the *Hypnerotomachia Poliphili* has helped us see more clearly. Griffo could not accept his own instrumentalization, or an ideology that separated invention from ingenuity. Soncino, however, appears also to have appreciated the opportunity that the model of Aldus provided to be not one of the craftsmen but instead their master.

[Hebrew column]

ראשית
ברא
אלהים
את

השמים ואת הארץ: והארץ
היתה תהו ובהו וחשך על
פני תהום ורוח אלהים
מרחפת על פני המים: ויאמר
אלהים יהי אור ויהי אור: וירא
אלהים את האור כי טוב ו
ויבדל אלהים בין האור ובין
החשך: ויקרא אלהים לאור
יום ולחשך קרא לילה ויהי
ערב ויהי בקר יום אחד:
ויאמר אלהים יהי רקיע בתוך
המים ויהי מבדיל בין מים
למים: ויעש אלהים את
הרקיע ויבדל בין המים אשר
מתחת לרקיע ובין המים א
אשר מעל לרקיע ויהי כן:
ויקרא אלהים לרקיע שמים
ויהי ערב ויהי בקר יום שני:
ויאמר אלהים יקוו
המים מתחת השמים אל
מקום אחד ותראה היבשה
ויהי כן: ויקרא אלהים ליבשה
ארץ ולמקוה המים קרא
ימים וירא אלהים כי טוב:
ויאמר אלהים תדשא הארץ
דשא עשב מזריע זרע עץ פרי
עשה פרי למינו אשר זרעו בו
על הארץ ויהי כן: ותוצא
הארץ דשא עשב מזריע זרע
למינהו ועץ עשה פרי אשר
זרעו בו למינהו וירא אלהים
כי טוב: ויהי ערב ויהי בקר
יום שלישי: ויאמר
אלהים יהי מארת ברקיע
השמים להבדיל בין היום
ובין הלילה והיו לאתת
ולמועדים ולימים ושנים: והיו
למאורת ברקיע השמים
להאיר על הארץ ויהי כן: ו

[Greek column]

Ἐν ἀρχῇ ἐποίησεν ὁ θεὸς
τὸν οὐρανὸν καὶ τὴν γῆν. ἡ
δὲ γῆ ἦν ἀόρατος, καὶ ἀκατα-
σκεύαστος. καὶ σκότος ἐπάνω
τῆς ἀβύσσου. καὶ πνεῦμα θεοῦ ἐπεφέρε-
το ἐπάνω τοῦ ὕδατος. καὶ εἶπεν ὁ θεὸς
γενηθήτω φῶς. καὶ ἐγένετο φῶς. καὶ
εἶδεν ὁ θεὸς τὸ φῶς ὅτι καλόν. καὶ
διεχώρισεν ὁ θεὸς ἀναμέσον τοῦ
φωτὸς καὶ ἀναμέσον τοῦ σκότους. καὶ
ἐκάλεσεν ὁ θεὸς τὸ φῶς ἡμέραν, καὶ
τὸ σκότος ἐκάλεσεν νύκτα. καὶ ἐγένετο ἑσπέρα καὶ ἐγένετο πρωὶ ἡμέρα
μία. Καὶ εἶπεν ὁ θεὸς γενηθήτω
στερέωμα ἐν μέσῳ τοῦ ὕδατος. Καὶ ἔστω
διαχωρίζον ἀναμέσον ὕδατος καὶ ὕδατος.
καὶ ἐγένετο οὕτως. καὶ ἐποίησεν ὁ θεὸς
τὸ στερέωμα. καὶ διεχώρισεν ὁ θεὸς ἀναμέσον τοῦ ὕδατος ὃ ἦν ὑποκάτω τοῦ στερεώματος, καὶ ἀναμέσον τοῦ ὕδατος τοῦ ἐπάνω τοῦ
στερεώματος. καὶ ἐκάλεσεν ὁ θεὸς τὸ
στερέωμα οὐρανόν. καὶ εἶδεν ὁ θεὸς ὅτι καλόν.
καὶ ἐγένετο ἑσπέρα καὶ ἐγένετο πρωὶ ἡμέρα
δευτέρα . Καὶ εἶπεν ὁ
θεὸς συναχθήτω τὸ ὕδωρ τὸ ὑποκάτω τοῦ
οὐρανοῦ εἰς συναγωγὴν μίαν, καὶ ὀφθήτω
ἡ ξηρά. καὶ ἐγένετο οὕτως. καὶ συνήχθη τὸ ὕδωρ
τὸ ὑποκάτω τοῦ οὐρανοῦ εἰς τὰς συναγω-
γὰς αὐτῶν, καὶ ὤφθη ἡ ξηρά. καὶ ἐκάλεσεν ὁ θεὸς τὴν ξηρὰν γῆν,
καὶ τὰ συστήματα τῶν ὑδάτων
ἐκάλεσεν θαλάσσας. καὶ εἶδεν ὁ θεὸς ὅτι καλόν. καὶ εἶπεν ὁ θεός. βλαστησάτω ἡ γῆ βοτάνην χόρτου σπεῖρον σπέρμα κατὰ γένος
καὶ καθ' ὁμοιότητα. καὶ ξύλον κάρπιμον ποιοῦν
καρπὸν οὗ τὸ σπέρμα αὐτοῦ ἐν αὐτῷ κατὰ γένος ἐπὶ τῆς γῆς. καὶ ἐγένετο οὕτως. καὶ ἐξήνεγκεν
ἡ γῆ βοτάνην χόρτου σπεῖρον σπέρμα κατὰ γένος καὶ καθ' ὁμοιότητα. καὶ ξύλον κάρπιμον ποιοῦν καρπὸν οὗ τὸ σπέρμα αὐτοῦ ἐν
αὐτῷ κατὰ γένος ἐπὶ τῆς γῆς. καὶ εἶδεν ὁ θεὸς ὅτι καλόν. καὶ ἐγένετο ἑσπέρα καὶ ἐγένετο πρωὶ
ἡμέρα τρίτη. Καὶ εἶπεν ὁ θεός. γενη-
θήτωσαν φωστῆρες ἐν τῷ στερεώματι τοῦ
οὐρανοῦ εἰς φαῦσιν ἐπὶ τῆς γῆς, τοῦ διαχω-
ρίζειν ἀναμέσον τῆς ἡμέρας καὶ ἀναμέσον
τῆς νυκτός. καὶ ἔστωσαν
εἰς σημεῖα καὶ εἰς καιρούς. καὶ εἰς ἡμέρας.
καὶ εἰς ἐνιαυτούς. καὶ ἔστωσαν εἰς φαῦσιν
ἐν τῷ στερεώματι τοῦ οὐρανοῦ. ὥστε
φαίνειν ἐπὶ τῆς γῆς. καὶ ἐγένετο οὕτως.

[Latin column]

IN principio creauit
deus cœlum, & ter-
ram. terra autê erat
inanis, & uacua, &
tenebræ erant super faciem abyssi,
& spiritus domini ferebatur super
aquas. dixitq; deus fiat lux, & facta
é lux . et uidit deus lucem, quod
esset bona, & diuisit lucem a tene
bris, appellauitq; lucé diem, & te
nebras noctem, factumq; est uespe
re & mane dies unus.   Dixit
quoq; deus fiat firmamentum in
medio aquarum, & diuidat aquas
ab aquis, & fecit deus firmamêtum
diuiditq; aquas, quæ erant sub fir
mamento ab iis, quæ erant super fir
mamêtu, & factum é ita. uocauitq;
deus firmamêtu cœlum & factum
est uespere & mane dies secundus.
Dixit uero deus, congregentur
aquæ quæ sub cœlo sût in locum
unum, & appareat arida, & factu
é ita, & uocauit deus aridam ter
ram, & congregationes aquaru ap
pellauit maria, & uidit deus qp eét
bonum, & ait germinet terra herbá
uirentem & faciétem semen, & li
gnum pomiferum faciés fructum
iuxta genus suú, cuius femen in se
metipso sit sup terram, & factum
é ita, & ptulit terra herbam uiren
tem, & faciétem femé iuxta genus
suum, lignumq; faciés fructum,
& habens unú quodq; femété se
cúdum speciem suam. et uidit de
us qp esset bonum . & factum é ue
spere & mane dies tertius.   Dixit
át deus fiant luminariain firmamê
to cæli, & diuidant dié, ac nocté,
& sint in signa, & tépora, & dies, &
ános, & luceant in firmamêto cœli
& illuminent terrá, et factú est ita.

THREE

Divine Impressions

his chapter presents what is a novel theme in a book on Aldus Manutius. None but the most timid or most stubborn of authors could resist being drawn in some form or another on the *Hypnerotomachia Poliphili*. By contrast, Aldus' monumental edition of the letters of St Catherine of Siena is mostly overlooked. This is despite the fact that it belonged to the very same transformative period of Aldus' production – was the very next publication, no less – and shared with Francesco Colonna's work the rare distinction of being undertaken with explicit backing from outside the firm. Like the *Polifilo*, Catherine's letters were also written in an Italian vernacular – as different as could be, though likewise distinct from the canonical *volgar lingua* that was soon to squeeze out literary alternatives. But whereas, with Colonna, the publishing privilege granted by the Venetian Signoria was held by Leonardo Crasso and Aldus was ostensibly silent except for the wry self-identification on the page of corrections, with Catherine Aldus held the ten-year privilege himself.[1] The volume even included a full dedicatory preface issued in Aldus' own voice. It represents an important stage in the textual tradition of the letters. The *Polifilo* is often taken as the paradigmatic work of Venetian Renaissance antiquarian culture, yet there is a case for seeing the Catherine edition as even more 'Venetian' than its counterpart: the city had been the driving force behind the cult.

24 Trial sheet for an Aldine polyglot Bible (before September 1504).

Why, then, has it been so overlooked? Frankly, I believe the answer is to be found in the role that religion still plays in the way we divide up the past. We struggle to account for its complexity and its non-linear nature, and therefore permit the character of religious practice and belief to carve those complexities into the simplified chunks we call Middle Ages, Renaissance and Reformation (or indeed early modernity). Humanists, we allow, were not necessarily, or not even very often, irreligious. They appreciated especially the Church Fathers for the example they offered of a Christianity compatible with eloquence, with the modes of expression, argument and thought of the ancient world. But they despised the style and methods of the medieval schoolmen. Their own methods were secular. When they thought about religion, they thought mainly in terms of morals and ethics. Some, like Lorenzo Valla, Erasmus and Thomas More, thought very seriously indeed about such things as ecclesiology (the nature and structure of the Church) or biblical scholarship, but as there is a qualitative difference between these matters and popular religious expression, their humanist credentials are undamaged, even enhanced, by their *apologiae* and invectives. If anything, and despite themselves, they herald the new religious world of a Reformation that those here named who lived to see it opposed. Did not Erasmus mock medieval popular devotions and the cults and legends of the saints as embarrassing superstition?[2] Meanwhile, for scholars of medieval (and early modern) religion in all its richness, the humanists are generally either a bunch of dyspeptic killjoys, an irrelevance (except in their capacity as educationalists or to the extent that their methods, honed on classical texts, led to wider critique), or an epiphenomenon (which, after all, didn't turn so many unlettered heads anyway). Often they and their works simply serve as the interface where power met popular culture, where commonly held beliefs were dressed up and made presentable. Like Vasari in his disappointment with the late Botticelli, we cultural historians of the revival of antiquity are often guilty of waning interest when our protagonists come down with old-time religion. In this respect, the pagan, erudite *Hypnerotomachia Poliphili* has the same advantages as the painter's *Primavera*. Source bases and skill sets all conspire to entrench these divisions and turn our fields away from what was shared. The result is that we underappreciate the humanists' investment not only in the pristine origins of their faith or the accuracy of their sacred texts, but in the living religious culture of their day.

This imagined divide has marginalized the Catherine edition from the rest of Aldine scholarship, and from the enterprise of humanist publishing more broadly. I myself have elsewhere argued for understanding Aldus as a sort of Christian humanist *avant la lettre*, promoting the notion that the reform and dissemination of letters by means of the printing press were prerequisites for the reform of religion and society in ways that influenced the ideas of Erasmus.[3] We saw how his first publication, the grammar of Constantine Lascaris, was prefaced by the invocation of the divine wrath that threatened Italy and the world, for which Greek language and scholarship would be antidote and salvation. In the early years of the press, he published a Book of Hours (1497) and a Psalter (before 1498), both in Greek, with either pedagogical motives or Venice's Uniate community (those Greek Christians in communion with Rome) in mind. His great unrealized project was the polyglot Bible, though it was the object of much anticipation in humanist circles and a trial sheet was produced (illus. 24).[4] A self-styled (if unlikely) successor to Pico della Mirandola, in 1501 he issued under his own name and as an appendix to his Latin grammar an introduction to Hebrew grammar, which may have been intended to signal a move to promoting and publishing a more philological, less esoteric kind of Christian Hebraism that ultimately never came. Gershom Soncino, who had been in Venice and was likely involved with the projected Bible around then, was later to claim that the grammar was his text too – adding further piquancy to the accusations of wrongful appropriation made against Aldus by Francesco Griffo, fanned by Soncino as the punchcutter's new employer.[5] Addressing himself to his fellow educators, Aldus regularly emphasized the importance of instruction in Christian morals, and in Christian literature as well. On a diet of good early Christian poets, the children in their charge would learn to distinguish truth from falsehood and, when it came time, know how to pick what was worthwhile from pagan poets and leave the rest, 'like roses from the thorns'.[6] This moral programme for humanist education does not entirely agree with what the *Musarum panagyris* suggested to us about Aldus' own methods in Carpi, but it would be echoed by Erasmus and by their fellow reforming educator John Colet (1467–1519), who, in his foundation statutes for London's St Paul's School (1512), insisted that the children be 'taught all way in good litterature both laten and greke, and goode auctors suych as haue the veray Romayne eliquence joyned withe wisdome[:] specially Cristyn auctours that wrote theyre wysdome with clene and chast laten other in verse or in prose'.[7] Many of those authors – Prudentius, Proba, Sedulius and Juvencus, among those on Colet's list – had been published by Aldus. Such an Aldus, with such publications, fits comfortably into a humanistic mainstream. Indeed, with respect to the mainstream of the early sixteenth century, he may be said to be one of its fathers.

Even so, Catherine is different. A fourteenth-century ascetic and mystic, a tertiary, or lay affiliate, of the Dominican order, Caterina Benincasa (1347–1380) was no humanist's model for moral education, exemplary behaviour, or 'veray Romayne eliquence'. Her charisma was entirely more bodily and visceral, defined by the physicality of her devotions and the scope and intensity of her activism. She did not write Latin; that she knew how to write at all was the product of a miracle. She experienced a mystical marriage to Christ, sealed with the ring of his foreskin. She practised extreme fasting, sucked a fetid sore and drank the pus from a cancerous ulcer, and campaigned incessantly for causes including the restoration of the Papacy from Avignon to Rome, the healing of the Western Schism, and the launching of a crusade, as well as an end to the so-called War of the Eight Saints (1375–8) between the Papacy and Florence and the suppression of the Ciompi revolt that broke out in that city afterwards. She was said to have received (invisible) stigmata. Controversial in her lifetime, she was canonized in 1461 by Pope Pius II – a humanist indeed, but more relevantly a fellow Sienese. Her most dramatic act, recounted in one of the very letters Aldus published, was comforting a condemned man on his way to execution, and then, at the foot of the scaffold, catching his severed head, becoming drenched in his blood.[8] She is a figure, perhaps the ultimate one, of the world of late medieval religious devotion and affective spirituality, associated with the mendicant orders and totally at aesthetic and ideological odds with the education- and philology-based reform movement promoted by Christian humanists. Martin Lowry saw the Catherine edition almost in a votive context, separate from the printer's programme in all but an instrumental way. He explained Aldus' publication of the volume as a form of 'atonement' for having printed the *Hypnerotomachia Poliphili*, and swiftly moved on.[9] In part, the point of this chapter is to remove the line between Renaissance humanism and medieval devotion that isolates the Christian humanist in Aldus from the medieval Christian and stops us from appreciating this edition within the ambit of his enterprise.

There is, of course, another thing that sets Catherine apart from almost all other writers published by Aldus Manutius, and that is her gender.[10] This near-solitary status is not altogether surprising in one sense, given the type of work Aldus tended to publish. Yet this break from the norm stands out further because the relationship between women and the humanist movement was such a vexed one. Despite the undoubted existence of 'learned ladies' in Renaissance Italy and the wider phenomenon of female patronage, humanism and masculinity were intrinsically bound. This is something that has been implicit in all our discussions so far with regard to humanism, printing and labour or work – and, indeed, the Carpi chapel fresco that we looked at showed how distinctions between different masculine types could be made with clothing – but it is time to address this issue more explicitly now. Though the relationship between humanism and maleness might seem self-evident, or at least determined socially and institutionally by the fact that it was encountered and promoted as an educational programme and that school (at least) was for boys, there was also an ideological element to it, which was intensified at the movement's more scholarly end. The rhetoric that emanated from the Aldine Press magnified the athletic heroism of the enterprise: Aldus' labours were 'Herculean', his burden like that of Atlas, his efforts and masculine activity standing in contrast to the enervated pleasure-seeking of the Assyrian Sardanapalus, byword for 'effeminacy'.[11] 'By Hercules!', exclaimed Erasmus in the 'Festina lente' essay, celebrating Aldus' achievement as he explained the dolphin-and-anchor device, 'an undertaking Herculean and worthy of a royal spirit, to restore to the world something so divine and almost entirely in ruins, to seek out what is hidden, to dig up what is concealed, to bring back the dead, to make whole the mutilated, to free from faults what has been in so many ways disfigured'.[12] The intellectual machismo behind the humanist project was stressed by Lisa Jardine, not only in her work on Erasmus – the humanistic Hercules par excellence – but also in her studies, sometimes undertaken alongside Anthony Grafton, on those few female humanists and the limits placed upon them, their treatment as wonders but not as colleagues, by dint of the fact that humanism, as educational programme and cultural practice, was gendered male: a male activity for male (professional and public) fashioning.[13]

This makes it all the more interesting that, in September 1500, Aldus Manutius used the work of a woman – and a modern (that is, a medieval) one at that – to launch the new typeface of humanism: the italic.

IN RECENT YEARS, Catherine of Siena has become the object of a major reappraisal. Now taken seriously as a writer (who surely dictated her works) and an activist, a fresh acknowledgement of her impact on the literary culture of the trecento has seen one leading scholar include her, alongside the traditional triumvirate of Dante, Petrarch and Boccaccio, and with the transplanted Bridget of Sweden, in an expanded 'Five Crowns' of fourteenth-century Italian literature.[14] The Aldine edition of her letters was certainly the primary way that later generations came to know her written legacy: it was this to which the Sienese *érudit* Orazio Lombardelli (1545–1608) was referring in his treatise on the sources of the Tuscan vernacular when he named the '368 letters of *la nostra santa Caterina* apart from those that have not yet seen the light' as evidence from the 'best age of the Tuscan language'.[15] And surely the prestige of the printer added to Catherine's suitability for inclusion on the reading lists of the literati, at least as far as the mid- to later sixteenth century was concerned.[16] In manuscript, too, the letters had previously circulated, often in the company of translations from ancient, tre- and early quattrocento Latin authors, in an arrangement that speaks to the sort of 'vernacular humanism' that existed alongside more consciously learned models in the fifteenth century, above all in Florence.[17] Some scholars have argued that this vernacular humanism, with its ethical commitment to the 'public life' reminiscent of a previous age, was what Aldus was trying to renew and promote in publishing these hortatory epistles. They have claimed that it represented a shift in his publishing programme 'from Greek and Latin texts to vernacular ones', with 'Catherine as an ideal authority by which to launch a transition from Latin to vernacular literature'.[18] The italic type, the small but significant appearance of which in the volume we will discuss shortly, is thus characterized as 'the type that would embody subsequent vernacular books'.[19]

Yet I would caution against understanding Aldus, his involvement in the Catherine project and its significance to him from the place of his edition on a continuum between the literary cultures of the fifteenth century and the later sixteenth. In the first place, it is not fair to characterize the period after the Catherine edition of 1500 as representing a shift to the vernacular. On the contrary, it represented a shift *to Latin* – which, as we saw, Aldus and his colleagues were ambivalent about. It is the very next publication, rather, that represents the underappreciated landmark: Lucretius' *De rerum natura* (On the Nature of Things, December 1500) was the very first classical Latin literary work published by the press.[20] Even this edition reveals some discomfort at the prospect of turning away from Greek. Dedicated, like the volumes of Aristotle, to Alberto Pio, with a letter that emphasized the importance of the text for understanding Epicureanism, it was in effect published as philosophy; the second Aldine Lucretius edition (January 1515), in octavo and with a longer disclaimer against his 'lies', would be published as literature.[21] Catherine was not even the first vernacular author Aldus published: that honour went, of course, to Francesco Colonna and his *Hypnerotomachia Poliphili*. It is true that she preceded her fellow Tuscans Petrarch (July 1501) and Dante (August 1502), but these authors followed Virgil (April 1501) and Horace (May 1501) in being published in octavo and in italic. This would, if anything, have been seen to integrate them into a classical canon, not a specifically vernacular one. The novelty of these two editions was in the work of Pietro Bembo, their editor, to restore the fourteenth-century texts on the basis of early manuscripts – Petrarch's own, they believed – and in that of Aldus to provide them (especially Dante) without commentary.[22] In this form they (especially Petrarch) would become models for the *volgar lingua*, though both that day and Bembo's treatise on the subject were yet to come.

Aldus was certainly curious about the vernacular and, as befit a man of Lazio who lived in Venice and had spent many years in the Po Plain, perhaps especially about the differences between Italian dialects. He likened the situation in the vernacular to that found in ancient Greek, which had multiple literary dialects, and contrasted this welcome diversity and sheer linguistic abundance (*copia*) with its lack in Latin: 'if only in Latin we had such abundance!' he once wrote.[23] This was a striking move because his comparison was not strictly between Greek and Italian literary dialects but rather between the Greek and what he called the 'common tongue'. It was also an opinion that set him apart from other leading voices – first among them, Poliziano's. In the *Miscellanea*, his collected writings on philological problems, Poliziano had asserted that Latin was more *copiosa*, or at least no less, than Greek, which was merely more *lasciviens* (playful, licentious, frisky).[24] His was a moral argument as much as a linguistic one; indeed, the worth of Latin letters versus Greek is one of the *Miscellanea*'s persistent preoccupations. This, along with the fact that he would publish the *Miscellanea* in his 1498 edition of its author's works, suggests that, in associating *copia* with Greek and the vernacular but not with Latin, Aldus was consciously distancing himself from an intellectual idol in this respect. At the same time, he was repurposing and redirecting an earlier argument of Lorenzo Valla (*c.* 1407–1457), to whom Latin's superiority had been in its unity, which made it the expression of an eternal Roman empire (though Valla was himself pushing back against Cicero's very different idea: that Greek was a universal whereas Latin was a local language).[25]

Vernacular languages, Aldus recognized, had their own integrity, with their own 'rules of speech' just as Latin had: that was why, he insisted to the readers of his Petrarch, he wrote *volgari* instead of the Latinate *vulgari*, and *canzoni* (songs) for the plural instead of *canzone*. 'Any simple Tuscan knows that in this language you don't follow Latin in every respect,' he said, and 'if people don't believe me [that *canzone* is used for the singular], let them at least believe the poet, in whose hand I've seen it written here this way.'[26] Some years later, he spoke of Petrarch's vernacular 'eloquence' in company that included the ambassador of King Ferdinand II of Aragon.[27] But neither Aldus nor Bembo was the textual editor of the Catherine volume and there is none of this linguistic sensitivity on display: her fourteenth-century Sienese dialect is given a modern makeover.[28] For their part, civic humanism and the active life are rarely subjects of great concern for the man of Alberto Pio. And despite the volume's impact in the very different climate of the later cinquecento, when in Italy's academic and literary cultures the vernacular had become pre-eminent, such potential would have been lost on Aldus, who could not have conceived of this world and never sought it. One contemporary Venetian tradition of depicting Catherine was in the guise of a theologian.[29] This identification would agree with the large, folio format in which the edition was issued – instead of, say, in multiple parts in quarto as for the Greek epistolographers (1499) – and better suits the way the text was handled. The long-term prospects of the 'common tongue' would have been far from Aldus' mind when he brought Catherine's letters to press in these transitional, intellectually productive years.

In his dedication of the volume to Cardinal Francesco Todeschini Piccolomini (1439–1503), nephew of the late Pope Pius II and soon to be pope in his own right for a month as Pius III, Aldus described the letters of St Catherine as having been 'suppressed' for around 120 years. That was a conventional humanist trope, and, in this case, it wasn't actually true: not only did they circulate widely in manuscript, but some of them had even been printed. Yet the Aldine edition was the first attempt to present the corpus in its entirety. Indeed, we need only compare the 368 letters that Aldus counted to the 31 printed eight years previous at Bologna, in an edition issued with this apologetic postscript: 'It's true that this glorious virgin Catherine wrote many other letters to different people – prelates, religious and laymen and -women of different stations – but these are the only ones at present to have been collected.'[30] The Aldine edition shared its humble predecessor's concern with the recipients' station: the letters were not organized chronologically but by correspondent hierarchically, from popes and cardinals down. The most frequent addressee, with seventeen letters, was Raymond of Capua (*c.* 1330–1399), Catherine's confessor and disciple, who became master general of the Dominican order and wrote Catherine's life, the so-called *Legenda maior*. Certainly women do not have a privileged place in this edition, though strictly speaking it is only laymen (including kings and princes) who come before laywomen (including Queen Joanna I of Naples): religious women preceded them both. The effect of this ordering is to take Catherine 'out of time': to dehistoricize the letters and make their message both eternal and immediate. Dehistoricizing meant de-emphasizing the conflict that, in large part because of her gender, almost always accompanied her public mission. It was not the first time that the men handling Catherine's legacy had had to take this matter into account, with what we shall see are important consequences for our understanding of Aldus' key intervention in the book.

The letters were a co-publication, undertaken by Aldus with and perhaps sponsored entirely by Margarete Ugelheimer. She was the widow of Peter Ugelheimer (d. 1487/8), a Frankfurt native who had been the business partner of the great Nicolas Jenson, and subsequently executor of the late printer's estate.[31] After her

25 Fra Bartolomeo, *God the Father with Sts Mary Magdalene and Catherine of Siena*, 1509, oil on panel (transferred).

husband's death, she stayed in Venice and remained in the book trade. Andrea Torresani had also worked with Jenson, so Margarete's link to the Aldine Press (or at least to one of its principals) would have gone back a long way. Both she and Aldus were signatories to the contract to borrow five manuscripts containing the letters from the Observant Dominican convent of San Pietro Martire on the Venetian island of Murano, 'per stampare per madona Margarita Oglemer'.[32] The manuscripts had been assembled, as the volume's title page declared, 'with exceedingly great diligence and effort over a period of around twenty years' by the convent's prior, Fra Bartolomeo d'Alzano of Bergamo.[33] In other words, he was the textual editor. He was also the patron of another, more famous Dominican Fra Bartolomeo, the Florentine painter (1472– 1517). In 1508, Prior Bartolomeo commissioned from the artist an altarpiece of *God the Father with Sts Mary Magdalene and Catherine of Siena* (illus. 25). To help raise the advance, he sold some of the ten copies of the edition of the letters that Aldus had provided to him and his convent along with the fee for the manuscript loan.[34] But the prior died that December, further funds were not forthcoming, and consequently Fra Bartolomeo never delivered the painting, donating it to a Dominican convent in Lucca instead. Still it bears the trace of its original commission; for beneath the levitating saint in the immediate foreground is this very volume – emerging from the picture towards the viewer, hovering above the prospective altar. If there is a case for seeing the Catherine edition as a kind of votive offering, it is here, and as its editor's.

The edition clearly meant a great deal to some people, Bartolomeo d'Alzano above all and likely Margarete Ugelheimer too – though, unlike the prior, she is not named in the volume itself. Perhaps, if she had not died earlier that year, we might have seen the first and only Aldine edition issued as a co-publication. The dedication to Cardinal Todeschini Piccolomini is nonetheless issued – for the first and, but for his addresses to the readers of his Petrarch editions, only time in the vernacular – in the voice of Aldus alone.[35] Crediting Christ with having inspired 'certain of his devoted servants' to have the letters put in print, he identified specifically the 'devoted servants of God of the Order of Preachers of the Observance' as having encouraged the dedication to the cardinal. This referred to Prior Bartolomeo and his (possibly less enthusiastic) brothers. Yet Aldus also offered reasons of his own. 'I supposed', he wrote, 'that giving you a fruit such as this, produced by a fruit-bearing plant from your illustrious city of Siena, would be a welcome thing for me to do for you.' There was also 'another reason', he continued:

> This virgin wrote many letters to supreme pontiffs and cardinals concerning the reformation of Holy Church and so that the standard of the Cross would be unfurled against the pagans. As these letters have survived until this time (by the will of God, I believe) somehow unknown and hidden, and are being published now that the infidels have equipped themselves with an astonishing army and magnificent array on sea and land for the purpose of destroying the faith of Christ, and, with terrible damage and slaughter of Christians, have already begun to put this desire into action, one could think them written rather for the pontiffs of our day than for those back then. Still another reason is because the saint was canonized by your uncle, Pope Pius II of blessed memory, by whom the Office in this virgin's honour was instituted. His Holiness was so desirous of campaigning against the pagans that he wrote a great and worthy letter to the Grand Turk [Sultan Mehmed II (r. 1444–6, 1451–81)] to try to convert him to the faith of Christ, and finally motivated all of Christendom to crush his pride and his forces. This would have come to a happy

conclusion had he not been taken from us amidst the preparations.[36]

We have heard of Aldus' concern for the state of Christendom from his prefaces before, though never articulated quite so fervently. In his first preface, to the Lascaris grammar of 1495, he held out Greek studies as the antidote to the worldly corruption so infuriating to a just God. Now, the corruption of the Church and the crimes of the world have reached such a point that 'everywhere there would be abundant material for writing satires and tragedies' – two genres he had not yet published, but would soon.[37] Today,

> there is nothing left in man but the form and the name; he no longer cares for honour or reputation, as if other men were so many paintings or statues. It is, however, greatly to be feared that, just as each malicious deed is committed publicly, so too will the wrath of God show itself, with whips and with scourges.[38]

The geopolitical turmoil of the moment – the Turkish threat, invasions of Italy by two successive French kings, the falls of the Neapolitan monarchy, the Milanese duchy and the Medici and Savonarola in turn – and the notorious reputation of Pope Alexander VI seem to drive Aldus deeper into this apocalyptic language. Its Savonarolan character perhaps reveals spiritual influences on one whose friend Gianfrancesco Pico was the Dominican friar's great believer and defender, and whose present editor, Prior Bartolomeo, would later commission his altarpiece from Savonarola's portraitist. Aldus refers to uncorrected vices and crimes so great that they demand the 'stones' (*pietre*) within and without the Church to raise their cry against them, and to a profound sickness that infects even the 'doctors' (*medici*) themselves: these may be read as comments on Florence's fallen leaders and the wayward

Dulce fignum charitatis
Dum amator caftitatis,
Cor mutat in Virgine.

iefu
dol
ce

iefu
amo
re

iefus

COR MVNDVM

CREA IN ME DEVS

SANCTACATHARINA DESENIS.

26 Woodcut from Catherine of Siena, *Epistole* (1500).

successor of Peter. Catherine's letters, 'full of the most holy teachings and of the Holy Spirit', are the remedy; they will bring people back to the love of God and restore the soul to health:

> Truly I dare say that whoever reads these holy letters with devotion will be unable to do anything but undergo complete reform, have the name of the crucified Jesus Christ enter into his heart, and become inflamed with love of God . . . They not only exhort one to do good, but also compel it in a wonderous way.[39]

Facing the collection's first letter (to Pope Gregory XI) is a full-page woodcut: it is Catherine, dressed in the habit of a Dominican *mantellata* (illus. 26). A gentle turn of the head to her right and a *contrapposto* stance slightly soften the imposing figure. In a general way the image conforms to a Venetian iconographic tradition, shared across manuscripts, panel paintings, small sculptures, single-sheet prints and even frescoes, as in a series of Dominican saints executed in the spandrels of the nave arcade at the Murano convent.[40] Above Catherine's head hover two angels bearing three crowns: these signify her sanctity as virgin, martyr and confessor, identified respectively by the lily, palm and crucifix she holds in her right hand together with an open book. This last represents a difference: elsewhere in this iconographic tradition, the book is depicted closed. The image shares the page with texts executed in a mix of woodcut and moveable type. That in capitals above the image, 'She has gone to the betrothal adorned with three crowns,' comes from a poem in praise of Catherine by Pope Pius II, which had been printed in a 1494 Venetian edition of her *Dialogue on Divine Providence*.[41] The lines in the cartouche, 'A sweet sign of charity,/ As the lover of chastity/ Changes the heart inside the virgin', are from a hymn for the saint, while the words on the banderole, 'Create in me a clean heart, O God', are from

Psalm 51.[42] These verses refer to Catherine's famous exchange of hearts with God, as that episode was related in the *Legenda maior* of Raymond of Capua, who reported that it was on this scriptural passage that she was meditating when the exchange took place. The radiant heart itself, bearing the name *iesus*, is in her left hand. Finally there is the text depicted as if written in the open book: *iesu dolce*/ *iesu amore*. Spread across the two visible pages, this is the valediction that Catherine used in her letters, and thus, in a sort of *mise en abyme*, identifies the book she is holding as the book we are reading. The cursive characters suggest the ur-prototype, linking the volume to the original epistles in the saint's miraculous hand. And yet they also represent the very first appearance of Francesco Griffo's italic type.

This italic is a work in progress, to be sure. No ligatures, in which Aldus would later take such pride, connect these isolated letters. But nonetheless the type of the Latin classics is here inaugurated with Catherine's transferred touch – the type of belles-lettres with the hand of one who, as her confessor–biographer admitted, was utterly 'ignorant of grammar', of Latin.[43] This raises a startling question: is a woman holding, as one scholar has claimed, 'the book of the future'?[44] We could, instead of agreeing, choose alternatively to write it off as a mere experiment, as what another scholar called a 'typographical *capriccio*'; indeed, if we maintain the position that 'the real Aldus' is present only in the publications that belong to his 'programme', it can be nothing more.[45] Yet these characters are used for the name *iesus* on the heart as well. And exactly what happened to Catherine's heart was a subject of disagreement between sources: between the legend of Raymond and the *Epistole* themselves. If we are at the very least to interpret the woodcut, the deployment of the italics becomes impossible to overlook.

The heart played a regular and important part in Catherine's thought, her mission and her description of them – and so too in the descriptions of them by others. She was versed in contemporary ideas derived from Aristotle about its function and nature, and understood Christ's heart as the source of his fertile, life-giving power in the world.[46] The most famous appearance of the heart in the Catherinian corpus, however, is the story told by Raymond of Capua of the removal of her own from her chest and its exchange for Christ's. This was the text at the core of the cult. It had circulated widely in manuscript and now in two printed vernacular translations – the first in 1477 by the pioneering press of the nuns of San Jacopo di Ripoli in Florence – and was associated with a visual iconography of the heart exchange that had from early in the fifteenth century been disseminated from Venice to other cult centres.[47] According to Raymond, recounting an event he claimed to have found recorded in a previous confessor's notebooks, the exchange of hearts took place in 1370, before Catherine had embarked on her controversial public mission.[48] As she meditates on that passage from Psalm 51, 'Create in me a clean heart, O God,' and prays fervently for Him to remove it and do so, she experiences a vision in which the Lord comes to her and opens her left side. Upon waking, she is struck by the sensation that there is no heart inside her body. Some days later, God appears to her with a heart in His hands. 'Behold, my dearest daughter,' He says, 'just as some days ago I took your heart away from you, now I consign to you my heart, so that you may live forever.'[49] A scar where God made the incision remains on her body as a 'sign of the miracle'.

Catherine's own account of this episode – transmitted in a letter to Raymond printed for the first time in the Aldine edition – differs drastically. In the first place, it occurs not at the start of her mission, but at the very end, less than three months before her death. It is Sexagesima, the second Sunday before Ash Wednesday.[50] Catherine is in Rome, called there by Pope Urban VI (r. 1378–89) to work for the end of the Schism, while Raymond is in France. Losing confidence in Urban, whom she had keenly supported, she is struck by a powerful vision. God visits her and reveals a sight of the Church abandoned. She asks Him to tell her how she can help remedy this, and He replies, 'Offer your own life once again, and don't ever give yourself rest.'[51] As the day turns to evening and she contemplates what this injunction means, the visions intensify. 'God set me before Himself,' she writes:

> This truth was reflected with such light that, in that abyss, the mysteries of Holy Church, and all the graces past and present I've received in my life, and the day when my soul was wedded in faith were made fresh again. Then with horrible violence the devils shrieked above me, seeking with their terror to obstruct and slacken my free and flaming desire; whence they struck against the barky exterior of my body. But my desire was further ignited as I cried out, 'O eternal God, receive the sacrifice of my life within this mystic body of Holy Church! I have nothing to give but what You have given me. Remove my heart, therefore, and squeeze it over the face of this bride!' Then, turning the eye of His mercy towards me, eternal God ripped out my heart and squeezed it out on Holy Church. Then the demons screamed all the more, as if they had felt intolerable pain, and made every effort to terrify me, threatening to make it so that I could not complete this task. But since, no matter how it joined forces and worked with fiery irons, Hell cannot withstand the virtue of humility enlightened by most holy faith, still I heard in the presence of divine majesty words that were so attractive and full of promises of happiness; and since truthfully I was so wrapped up in this mystery, my tongue is at this point no longer able to talk about it. Now I say, Thanks, Thanks be

to eternal God the Most High! He has set us like knights
on the battlefield to fight for His bride with the shield of
most holy faith.[52]

Nothing like this exists in Raymond's account. He tells indeed of
violent visions and bodily torments that continue from Sexagesima until her death; yet, though he was the recipient of the letter,
on the matter of the heart he is completely silent.[53] There was a
good motive for his subterfuge: he was trying to pave Catherine's
way to sainthood. A woman's exercise of political agency and
public mission was potentially problematic, and this keen curator
of his spiritual guide's life and legacy had to justify it.[54] Insofar
as Raymond's Catherine acts, then, it is because she is, quite literally, powered by Christ. But this stands in contrast to the testimony of Catherine's letter. For there, it is *her* heart that fights off
the devils; *her* heart – torn from her chest at her command – that
defeats Hell.

We might expect the Aldine woodcut to agree with Catherine's
version: the saint, we determined, is after all holding a volume of
the *Epistole*, and this volume represents the printed edition itself.
The banderole is the clue, however, that things are otherwise:
Catherine's meditation on the Psalms – the precise passage found
on it in the woodcut – belongs to the exchange story that comes
from Raymond alone. The narrative to which it refers, which the
image evokes, is at odds with that in the letters the woodcut intro-
duces and purports to depict. What we have before us instead
is an overwriting of Catherine's testimony – an overwriting to
rival, in nature if not extent, any that the author of the *Legenda
maior* attempted. The material structure of the Aldine volume, with
the woodcut immediately preceding the letters, conspires to
assert that they come, physically and temporally, *after* the heart
exchange, not before. All this means consequently that we are
not presented with Catherine's heart that defeated the devils

(absent from Raymond's account), but rather with a heart impressed by the same force that was driving her when she wrote the epistles.

A plain reading would make the woodcut heart that of *iesus* Himself: the heart Catherine received rather than the one she lost. Yet the hymn of Pius II in the cartouche and Aldus' dedication to Pius' nephew together suggest still another possibility. Echoing the hymn's reference to the heart's 'mutation' or *change* rather than necessarily its *exchange*, Aldus claimed that the reforming effect of the letters he was publishing would be to cause the name of the crucified Christ to enter the hearts of those who read them. Viewed in this light, the heart Catherine is holding may be the reader's. The novel characters in which the name on the heart and the words in the book are printed directs our attention to the joint source of these divine impressions. This is finally what makes Aldus' new italics so crucial, and their inaugural deployment as audacious ideologically as Griffo's type was technically: only one printer printed letters like this; and here that printer is placed in the position of God.

WHAT, IN THE END, can the Aldine edition of the letters of Catherine of Siena tell us about the relationship between women and humanism? Certainly nothing that would make Aldus a trailblazer of any sort. Socially speaking, and as we have seen before and will yet see again, Aldus was always more interested in building barriers up than in taking them down. It was to defend his chosen place and identity among various possible *masculine* types – the teacher, the scholar, the tradesman, the capitalist, the landowner – that he expended his thought and effort. But the edition of Catherine is not without its importance here, and, though in a different way than possibly expected, her gender too may be relevant. Our reading of the woodcut shows the caution with which the attribution to Catherine not only of her own religious message but of the type then being primed for Virgil, Horace and an elite male readership was handled. With Raymond's chronology imposed, the epistles as printed by Aldus are the product of an instrumentalized woman, with an agency not her own. Less than five months later, when the italic type received its formal launch in the octavo Virgil, it would be a very similar interpretation that Aldus, in his introductory epigram, imposed on Francesco Griffo. The decisions made in relation to the woodcut reinforce our sense that the question of agency in matters of word and type was at the heart of Aldus' project of invention in these years.

What of the Catherinian epistles themselves? Raymond of Capua had also struggled to reconcile what he insisted was a 'high style' and profundity that his Latin could hardly match with Catherine's use of the vernacular: awkwardly he compared her writings and letters to those of Sts Paul and Augustine – the latter who often eschewed high style, the former who wrote neither in Latin nor in his vernacular.[55] Although the letters may nevertheless have been and would become again a model for a kind of vernacular eloquence, this was not the future Aldus envisioned for them; indeed, this was not a future that Aldus, seeking to preserve his reputation as a printer of Greek while managing a delicate transition to the Latin literary classics, envisioned at all. The subsequent publication as 'classics' of Petrarch and Dante also rendered any precedence that Catherine had a short-lived victory, and she would go uncited in Pietro Bembo's *Prose della volgar lingua* (1525), the most substantial treatment of the Italian vernacular produced by anyone close to Aldus. There is no sign that Aldus, or for that matter his male and female collaborators in the edition, conceived of eloquence as anything other than fundamentally male and, if not necessarily Latin, then rooted nonetheless in grammar and rhetoric.

If we finish by returning from questions of gender to those of religion, however, we can probably make some more significant observations. The Catherine woodcut offers an equation of the physical, printed word of the humanist press with the divine word. In his prefaces, Aldus was adamant that philological accuracy and classical eloquence, as expressed by his metallic types, were the accessories to truth and prerequisites for religious renewal. This was a stance he shared with the man who, in 1508, would become his colleague in Venice, and who will play a bigger role in the next chapter: Erasmus of Rotterdam. Erasmus ultimately came to Venice to have his *Adagia* published, but, in the first, unsolicited letter he sent to Aldus, he spoke mainly of his interest in a Greek Plato and a polyglot Bible, two Aldine projects he had heard of from mutual friends.[56] Greek philosophy and biblical Christianity: for Erasmus, true Christianity was the philosophy of Christ, and the basis of reform was philology. The accessory to philology was printing. This chapter has explored the investment of one leading humanist in medieval religious devotional culture, and also come upon its limits. Catherine's goals for the reform of Church and society were shared by humanists like Aldus, and her words could change hearts. Their words, they thought, could change the world.

FOUR

The Printer as Prince

't is our intention to produce henceforth all the best authors in the same type': the book printed in Francesco Griffo's italic, which Catherine of Siena had so tantalizingly foreshadowed, was soon a reality (illus. 27).[1] And the reforming sense of purpose that the cursive letters' launching imparted to the new Latin publishing programme remained, at least at first. It was April 1501, the volume was Virgil: *Eclogues, Georgics* and *Aeneid*. In his brief introduction, printed above the celebratory epigram with which he bestowed upon the Latins the work of Griffo's Daedalean hands, Aldus explained that he had not included either the juvenilia or 'the obscene poems'. By this he meant a collection now considered to be of mixed authorship and known as the *Appendix Vergiliana*, which contains a series of *Priapea*, or 'Priapus poems', spoken by the phallic fertility god whose rites were so vividly celebrated in the *Hypnerotomachia Poliphili*. These works, he said, 'we have judged unworthy of an *enchiridion*'.[2]

An *enchiridion*, often translated as a 'manual', is literally a 'handbook': the Greek word originally referred to a dagger. Writing later in 1501 from a castle near Saint-Omer in what is now northern France, Erasmus of Rotterdam would use it as the title for *The Handbook of a Christian Knight*. This was a guide to living a Christian life in the world. His audience was not one of priests and theologians but of the laypeople whose active lives he sought to make

ALDVS STVDIOSIS
OMNIBVS ·S·

P·V·M·Bucolica. Georgica· Aeneida quam emenda
ta, et qua forma damus, uidetis. caetera, quae Poe
ta exercendi sui gratia composuit, et obscena, quae ei
dem adscribuntur, non censuimus digna enchiridio.
Est animus dare posthac iisdem formulis optimos
quosque authores· Valete.

IN GRAMMATOGLYPTAE
LAVDEM·

Qui graiis dedit Aldus, en latinis
Dat nunc grammata sculpta daedaleis
Francisci manibus Bononiensis,

P·V·M·MANTVANI BV
COLICORVM
TITYRVS·

Melibœus· Tityrus·

Tityre tu patulae recubas sub Me.
te gmine fagi
Siluestrem tenui musam meditaris
auena·
Nos patriae fines, et dulcia linqui
mus arua,
Nos patriam fugimus, tu Tityre lentus in umbra
Formosam resonare doces Amaryllida syluas·
O Melibœe, deus nobis haec ocia fecit· Ti.
Namq; erit ille mihi semper deus, illius aram
Saepe tener nostris ab ouilibus imbuet agnus·
Ille meas errare boues, ut cernis, et ipsum
Ludere, quae uellem, calamo permisit agresti·
Non equidem inuideo, miror magis, undiq; totis Me.
Vsque adeo turbatur agris· en ipse capellas
Protinus aeger ago, hanc etiam uix Tityre duco·
Hic inter densas corylos modo namq; gemellos·
Spem gregis ah silice in nuda connixa reliquit·
Saepe malum hoc nobis, si mens non leua fuisset,
De caelo tactas memini praedicere quercus·
Saepe sinistra caua praedixit ab ilice cornix·
Sed tamen, iste deus qui sit, da Tityre nobis·
Vrbem, quam dicunt Romam, Melibœe putaui Ti.
Stultus ego huic nostrae similem, quo saepe solemus

a ii

expressions of faith, and for whom his counsel was one of personal
reform over empty ritualism. What he did not mean to empha-
size at that point was the book's portability: his *Enchiridion* – not
published as a stand-alone until 1518 – was a title to have 'to hand',
rather than a book specifically fashioned for it.[3] Many scholars
have understood Aldus' concern over content as being primarily
about decorum and managing readers' expectations. Before this
Virgil edition, a personal, portable volume was most often associated with that instrument of private religious devotion, the Book
of Hours, though Aldus himself would credit his encounters with
similarly sized manuscript volumes of literature in Bernardo
Bembo's library for the inspiration.[4] Yet his choice of word, seen

27 Pages from *Vergilius* (1501), in octavo, with Aldus' address to readers and
epigram 'In Praise of the Punchcutter'.

in the context of his published statements on education and in light of the reforming agenda with which he associated the new type in the Catherine edition, suggests that his concern, and therefore his meaning, might have been closer to that of his future colleague: the purpose of his press was moral because good literature in the hands of the Christian people at large was a weapon of reform.

Thus octavo format, cursive type and the choice of text itself – all addressed explicitly on the brief introductory page – were intended to condition the reception of this book and of the new Aldine publishing programme. The Virgil followed Aldus' publication of his first volume of early Christian poets, a work he proposed as a wholesome and orthodox alternative with which 'the tender years may be saturated' instead of with 'pagan fables and books' (as he had done to Alberto's).[5] And yet Virgil, as Aldus well knew, was the most important Latin author in the school curriculum: there was a reason he could feel confident issuing an initial print run of some 4,000 copies, an enormous number even taking into account the physical volume's novelty factor. Over the centuries Virgil had been subject to various Christianizing treatments, but Aldus did not rely on these. He supplied a market of students and teachers – and we know that these volumes, published with much white space and without commentary, were regularly annotated for school use – as well as educated laypeople: *studiosi omnes* ('all those devoted to learning'), to use what became a common form of address in his prefaces.[6]

Yet with Aldus, as with Erasmus, there is always a tension between accessibility and exclusivity. For the Dutch scholar, it manifested itself most evidently in his complex views on language and the sacred text: in his stated desire to have the Bible put into Christians' common tongues while limiting his own output and entire textual presence to learned languages, and even in his fantasies, perhaps inspired by his encounter with the *Polifilo*, of a perfectly encoded hieroglyphic language for containing and transmitting sacred wisdom.[7] For Aldus, it was between bringing the liberal arts to more ears and putting good literature in more hands, and preserving an ennobling, anti-democratic ethos and a reputation for excellence, rarity and quality. This became even more important once he was no longer operating primarily on the near-exclusive terrain of Greek philosophical and lexicographical publishing, but instead dealing in the same texts that were many printers' stock-in-trade: from the first in 1469, there had been 179 printed editions of Virgil by the end of the fifteenth century.[8] But Virgil was also sure to sell, and a healthier turnover was now required. The Catherine of Siena edition, perhaps even the pious prefaces to the contemporary editions of the Christian poets and of his Latin grammar, had prepared the ground for the transition, sanitizing the turn towards the bigger market. Printing was never *not* business, even if, for Aldus, it could never be business alone.

The literary octavo was, however, a formal innovation that expanded the possibilities of reading, away from the classroom or the study. At the beginning of this book, we saw two paintings, selected from an extensive potential corpus, which depicted lay sitters holding volumes of this sort (both volumes of Petrarch, as it happens: see illus. 6 and 7). In December 1513, Niccolò Machiavelli (1469–1527) gave perhaps the most memorable written testimony we have to the kind of revolution that Aldus brought about. In a letter to Francesco Vettori, Machiavelli, then in exile from Florence, described to his friend how he passed the days on his farm near San Casciano. After a morning of overseeing the work and chatting with the labourers chopping firewood, it was time to relax:

> Leaving the wood, I go out to a spring, and from there to my aviary. I have a book under my cloak, either Dante

or Petrarch, or one of the minor poets, such as Tibullus, Ovid, and the like: I read of their amorous passions and of their loves, recall my own, and take a little pleasure in this thought. Then I shift myself down the road to the inn . . .[9]

All of these authors had been published in octavo by Aldus, though even in Italy by this date there is no guarantee that in every case they or the other 'minor poets' (Aldus had published Tibullus together with Catullus and Propertius) were Aldine editions. Indeed, apart from Ovid, by the date of this letter the titles named had also been printed by the Florentine Filippo Giunta, who had copied the Aldine texts, type and format almost exactly, while we met Gershom Soncino and his Petrarch before.[10] What is clear enough, though, is that what Machiavelli was enjoying – what made this pastime possible – was the portable book: a small volume of good literature that could fit in the pocket under his cloak, to help fill the lazy hours before going to the inn. Nothing too serious: *that* he saved for the evenings, when he returned home, replaced his outdoor clothes with 'regal and courtly garments', entered 'into the ancient courts of ancient men', grazed on 'that food which alone was his, for which he was born' and wrote *The Prince*.[11] In contrast to that, this – with his *enchiridion* by his spring or in his aviary – was reading for leisure.

And Aldus knew it. Already with his second octavo edition – the works of the hardly less canonical Horace, published just one month after the pioneering Virgil – he was positioning his product accordingly. His dedicatee was a patrician, not a prince; a learned statesman rather than a professional scholar:

We send him then as a gift to you, Marin Sanudo, most sophisticated man of all, so that to the books of which we have seen your library is full Horace printed in this very small format may also be added, to invite you with his petiteness to read him whenever you can take a break from public duties or from writing the history of the Venetian state.[12]

Many of the classical Latin titles of those years – Juvenal and Persius, Ovid, Cicero's *Letters to Friends* among them – featured similar suggestions for how these books were to be received and by what sort of person, despite the large print runs (another 3,000 or more for Catullus) that indicate a less-than-exclusive circulation in reality. Sanudo was a multiple dedicatee of these new volumes, as he proudly noted in his diary.[13] Other recipients of dedications included his fellow Venetian patrician Marcantonio Morosini (1434–1509), who had loaned Aldus the manuscript copy of Lucan on which the volume dedicated to him was based; Jan Lubrański (1456–1520), Bishop of Poznań and counsellor to King Sigismund I of Poland; and Zsigmond Thurzó (d. 1512), scion of a great merchant-entrepreneurial family, then provost of the church of Transylvania and secretary to King Vladislaus II of Bohemia and Hungary: 'so that, since you are extremely busy with your own and royal affairs and are not free to devote yourselves to more refined studies at home in your libraries, you have at your disposal these little books from us to read conveniently out of doors'.[14] There were also the editions of Petrarch's *Cose volgari* (*Rime* and *Trionfi*) and Dante's *Commedia*, works in the vernacular, edited by Pietro Bembo and integrated seamlessly into the publishing programme, as classics among classics. The volumes 'in forma picola, de littera minuta et quasi cancelleresca', caught the attention of the acquisitive Isabella d'Este: from Mantua the marchioness wrote to her agent in Venice to obtain a Virgil, an Ovid, two Petrarchs and a Dante, all printed on *cartha bona*, on vellum (illus. 28).[15] Over time, and once Francesco Griffo had cut a small Greek fount (his last Aldine type), some books in that language started to appear in octavo too: the *editio prínceps* of Sophocles (1502), then of Euripides (1503). Homer, including the *Iliad* and the *Odyssey*, as well as the Homeric Hymns and the *Battle of Frogs and Mice*, and a rare instance of a major Greek corpus for which Aldus' was not a first edition, followed in 1504. Eventually the prefaces of the Latin editions began to host learned discussions and philological inquiries as well, even if the scholarly agenda never matched that of the Greek programme: collation could be slapdash, and the only *editio prínceps* of a major ancient Latin author Aldus ever published was the complete letters of Pliny the Younger, in octavo, in 1508.[16]

Relatively late to arrive in this format was contemporary writing. In 1502, Aldus asked the Neapolitan poet Jacopo Sannazaro

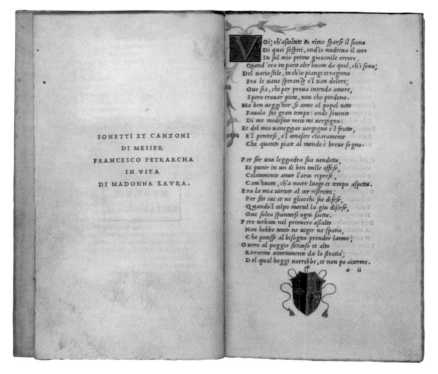

28 The Aldine Petrarch on 'charta bona', with the arms of Isabella d'Este:
Le cose volgari di Messer Francesco Petrarcha (1501).

(1458–1530) to send his Latin and Italian works for printing, but did not specify in what size or type.[17] In 1505, he printed the verses of Giovanni Aurelio Augurello (1441–1524), Bembo's former tutor, in an octavo italic edition that included a printer's mark but no dedication (understandably: it not only included odes to various addressees, but also the poet's commendation of the book to Aldus!).[18] This is a curious choice, more akin to the various short pamphlets he also produced, mainly for friends. He published the *Urania* and other didactic poems by Giovanni Pontano (1426–1503) in this format in the same year, and Latin translations by Erasmus of Euripides' *Hecuba* and *Iphigenia at Aulis* in 1507. But fundamentally he came to think of this as a series that comprised the literary authorities of the ancient and (in the case of Petrarch and Dante) vernacular languages.[19] With Sannazaro's *Arcadia* in 1514, the series received its first 'modern' work in the Tuscan tongue. Books for language learning or primarily for student and classroom use – like the grammars and the early Christian poets – remained in quarto. The explicitly moral connotations of the *enchiridion* had served their purpose at the start and did not last: when a new edition of Virgil appeared in 1505, the *Priapea* was included. This was now the domain of literature.

Yet, despite a seemingly reimagined sense of purpose, for Aldus these were anxious, increasingly unsatisfying years. 'Such a burdensome task it was to found the Roman tongue!' he declared, repurposing in his warning against the printers of Lyon what Virgil had claimed for those Trojans destined to found the Roman people in the face of Juno's wrath; he was not wrong.[20] He faced the loss of his punchcutter and the challenge of those counter-feiters, and we have already heard the disapproving chorus of his scholarly friends: you migrated from Greece to Italy for profit, teased Janus Lascaris; Andrea d'Asola won't let him print Greek books one after the other anymore, said Johannes Cuno, turning up his nose at volumes like Augurello and Pontano. The words of others are all very well, but the dedications tell their own story. Until the Lucretius of 1515 – the final book printed in Aldus' lifetime, a second edition of a fundamentally philosophical text – not one of these octavo volumes was dedicated to Alberto Pio. It is not that Alberto had no taste for literature: Ovid was no 'outcast quite abjured' to this devotee of Aristotle's checks. He owned these books himself; he had Petrarchan frescoes on the walls of his palace and commissioned a scheme dedicated to the Muses for his *studiolo*; Aldus had certainly drilled him in the Latin poets; a portrait of 1512 attributed to his court painter, Bernardino Loschi, depicts him in ambassadorial attire with an open copy of a hand-held *Aeneid* (illus. 29).[21] But a prince's preserve, according to Aldus, was philosophy: it had been so for Pico della Mirandola and was too for his nephew. Aldus had shown his hand in this regard many times over, in his Aristotle dedications to his patron: 'republics would truly be governed best if either philosophers ruled or princes philosophized.'[22] Even Loschi's portrait acknowledges this distinction, for if this is an image of Alberto as a cultured man of affairs, then the artist has nevertheless depicted him reading that most philosophical passage of Virgil's epic (6.724–47), where the shade of Anchises explains to his son the transmigration of souls. A true prince is always pursuing wisdom. The Aldine Latin octavos are dedicated to senators and statesmen, to courtiers and counsellors, to poets and even prelates, but not to princes. The only partial exceptions were made for an epyllion, or short epic, on the Holy Roman (that is, German) Emperor Frederick III (1415–1493) and his son Maximilian I (1459–1519), a 1504 publication we will look at shortly but which was dedicated to Maximilian by a Vienna theologian and not Aldus, and for the works of the two Ferrarese poets, father and son Tito Vespasiano and Ercole Strozzi, dedicated in 1513/14 to Lucrezia Borgia (1480–1519). It was Lucrezia, Duchess of Ferrara and the late pope's daughter, who seems at least formally to have asked Aldus to take

on the project – a detail which, combined with her gender and the content (she herself is an object of Ercole's praise), may make this a special circumstance.[23] By contrast, even the vernacular *Asolani* (1505), a philosophical dialogue on Platonic love at which Johannes Cuno had also looked askance but which was written by Lucrezia's admirer Pietro Bembo and dedicated to her, was printed in quarto; only after Aldus' death was an octavo edition issued. Other more serious works with princely dedicatees – Gianfrancesco Pico's *De imaginatione* (1501), with a double dedication

29 Bernardino Loschi (attrib.), *Portrait of Alberto Pio*, 1512, oil on panel.

by Aldus to Gianfrancesco's cousin Alberto Pio and by the author
to Maximilian; the first edition of Plato (1513), dedicated to Pope
Leo X – received more serious formats.

Where Aldus' anxieties lay should be clear from what we have
learned about him so far. As a publisher of Greek and as an educator, he was a benefactor of learning; as a printer of the portable
Latin literary classics, however, he was the intelligent inventor of
a mass-produced accoutrement of aspiration and status. Cuno was
right, to an extent: it did not take an Aldus to print an Augurello.
Though the Aldine printed product remained distinctive, the
publishing programme had become less so. The product quickly
contributed to a culture of *otium* (leisure) that was growing rap-
idly among Italian urban sophisticates, not least in Venice. But
this always remained a culture foreign to Aldus' background and
ethos. Though Venice may have been, in his memorable words,
like 'another world', beyond business it had no great hold on him:
he was no Venetian, and no republican. Remarry someone from
either Carpi, Asola or Ferrara, and nowhere else; otherwise become
a nun: these were the bracing instructions he gave his new wife in
his (first) will, written shortly after their marriage.[24] The Venetians would not look out for a foreign woman with children and
no protection. It was anyway the *agri*, the fields of Carpi with
which he was endowed, that guaranteed his particular forms of
dependence and independence.

Making class distinctions – differentiating scholars from workers, like architects from craftsmen and masters from slaves – was
part of the Aldine toolkit already. But as the publishing enterprise
evolved by necessity further away from the programme and values
by which it was first distinguished, and further from the preoccupations of his ideal philosopher-prince, a political edge began to
appear in Aldus' project of self-invention. An intensification of
European contacts, with Italy as a focal point, provided the context
and inspiration for some of his next moves, as he sought to maintain

his enterprise and preserve the status and reputation he had attained. That is where the rest of this chapter picks up the story.

IN 1508, ERASMUS OF ROTTERDAM presented his printer to the world as a prince. His essay on Aldus' motto, 'Festina lente', and mark, the dolphin and anchor, published in the Aldine edition of the *Adagia*, made remarkable claims, some of which we have already seen. Suetonius and Aulus Gellius had asserted that 'Make haste slowly' in its Greek form had regularly been on the lips of Caesar Augustus; the symbol had appeared on coins of the emperor that Erasmus identified as Vespasian; the evidence that the motto and symbol had meant one and the same thing all along was in an ancient book on hieroglyphs (by which he really meant the *Hypnerotomachia Poliphili*).[25] It was clear:

> This saying, σπεῦδε βραδέως, arose then out of the very mysteries of ancient philosophy, whence it was adopted by the two most praised emperors of all. Just as for one it had the status of an adage, for the other it took the place of his insignia, wonderfully agreeable it was to the character and nature of both. Now, however, it has come down to Aldus Manutius of Rome, as to a third heir.[26]

In fact, the dolphin and anchor's existence as a printer's mark was more distinguished than its previous life on a coin:

> And nor do I believe that this symbol was more illustrious then, when it was carved [*inscalptum*] upon the imperial coinage and passed around, getting worn out by the hands of merchants, than now, when everywhere on earth, even beyond the limits of the Christian empire, together with books of every kind in both languages it is disseminated,

recognized, safeguarded and celebrated by all who revere
liberal studies.

If, as an imperial symbol, it suffered the clasp of merchants' grubby
paws, only now, Erasmus informs his reader, has it transcended
trade. Harnessed by the humanist, it was a sign of 'the extraordin-
arily beautiful and plainly royal desires of our friend Aldus'.[27] Not
even the Egyptian king who built the Great Library of Alexandria
could match him:

> However much you heap praises upon those who by
> their own strength either preserve their states or even en-
> large them, they are dealing in matters that are at any rate
> profane and confined to narrow limits. But he who res-
> tores a literature fallen into ruins – almost harder than to
> have begotten one – is in the first place building some-
> thing sacred and immortal, and furthermore pursues what
> concerns not just one individual province, but everyone,
> everywhere, for all time. Lastly, this was once the duty of
> princes, amongst whom particular glory belongs to Ptol-
> emy. Nevertheless, his library was enclosed by constrictive
> palace walls. Aldus is building a library which has no walls
> save those of the world itself.[28]

This noble work was set fundamentally apart from that of 'those
common printers', 'to whom the slight profit of a single gold coin
is more important than the entirety of literature'.[29] Truly nothing
could better befit a princely spirit than Aldus' Herculean labours.
Reading this text, one would struggle to believe that the everyday material reality of the dolphin and anchor was surely to
swing outside a Venetian printing shop like a pub sign.

Erasmus' derogatory reference to the 'common printers' –
vulgares excusores, based on a verb (*excudo*) that Renaissance writers

used in a transferred sense for putting books in print but literally meaning 'metalworkers' and employed derogatorily by Poliziano too – surely drew upon the sentiment of Aldus' prefaces.[30] It also suggests his familiarity with some of the distinctions between the arts and the denigration of the manual and mechanical that we encountered around Aldus in our discussion of the *Hypnerotomachia Poliphili*. That the *Polifilo* was the source of the dolphin and anchor in the first place is something we have seen Erasmus slyly acknowledge with his cryptic reference to the book on hieroglyphs. We have also seen why, contrary to what he implied, the source would not have been the ancient coin given to Aldus by Pietro Bembo: that gift was probably made around 1501/2, when Bembo and Aldus were collaborating on the Petrarch and Dante editions.[31] But as Erasmus famously did not know the Italian vernacular and would have struggled even more than most to read the *Polifilo* for himself, the references to both the book and the coin are evidence of the conversations he must have had with either Aldus or someone close to him, and therefore of his understanding of the mark's real origins. He knew that, rather than reconstructing a lost history, in narrating a tale of emperors and kings he was making up an illustrious succession story that would flatter his publisher while serving mutual aims – for the propagation of good literature per se was an Erasmian concern as much as, or even more than, an Aldine one, even as associating the real business of the publisher with a humanistic, scholarly agenda was an Aldine project before also being taken up by his Dutch friend.[32] The impact of this story – like the impact of Erasmus' *Adagia* on humanist Europe – is unquestionable: when Aldus, in Milan in 1511, met the French bibliophile Jean Grolier (1489/90–1565), he gave him a replica of the dolphin-and-anchor coin, which Grolier sketched alongside the 'Festina lente' essay in his copy of the *Adagia*.[33] Aldus was in effect endorsing an account which, while concealing a reference to the *Polifilo* for the benefit of real initiates,

attributed to the ancients what he and Francesco Colonna had
come up with sometime around 1499!

Erasmus' tale thus became the approved version. He was not,
however, the first to take on board the imperial coin and respond
to its possibilities. Probably in late 1503 or early 1504, the bronze
portrait medal of Aldus was cast, featuring the dolphin and anchor
and the Greek motto on the reverse (illus. 30 and 31).[34] Here the
symbol at last was modelled on the coin. Yet on the obverse (the
side with the portrait bust) was something still more surprising:
Aldus' name. Previously *Altus Cato* and *Aldus Mannuccius* had mor-
phed into the celebrated *Aldus Manutius Romanus*, Aldus Manutius
of Rome. Now he sported the name of his patron too: ALDVS PIVS
MANVTIVS R(OMANVS). In the dedication to Alberto Pio of the
commentary on Aristotle's *De interpretatione*, published in October
1503, Aldus, showing off the name for the first time, explained
to the world:

> With the present letter to you, we acknowledge publicly
> that three years ago you gave us not insignificant resources
> and adorned us with the *gentilitium* of your family. [We do

30, 31 Medal of Aldus, obverse: ALDVS PIVS MANVTIVS R(OMANVS);
reverse: ΣΠΕΥΔΕ ΒΡΑΔΕΩΣ ('Make haste slowly'), after 1503, bronze.

so] that all who read this know how much we owe you; and also that they not be astonished if, after this, they read or hear of me called Pio as a *cognomen*.[35]

Thus our scholar, petty landlord and bourgeois now possessed a noble name of the military aristocracy, almost as if he had been adopted into the family – though he retained some ambiguity on this point: referring to the name given as a *gentilitium* (the second part of a Roman name, denoting the *gens* or clan to which one belonged) implies he was; calling it a *cognomen* (the third part, often after something for which one was known) suggests he wasn't. He was never ennobled. Yet the appearance of the new name on the medal – a quintessentially Renaissance art form with unmistakably imperial connotations – seems to turn the dolphin and anchor and Greek inscription into a coat of arms and chivalric motto. It represents a function distinct from that as guarantee of scholarly excellence and quality, which, as Aldus insisted in his contemporaneous warning against the *Lyonnais*, the woodcut device had. Combined with the transformation of the symbol in line with the imperial prototype, it all points to someone pushing at the limits of his status.

But, if we are to believe Aldus' words, three years had gone by since the grant. So why only start using the name now? Aldus claimed in that same dedication than he had not publicly adopted it earlier so as not to cheapen the honour by appearing superficial: he had preferred to wait until the opportunity of dedicating a (Greek philosophical) book to Alberto arose. Yet there is also another factor that may have contributed to this desire to promote his new name and status on paper and in bronze. A plan was afoot to move Aldus to Germany. There he was to found his *Neakademia* as both a printing enterprise and a school of arms and letters for noble youths. All this was to be under the patronage of Caesar himself: Maximilian I.

The likelihood of such plans ever materializing – and under Maximilian, a man of great cultural enthusiasm, often impecunious, of much ambition and many half-baked or never-realized schemes – has struck more than one scholar as far-fetched.[36] The idea of Aldus establishing a programme of military training for *pubes Germanica* (young German manhood) sounds about as probable as his supposed dissection of the pig at Carpi; though, it must be said, the plan as articulated was for others to see to the teaching and for Aldus to stick to the printing. Yet this is precisely what Johannes Cuno reported from Venice to Willibald Pirckheimer in that same December 1505 letter where dissatisfaction with the diminished ambitions of the Aldine printing programme was laid bare. According to Cuno, Aldus, having finished work on his second edition of Virgil, was going to Carpi to wait with Gianfrancesco Pico for the impending summons for which he and others had been working.[37] Close Italian friends had been expecting news for more than a year. 'What are you intending?' wrote Scipione Fortiguerra from Florence. 'What of your wedding? What of the emperor? And what else?'[38]

The precise details of the plan are in some respects the least important part. What is clear is that Aldus had been cultivating leading German humanists for some time, and they him. Already in 1497 he was in correspondence with Conrad Celtis (1459–1508): 'if you are still possessed by the desire to see Italy, not only am I eager for you to come, but I also beg it of you, as much as I can beg.'[39] Johannes Reuchlin (1455–1522), meanwhile, had met Aldus in 1498 on his return from Rome, where he had given an oration on behalf of Philip, Elector Palatine, before the pope. The wealthy Pirckheimer of Nuremberg, patrician humanist and close friend of Albrecht Dürer, wrote to Celtis and to German contacts at his old alma mater of Padua for news of the latest Aldine publications, including the much-anticipated polyglot Bible.[40] While Latin Aldines could, depending on dealers' stock levels, sometimes be found at better prices in Germany, the Greek volumes were best sourced from Aldus directly.[41] Pirckheimer's library would eventually include 32 Aldine titles, thirty published in Aldus' lifetime, mainly Greek.[42]

In part this is evidence of the way humanist networks functioned around the year 1500, when Italian travels were still tantamount to visiting the Pierian Spring, and before print culture had more fully severed the link with place: personal contacts, recommendations, occasional journeys. 'Finding a safe haven at last in Venice,' wrote the poet Vincenz Lang (*c.* 1475–1502/3) to Celtis,

> We made for the famous man restoring Greek antiquity, Aldus Manutius. When I greeted him in your name, he received me with the most gracious expression and right away presented me with two recently printed little volumes of the most ancient poet Musaeus with Latin translation: one to bring to your civilized self; and the other volume indeed he gave to me.[43]

Lang was excited by a volume that was by this point over three years old, but others were on top of the latest publications. Johannes Cuspinianus (Speißheimer, 1473–1529) – friend of Celtis, rector of the University of Vienna – wrote to Aldus upon hearing that he was publishing the Roman anecdotalist Valerius Maximus: he had seen some exempla in an ancient manuscript which he suspected (rightly) would be missing from those Aldus had. Although he received the letter too late for the 1502 issue, Aldus asked for them anyway, and a note of thanks to Cuspinianus and the missing exempla were added to the reissue of 1503.[44] Cuspinianus also sought to obtain for Aldus the (largely honorific) title of count palatine. Aldus praised Celtis for writing poems that seemed to have sprung more from the heart of Rome than from amidst the

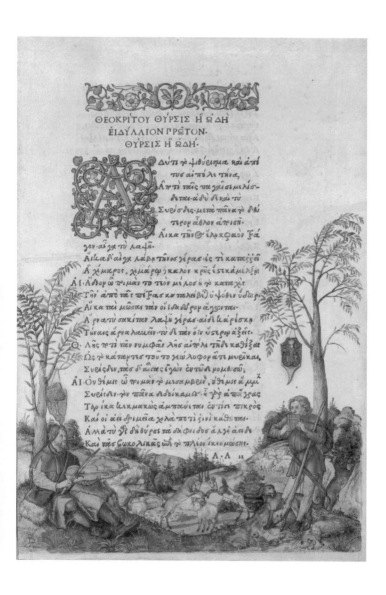

32 Albrecht Dürer, 'A pastoral landscape with shepherds playing a viola and panpipes', page from Theocritus, *Idylls* (1496), watercolour and gouache heightened with pen and ink and gold.

barbarians, and lauded his appointment to the presidency of
Maximilian's new College of Poets in Vienna as a sign of the dev-
elopments that were fast making Germany 'another Athens for
our sort of people'.[45] He entreated him for the titles of Greek
books he had encountered and even sent him the trial sheet for
the polyglot Bible.[46] If not in Venice, where he travelled at least
once and possibly twice, then Dürer, who was close to Celtis as
well, certainly encountered Aldus in Pirckheimer's library: a splen-
did pastoral scene on the opening page of Theocritus' *Idylls* (1496)
is the finest of the miniatures he executed for his friend's Greek
Aldines (illus. 32).[47] He also had an Aldine of his own: the master
woodcut artist, co-designer of the fantastical, monumental *Triumphal Arch* for Maximilian, possessed a copy of the *Hypnerotomachia
Poliphili*.[48]

Praise and public recognition from Aldus meant a lot to this
pioneering generation of German humanists – this despite his
never publishing even one of their learned or poetic works. There
was no market, apparently, for Celtis' Greek grammar, which its
author had sent him lacking in accents, or for the bilingual dictionary, which Celtis claimed to have come upon 'in the Hercynian
Forest among the Druids' (that is, at the abbey of Sponheim in
western Germany, home of the 'druidic' Abbot Trithemius and
his impressive library).[49] But the way Aldus put his press in his
German visitors' service still shows that the benefits were mutual.
In September 1498, he printed Reuchlin's Roman speech – only
twelve leaves long, a piece of diplomatic oratory concerning a
princely marriage: it was by far the least significant thing he had
yet published under his own name.[50] Returning to find Maximilian
at Metz, Reuchlin immediately pursued what he referred in a
letter to Aldus as his friend's 'case'.[51] While it no doubt enhanced
Reuchlin's reputation, the printed oration might also have been
seen by both as a means of smoothing Aldus' path to the imperial
court, where his more erudite editions would have less immediate

purchase. Indeed, Aldus may have had this lesson in mind when, at what seems to have been the height of anticipation around 1504–5, he chose which works to dedicate to those court figures whose support he believed he had. To Matthäus Lang (1469–1540), secretary to Maximilian and provost of Augsburg, later cardinal and prince-archbishop of Salzburg, he dedicated a volume of Aristotle and related texts in Latin, translated into that language around thirty years earlier by Theodore Gaza (*c.* 1398–1475). With most of these texts already published in Greek (and naturally dedicated to Alberto Pio), this was a rare instance of a stand-alone translation, and surely reflects what Aldus judged would be received as a highly learned publication in a society and milieu less intellectually restricted or advanced.[52] To Johannes Collaurius (Kollauer, 1459–1519), another imperial secretary, he dedicated Pontano's didactic poems – likewise a concession, this time to the contemporary, though perhaps a smart choice if we consider promoting the prestige and purchase of specifically Italian humanism (and Italian humanists) at court to have been a priority.[53]

Amidst these publications in August 1504 was issued the short epic on Maximilian, called *Encomiastica* and written by the Vicenza-born, Friuli-based Giovanni Stefano Emiliano, alias Helius Quinctius Aemilianus Cimbriacus (*c.* 1449–1499).[54] The work was dedicated to Maximilian by Giovanni Ricuzzi Vellini (1468–1546), a humanist, Franciscan and professor of theology at Vienna, called Camers after his Italian home town of Camerino in the central Apennines. In order that the scholarly community could read and learn of the great deeds of Frederick and Maximilian – the high point in this specific work being the liberation of the young king of the Romans (Maximilian's title as co-ruler and before official papal recognition as emperor) from captivity in Bruges in 1488 – Camers had travelled from Austria to Venice to have a copy of these verses made. 'I made my way to the Academy of Aldus of Rome,' he wrote in the dedication, 'so that they could be printed accurately and fully free of fault': 'this was done exactly so, for nothing more welcome, nothing more agreeable could have befallen Aldus than that he should release the deeds of the divine Caesar, put into print under his direction on account of his incredible devotion to Your Majesty, into the hands of men.'[55]

The publication of Cimbriacus' *Encomiastica* was a means of advertising the link to Aldus that these German and Viennese humanists enjoyed. The author was not unknown to Venetians: he had dedicated a collection of shorter poems to Nicolò Donà (1434–1497), Venetian patriarch of Aquileia, and wrote the epitaph for his tomb.[56] Nor was it an unknown text in Vienna; Cuspinianus had a copy.[57] But for this august purpose it would be surprising for the work of a deceased Italian poet of essentially regional importance with no evident connection to Aldus to be the best they could get. A clue as to what Camers might have initially had in mind comes in a letter Aldus wrote in September 1504 to their mutual friend Conrad Celtis. Full of praise for Celtis, of whose recent book-hunting adventures he had heard so much, Aldus nevertheless wished to follow up on something his correspondent apparently already knew from Camers, namely that Aldus had declined the opportunity to print some poems in praise of Maximilian written by Celtis and his students from the College of Poets, which had been recited before the monarch that March. 'Of course I would as gladly gratify your wishes as anyone else's,' Aldus wrote, 'but one must beware of kings; for I am not unmindful of that line from Ovid: "Or do you not know that kings have long arms?"'[58] It is not hard to see what Aldus meant. These panegyrical poems – particularly Celtis' – revel not only in the revival of the arts on German soil but in a victory of German forces led by Maximilian over Bohemian mercenaries: as published in Augsburg the following year, the collection is blatantly nationalistic.[59] The events in Cimbriacus' encomium were, like the poet, safely in the past. Given his humanist friends and patrons in other Central European realms, serving monarchs it was unwise needlessly to antagonize – like Vladislaus II of Bohemia and Hungary, whose soldiers had been defeated – printing this work of Celtis and collaborators may have been a bridge Aldus was unwilling to cross.

But there is another sense to Aldus' remark as well. The long arm of kings was not just evident in their power to harm; it was also manifest in their ability to suffocate with their embrace. Aldus was wary of republics, or rather of what they could do to their non-citizens; he had long associated with princes, and associated princes with Greek philosophy. Now he was pursuing imperial patronage, to bring his projected *Neakademia* north. Yet still he feared it being compromised by that long reach. In autumn 1505, he actually dispatched Cuno from Venice to pursue his business, with letters for the three dedicatees: Matthäus Lang, Collaurius and Maximilian.[60] As Cuno's letter to Pirckheimer, written on his return to Venice, informs us, Aldus was ready to move: the prospect of becoming a court printer and the importance of avoiding it must have loomed large in Aldus' mind.

Reuchlin despaired of his attempt to raise Aldus' cause with a prince distracted by military matters and lamented how Germany 'never stopped being uncivilized': 'what can be said of letters in the midst of war, of Apollo in the belly of Mars, of Helicon in the camp?'[61] Nothing came of the assurances Cuspinianus once made that the title of count palatine was at hand. For his part, Pirckheimer, perhaps more clear-eyed about Maximilian than those required to jostle for his patronage, was not surprised that the Academy plans went nowhere.[62] Nevertheless, and given the long-term investment in these connections, the effort expended and the pride swallowed, for Aldus their failure was a source of frustration. By late 1506 he had, Cuno wrote, 'girded himself again for the printing of Greek texts', disappointed in those hopes

ΕΥΡΙΠΙΔΟΥ
ΕΚΑΒΗ·

HECVBA·
EVRIPIDIS TRAGICI POETAE
HECVBA: LATINA FACTA
ERASMO ROTERODA-
MO INTERPRETE·

POLYDORI VMBRA·

encouraged, as his friends believed, from the top.[63] The Alsatian
Jakob Spiegel (1483–1547), another of those who had tried to
further his cause, would later recall Aldus as 'thoroughly devoted
to Caesar especially and to the Germans', but there was to be no
future *in media barbaria* (as he had called it to Celtis) for him.[64]

This is where Erasmus comes back into the picture. He was
in Bologna in October 1507 when he first wrote to Aldus, touting
his recommendations from mutual friends in England and offering
up his Euripides translations – which, he revealed, he had based
on Aldus' Greek edition – to be published (illus. 33 and 34).[65]
Aldus had returned to Venice where, buoyed by the successful
conclusion to a lawsuit against the piratical Filippo Giunta, he

33 Euripides, *Hecuba* (in Greek), from Εὐριπίδου τραγῳδίαι ἑπτακαίδεκα (1503).
34 Euripides, *Hecuba* (in Latin, trans. Erasmus of Rotterdam), from *Hecuba et
Iphigenia in Aulide Euripidis tragoediae . . .* (1507).

was preparing to throw himself back into a number of interesting projects: the younger Pliny, Plutarch, even Plato. A ready-made publication opened the door but, once invited to join Aldus in Venice, Erasmus set himself to putting the finishing touches on what must have been his real object all along: the vastly expanded edition of the *Adagía*, published by Aldus in September 1508. It was plainly the most important 'modern' Aldine since Poliziano ten years previous. The Dutch visitor spent those months lodging in the house of Andrea d'Asola and working in the frenetic atmosphere of the print shop that had now relocated across the Grand Canal to San Paternian, where top scholars, rare manuscripts and fresh copy rubbed up against correctors, compositors and pressmen; the most vivid testimonials to it are those found in his writing, especially the essay on 'Festina lente'. Erasmus does not address the failed imperial ventures, or the idea of the Academy, a title which by now Aldus had ceased to use for his printing operation. In additions made to the text eighteen years later, he mentioned the manuscripts and gifts that arrived from Hungary and Poland but said nothing about Germany.[66] Yet in the context of living in such close quarters and on such intimate terms, Erasmus' insistence in his exposition of the printer's mark on the superiority of the eternal empire of letters to the worldly empire of material things takes on even greater significance. A book stamped with the Aldine anchor was truer currency than any emperor's coin.

ON 11 AUGUST 1508, THE CHURCH OF San Bartolomeo in Venice was host to a remarkable gathering. The famed mathematician Luca Pacioli (*c.* 1447–1517) was giving a public lecture on Book 5 of Euclid's *Elements* and, joined by the pope, the emperor and the other distinguished figures (including the artist) depicted in Albrecht Dürer's *Feast of the Rose Garlands*, painted for that church two years before, the leading men of Venice were all in attendance. Ambassadors, theologians, doctors, patricians, artists, scholars – and among them, *Aldus Manutius Romanus*. Of the 92 people present whose names were recorded are many one would have encountered at Aldus' shop a five-minute walk away: Janus Lascaris, in Venice as ambassador of the French king; Bernardo Bembo and Marin Sanudo, two of Aldus' most important and most longstanding patrician backers; Fra Giovanni Giocondo (*c.* 1433–1515), architect and scholar, who had found the complete ten-book version of Pliny the Younger's letters in France and copied the manuscript for Aldus to print; and the humanist Giambattista Egnazio (1478–1553), Aldus' close friend (illus. 35).[67] Erasmus was not named, but he named Egnazio and Lascaris among those who had helped him, sharing manuscripts of yet-unpublished texts, in those final frantic months before the *Adagia*'s publication. Aldus, it seemed, was at the heart of a new 'School of Athens'.

But the long arm of kings – a fact of life of which Aldus once reminded Conrad Celtis – would intrude on this world too. The political disquiet and wars of Italy, which had so disturbed Aldus in the early years of the Aldine Press, were now closing in. In December 1508, at Cambrai, an alliance for the destruction of the Venetian state was agreed between Louis XII of France, Emperor Maximilian I and Ferdinand II of Aragon, joined in March the next year by Pope Julius II. One of the key negotiators, acting on behalf of the French king, was Alberto Pio. Early in 1509 Aldus, who one year earlier had been tasked with obtaining a Venetian *condotta* for Alberto's brother, was still trying to ride things out: in March and April he dedicated the successive volumes of Horace and Sallust respectively to Geoffroy Carles, president of the Senate of French-occupied Milan, and to Bartolomeo d'Alviano, then lord of Pordenone and second in command of the Venetian army.[68] On 14 May, however, D'Alviano's forces were crushed by the French east of the river Adda at a place called

35 List of attendees at Luca Pacioli's lecture at San Bartolomeo, Venice, on 11 August 1508, printed in his edition of Euclid's *Opera* (1509). Aldus Manutius Romanus is in the 12th line from the bottom.

Mnes hi funt qui interfuere. In diui Bartholomei æde: cũ ego Lucas Paciolus Burgenſis Sancti Sepulchri Ex mino ritana Francisci familia Quintum Euclidis profiteri ſolẽ niter cæpi præfatione hac prius habita. M.D.viii . Au guſti.die.xi.Et in primis..

¶ Clariſſimus Vir. Ioãnes Lascares ad ſenatum Venetũ chriſtianiſſimi francoꝛ Regis Orator . ¶ Vir clariſſimus Philippus fer rerius Barchinonenſis Catholici Hispaniarum Regis ad eundem Sena tum Orator. ¶ Reuerendus Apoſtolorum preſul Iſidorus bagnolus Se reniſſimi Principis Cancellarius. ¶.ꝗ. Ioannes Baptiſta Egnatius Vir omni litteraꝛ genere præſtans. ¶.ꝗ. Vincentius Dulcius.

¶ Reuerendi Sacre Theologie Profeſſores.

¶ Magiſter Gabriel Venetus Eremitãiæ Fæmilie teruiſinæ prouinciæ præſes. ¶.M. Gabriel Brunus Venetus Minoritanæ Familiæ Romaniæ Prouinciæ Miniſter. ¶.M. Petrus Lucignanenſis eius dem familie. ¶.M. Iacobus fauentinus eiusdem familiæ. ¶.M. Ioannes Andreas de ciuitali. ¶.M. Petrus de cruce Hispanus. ¶.M. Antonius foroiu lienſis. ¶.M. Germanus Guardianus. ¶.M. Nicolaus Mutinenſis. ¶.M. Angelus Venetus. ¶.M. Simon Venetus Regens. ¶ Sacre Theo. bacalarius formatus. Frater Petrus terrenouanenſis. ¶.S.Theo. Bacalarius Frater Bartholomeus montalcinas . ¶ Frater Iocundus Veronenſis Antiquarius. Omnes prelibati Eiusdem Minoritanæ Fa miliæ. ¶ Hieronimus Riginus Mantuanus Eremita. ¶ Sebaſtianus Leonardus Cosmographus.

¶ Magnificus Vir Bernardus Bembus Doctor ꝗ æques. ℣.M.V. Mari nus Georgius Doctor. ℣.M.V. Sebaſtianus foscarenus Philoſophie p̃ feſſor Clariſſimus. ℣.M.V. Gabriel Maurus æques. ℣.M.V. Franci scus donatus æques. ℣.M.V. Vincentius Quirinus Doctor. ℣.M.V. Petrus pascalicus Doctor ꝗ æques. ℣M.V. Nicolaus Teupul⁹ Doctor ℣.M.V. Daniel Rainerius aduocator comunis. ℣ Excellens Vir Joan nes Baptiſta Brocardus.

Medici Illuſtres.

℣ Benedictus Thedaldus. ℣ Marinus Brocardus. ℣ Franciscus Valen tinus. ℣ Alexander Veronenſis. ℣ Ambrosius Leo Nolanus. ℣ Ro dulfus Cæmertes. ℣ Matheus Feltrenſis. ℣ Cæſar Optatus. ℣ Ascanius Eſinus. ℣ Excellens ſtudiorum humanitatis profeſſor Hieronimus Ma ſerius Foroliuienſis. ¶.M.V. Hieronimus Sauorgnanus. ℣.M.V. Frã ciscus Duodus. ℣.M.V. Vincentius Grimanus. ℣.M.V. Franciscus ꝗ Iacobus fratres Cornelii. ℣.M.V. Thomas Iuſſinianus. ℣.M.V. Mar cantonius Cornerius. ℣M.V. Federicus Molinus. ℣.M.V. Petrus Do natus. ℣.M.V. Petr⁹ Contaren⁹. ℣.M.V. Donat⁹ Legius. ℣.M.V. Lau rentius Bragadenus. ℣.M.V. Marinus Sanutus. ℣.M.V. Angelus Pi ſaurius. ℣.M.V. Petrus Mocenicus. ℣.M.V. Sanctus Tronus. ℣.M. V. Laurẽtius Memmus. ℣.M.V. Carolus Contarenus. ℣.M.V. Domi nicus priolus. ℣.M.V. Ioannes Bembus. ¶ Flaminius poeta calenus ℣ Aldus Manutius Romanus. ℣ Palladius Soranus poeta. ¶ Leonar dus Auguſtini pratenſis. ℣ Petrus Zianus. ℣ Iacobus draganus. ℣ Ma theus Cinus Florentinus. ℣ Bartholomeus. Franciscus ꝗ Paulus fratres Rompiaſii. ℣ Nicolaus Sapa. ℣ Lucas Carolus. ℣ Bartholomeus Pe dretus. ℣ Laurentius Papienſis Muſicus. ℣ Franciscus maſſarius. ℣ Ia cobus Coccus. ℣ Marcus Antonius Bragadenus. Hi tres adolescẽtes ſũm me indolis. ℣ Petrus Priolus. ℣ Sebaſtianus Priolus. ¶ Bernardus rocelaius ꝗ Ioãnes eius filius Florentini. ℣ Iacobus Georgius Mathema ticæ Sectator. ¶ Georgius Tragurinus eiusq. filius Marcus. ℣ Alexius Bergomenſis. ℣ Ioãnes Marcus Canotius Patauinus. ℣ Petrus Lom bardus. Hi quatuor prefati Architectonica Clari. ¶ Bernardinus Pe rulus Vrbinas. ℣ Alexander francius ꝗ Vanotius Pauli Senenſes. ℣ Ot

Agnadello. In short order, the entire mainland state of Venice evaporated, its armies driven back to the lagoon. Aldus' premonitions had been correct: a republic under siege was no place for a foreigner, and especially not for Alberto Pio's man. If he ever resented his patron for this, he never showed it. The shop closed again, and Aldus took his family to Ferrara.[69] The Pio were anxious for him and advised on how he and Andrea d'Asola ought best to divide and preserve their business and property interests. Leonello Pio even offered to share his living quarters in the castle at Novi to accommodate him. But evidently Aldus did not think Carpi was safe either. Instead, during the years of this great hiatus, he wandered. He went to Bologna and from there down to Siena for a final meeting with Erasmus, then serving as tutor to two natural sons of the king of Scotland. In Milan he had his meeting with Jean Grolier, who would become the sixteenth century's most renowned collector of Aldine books. The emperor Maximilian wrote to Isabella d'Este, asking that properties belonging to Maria Torresani's dowry in Asola, which town had (temporarily) fallen from Venetian to Mantuan control and was held by the marchioness herself, be restored to 'our faithful, beloved' Aldus, *familiare nostro*; Aldus later passed through Mantua to see Isabella as well. A previous conflict had seen his own faraway home town of Bassiano pass in and out of the possession of Lucrezia Borgia. Now he returned to Ferrara, where she pledged to house and fund his Academy (at some indeterminate acceptable time), and where, in a new draft of his will, he named her – likely the only person at this level of society to know at first hand both him and his place of origin – an executor of his estate alongside Andrea and the Pio brothers. As alliances shifted, the Venetian position eventually recovered. With his mainland affairs largely in order and the immediate threats to the Republic averted, Aldus took advantage of a temporary peace in the spring of 1512 to return his family to Venice and himself, again, to work. Alberto Pio switched from

French to imperial service, and finally established himself as
Maximilian's ambassador in Rome to the new pope, Leo X. The
War of the League of Cambrai, waged in a bewildering array of
different alliances, would continue until the end of Aldus' life.

His last years were among his most productive. The Greek
programme, largely under the direction of the Cretan Marcus
Musurus (*c*. 1470–1517), realized one of its most monumental
achievements, the *editio princeps* of Plato, and the Latin programme
was re-energized too, with the contributions of Egnazio, Giocondo
and the patrician humanist Andrea Navagero (1483–1529) resulting in increasingly scholarly editions. Yet the prefaces also capture
the impatient voice of someone who felt very deeply just how
much work there was still for him to do. In the dedication to
Alberto Pio of the Lucretius edition issued in January 1515, Aldus
mentioned the poor health he had been suffering for some months,
which was getting worse.[70] This would be the last volume published
in his lifetime. He died in Venice on 6 February 1515. His death
was announced in April in the manner of most Aldine announce-
ments. In the preface to Lactantius, Giambattista Egnazio wrote
movingly of the 'grievous wound' (*grave vulnus*) his friend's departure
had inflicted on him personally and on the entire republic of
letters. 'There is in the whole of Europe scarcely anyone of even
moderate learning', he said, 'who has not been touched by some
singular kindness of Manutius.'[71] On the morning of 8 February
his obsequies were held at the church of San Paternian. The funeral oration was pronounced by Raffaele Regio, one of the city's
official public lecturers. His body was laid out surrounded by
books; it was then put into storage. He had stipulated that it
was to be taken to Carpi, to rest in a tomb to be determined by
the Pio.[72]

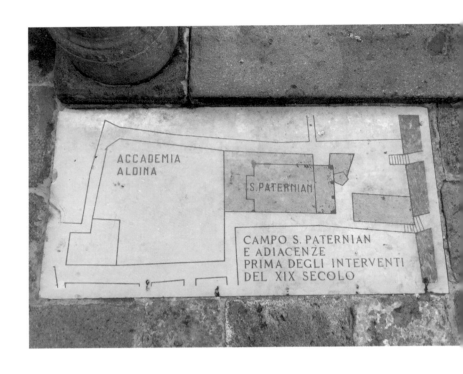

ACCADEMIA
ALDINA

S. PATERNIAN

CAMPO S. PATERNIAN
E ADIACENZE
PRIMA DEGLI INTERVENTI
DEL XIX SECOLO

Utopia

'ithin the bounds of Europe today, there is no race so barbarous or so remote that it does not know and revere the name of Aldus': in December 1516, the continent's educated readership learned that these words, from Giambattista Egnazio's printed eulogy, were, if anything, too modest.[1] A marvellous island had been discovered, somewhere in the New World, and its inhabitants were found to have the most remarkable customs and means of governing themselves. The place was called Utopia, and, through the account of Raphael Hythlodaeus, the traveller who related his journeys and observations to Thomas More (1478–1535), who then wrote up the whole episode and published it with the help of his friend Erasmus, Europeans were made to consider a society without private property, political tyranny, religious intolerance or lawyers. Among the pleasantest findings was the Utopians' aptitude and love for Greek, so great that in a short time they had mastered the language and eagerly read the philosophers and poets. Raphael had brought them Lascaris' grammar, Plato, Aristotle and Theophrastus; 'of the poets,' he said, 'they have Aristophanes, Homer and Euripides, also Sophocles in the smallish type of Aldus,' referring not to the italic (the Utopians would have little interest in Latin things, the travellers were sure) but to Griffo's last Greek fount.[2] They had no previous knowledge of printing and the European visitors had never practised it either, but, given a general idea

36 Plaque in Campo Manin, Venice, indicating the former church and campo of San Paternian and the location of the Aldine 'Academy'.

and especially the example of these Aldine books, they quickly taught the art to themselves and perfected it. Already they had turned out thousands of copies.

In Thomas More's time, as in ours, Utopia – as the name of his fictional island and the title of his book – was often pronounced by English speakers as YOU-*topía*, as if it were from the Greek εὐ-τόπος (*eu-topos*) or 'Good Place'. But it actually comes from οὐ-τόπος (*ou-topos*) or 'No-Place'. As a good place that is really a no-place, however, it has remained a powerful idea. The same could be said of Aldus Manutius. The press continued to operate in Venice: it would eventually pass into the hands of his son Paolo (1512–1574) and grandson Aldo 'the Younger' (1547–1597), becoming distinguished in the hands of Paolo for its service to Latin scholarship and then to the Catholic Counter-Reformation, and surviving until the end of Aldo's life. In 1515, however, the Manutius children returned with their mother to her home town of Asola. While the dolphin and anchor and the name ALDVS continued to grace the publications, it was their grandfather Andrea Torresani and uncles Gian Francesco and Federico who ran the press as 'Aldus' heirs'.[3]

Upon hearing the news of his death, Willibald Pirckheimer in Nuremberg wrote what he called 'Aldus' Epitaph':

> Since there was no place in the world for Aldus
> Where at last the Academy he conceived could be
>   founded,
> 'Foolish age,' he said, 'and unworthy Earth, farewell!',
> And carried off the enterprise to the Elysian Fields.[4]

To the end, then, and despite over a decade of plans and promises, and even a brief period of existence as a gathering of philhellenes and drinking companions, the Aldine Academy also remained more an idea than a place. As far as we know, moreover, this paper epitaph was the only one Aldus ever received – just as the ephemeral show of books arrayed around his body for the funeral at San Paternian would be his only monument. His last will stipulated a burial in Carpi, whereas the previous draft had indicated a preference for a church of the Observant Franciscans, leaving the final decision in the hands of Alberto and Leonello Pio. The Observant Franciscan church of San Nicolò in Carpi was intended for the Pio funeral chapel, which suggests that this was where he had in mind. Yet the church – part of Alberto's scheme for monumentalizing himself and his statelet – was under major renovation when Aldus died; the funeral chapel would ultimately never be realized.[5] Aldus' body probably never left Venice and was probably forgotten. There is no sign it ever received a formal interment. If it did, the interment left no record and no trace. The church of San Paternian was closed in 1807 during the Napoleonic suppressions. In 1871 it was finally demolished, along with the neighbouring property which had

37 Giovan Francesco Rustici, *Tomb Effigy of Alberto Pio*, 1535, bronze (with traces of gilding).

been home to the Aldine Press. Today a plaque commemorates what once stood there, but the site is taken up by the open space of Campo Manin and a 1970s edifice now housing the Intesa Sanpaolo bank (illus. 36).

The reason the funeral chapel was never finished is that Alberto Pio ended his life in exile. After Maximilian's death in 1519 he had become politically estranged from the emperor's successor, Charles V, and eventually returned to his old French

38 Detail from Giovan Francesco Rustici, *Tomb Effigy of Alberto Pio*.

allegiance. The defeat of the French by Charles' forces in the Battle of Pavia (1525) and then the Sack of Rome (1527) by a renegade imperial army – during which Alberto remained with Pope Clement VII, joining the besieged pontiff in the Castel Sant'Angelo – sealed his fate. Carpi was taken by the Este of Ferrara; in September 1527, Alberto, compensated for his service and given a large pension by King Francis I (r. 1515–47), left for France. He established himself at court and, from a palace in the rue Saint-Antoine, became an important figure in Parisian intellectual life and for the Italian artists who were migrating north, but he would never return to Italy. His death in Paris on 8 January 1531 was preceded by his taking of the Franciscan habit and followed by his burial with sumptuous ceremony in the presence of the king at the Observant convent of the Cordeliers.[6]

Four years later, a funeral monument with an effigy of Alberto in bronze was erected in the nave of the same church. Commissioned by his nephew Rodolfo Pio – once the child on whose education Leonello had sought advice from his former tutor, now papal nuncio to France, soon to be made a cardinal, an exceptional collector – from the Florentine sculptor Giovan Francesco Rustici (1475–1554) and found today at the Louvre, the depiction of the late prince *gisant-accoudé* (semi-recumbent, supported by a single elbow) was the first of its kind in France (illus. 37).[7] Accoutred *all'antica* in military costume, with muscle cuirass, pteruges and greaves, Alberto sinks into the soft bed and tasselled cushion adorned with arabesques – a brilliant effect in bronze that simultaneously gives life and bespeaks an eternal sleep. Deep in contemplation, his head rests on a closed right hand as he looks intently into an open book. At his feet lie two more books, large folio volumes, their covers decorated in moresque patterns (illus. 38). These specific patterns were developed locally by Francesco Pellegrino, an Italian artisan Alberto had protected in Paris. But they may have also been intended to evoke some of the prince's prized possessions. We know that moresques adorned the cover of one of the trophies of his book collection. This was the dedication copy of the first volume of the Aldine Aristotle, printed for Alberto on vellum. Aldus had it bound in Venice and decorated: inside with the Pio arms, outside with a plaquette of Julius Caesar in profile (illus. 39).[8] Thus the moresques and the philosophical folios together refer back to the beginning – to the monuments more lasting than bronze. While the combination of active and contemplative elements in the sculptural depiction indicates a man distinguished by arms and letters, Rodolfo Pio, who inherited his uncle's library, knew he was having commemorated one who had been made famous as philosopher-prince by Aldus Manutius. The now-lost inscription on the monument's pedestal identified him as prince of Carpi, but also as a 'follower of the fate of King Francis', both bereft of their Italian possessions.[9] The Albertine city was yet another no-place, never fully built and then summarily abandoned, more real in those texts and relationships than in any actuality.

Posthumously placeless, Aldus instead became contested territory. The earliest sign of this was in Germany, in the first great religious and intellectual controversy of the 1510s: the campaign to destroy Jewish books and the battle to defend them waged by Aldus' old friend Johannes Reuchlin. A group of Reuchlin's humanist backers published a satirical collection of letters purporting to be exchanges between his enemies, which they titled *Letters of Obscure Men*. Keeping the real identities of their printers to themselves, they released the book with a colophon that named the place of publication as Venice and the printer as 'Aldus Minutius'.[10] This spelling appeared in multiple editions, and, as *minutius* is Latin for 'lesser' or 'more insignificant', it was surely intentional. The first impressions were made in blackletter type, so there was no actual attempt to pass it off as an Aldine book. The implication was that the 'greater Aldus', advocate of real learning, would

39 Cover of the dedication copy of the Aldine Aristotle, vol. 1 (1495), given
by Aldus to Alberto Pio.

INDEX

LIBRORVM PROHIBITORVM,

·cum Regulis
confectis per Patres a Tridentina Synodo
delectos, auctoritate Sanctiss.
D. N. Pii IIII, Pont. Max.
comprobatus.

ROMAE,
Apud Paulum Manutium, Aldi F.
MD LXIIII.
IN AEDIBVS POPVLI ROMANI.

j.s. V. V. V. z ?
Ex lib. Joannis Jacob de Loberg - S. C. S. E. D.

40 Title page of *Index librorum prohibitorum* (Rome, 1564).

have been on their side. Erasmus, who supported the pro-Reuchlin cause, may have been thinking about this episode when, in his expanded treatment of 'Festina lente', he raised the spectre of false Venetian imprints and bewailed the deleterious impact that dishonest printers were having, above all in Germany.[11]

But by now it was 1526, and Erasmus had not only rejected but become increasingly alarmed by the direction of the Reformation that many of Reuchlin's other champions and followers supported. This would not save him, though: to many in Rome and around the Sorbonne in Paris, Erasmus had paved the way for Martin Luther and even came close to holding the same ideas. The man who took up the cudgels against him on behalf of this party was none other than the philosopher-prince, Alberto Pio. In a series of vicious critiques, rebuttals and invectives, and alongside their theological combat, the two men who owed so much to it traded blows over the legacy of Aldus Manutius. To Alberto, a reference Erasmus had made in *The Praise of Folly* to Aldus having republished his Latin grammar several times had been meant to mock and represented the utmost ingratitude towards a man who, 'whether you like it or not', had been his boss; Erasmus retorted with the signs of Aldus' esteem.[12] The last volleys were still being exchanged in print after Alberto's death. Even then, Erasmus could not let the matter rest. He satirized Alberto's ostentatious obsequies and religious traditionalism in a colloquy called *The Seraphic Funeral* and, by now losing his cool with much of Italy and ever the dyspeptic, mocked the mean fare on offer at Andrea d'Asola's house in another called *Squalid Opulence*.[13]

From all these controversies and exchanges, however, Aldus himself emerged unscathed. As scholars increasingly saw themselves divided by religion, he could still be claimed by everyone. In a sense he was saved for all of them by dying when he did: before 1517, before Luther's 95 Theses and the outbreak of the Reformation. This should not obscure the fact that Aldus was evidently worth fighting for: reputations depended on his authority. To those of us studying the decades around 1500, the consequences of these later religious rifts for those who lived too long can be bitterly ironic. When, in 1564, the *Index of Prohibited Books* agreed at the Council of Trent upheld a Catholic ban on many of the works of Erasmus, it made an exception for the edition of the *Adagia* then being revised by Paolo Manuzio.[14] The irony is not merely that the original had been published by Aldus, but that it was the same Paolo who published the *Index* (illus. 40).

Nowhere, and everywhere. The idea of the 'library without walls' – a common repository of reproducible texts shared by a European republic of letters – which Aldus and Erasmus had crafted and promoted was an undoubted success, ensuring Aldus' place as a humanist hero in the cultural history and memory of the Renaissance. And yet we have seen how this idea was developed as a solution in the wake of disappointment. The story of the invention of the publisher is one of many such solutions. The intellectual character of his labour, the reforming nature of his mission, the elevated status of his vocation: each was an argument to hold an alternative at bay. 'Others will better forge the breathing bronze,' says the shade of Anchises to Aeneas: you, Roman, are made to rule.[15] It was an idea to which Aldus held even as he struggled to effect it; and yet it inspired others to join and emulate him, and transformed the culture and nature of both the book and the press.

CHRONOLOGY

c. 1450	Born in Bassiano (Lazio), a small hill town south of Rome
1467–75	In Rome, studying under Domizio Calderini and Gaspare da Verona
From 1475	In Ferrara, where he attends the school of Battista Guarini, a centre for Greek studies, and meets the young philosopher-prince Giovanni Pico della Mirandola
23 July 1475	Alberto III Pio di Savoia born at Carpi to Leonello I Pio and Caterina Pico della Mirandola (Giovanni Pico's sister)
1482	War between Venice and Ferrara; Aldus leaves Ferrara for Mirandola; en route to Carpi
1483–9	At Carpi as tutor to the Pio
1484	Exchanges letters with Angelo Poliziano, leading Florentine humanist and intimate friend of Giovanni Pico
1489/90	Aldus relocates to Venice, apparently to establish a printing enterprise; his *Musarum panagyris* and other poems are published together with a letter to Caterina Pico, setting out views on the importance of the study of Greek
1491	'Alto Mannuccio' named among the many scholars met by Angelo Poliziano on his manuscript-hunting visit to Venice made with Pico
1494	Invasion of Italy by King Charles VIII of France; rise of Savonarola in Florence; deaths of Poliziano and Giovanni Pico della Mirandola

February–March 1495	Constantine Lascaris, *Erotemata*, is the first publication of the Aldine Press
1495–8	The first edition of the works of Aristotle published in Greek: Aldus' most substantial editorial achievement
July 1498	Aldus publishes the works of the late Angelo Poliziano: their correspondence is included
c. September 1498	Granted agricultural estates in the district of Novi by Alberto Pio
1499	Death of Pierfrancesco Barbarigo, silent partner of Aldus Manutius and Andrea Torresani d'Asola and largest backer of their firm
December 1499	*Hypnerotomachia Poliphili*, its mysterious author and artist(s) left anonymous, printed at Venice by Aldus Manutius, '*accuratissime*'
1500	Aldus given the name 'Pius' by Alberto, though he only starts using it three years later
19 September 1500	Publishes the *Epistole* (Letters) of St Catherine of Siena in partnership with Margarete Ugelheimer: the first appearance of italic type
December 1500	Lucretius, *De rerum natura*, the first classical Latin literary work published by Aldus
April 1501	The works of Virgil, published as an *enchiridion* (in octavo) and in italic, the model for subsequent literary publications; contains Aldus' epigram in praise of his punchcutter Francesco Griffo of Bologna
July 1501	Petrarch's vernacular works, edited by Pietro Bembo; Dante follows in August 1502
c. 1502	Together with his Greek and philhellenic friends, Aldus draws up the statutes for a *Neakademia*, dedicated to camaraderie and improving their spoken Greek
June 1502	The dolphin-and-anchor device first used as Aldus' printer's mark

16 March 1503	Aldus issues a warning against the printers of Lyon counterfeiting his books
7 July 1503	Aldus' relationship with Griffo having disintegrated, Gershom Soncino publishes an edition of Petrarch in a new italic type produced by the latter, said to have made all the types Aldus had ever used
1504–5	Plans to bring Aldus to Germany to establish an 'academy' under Emperor Maximilian I intensify, but ultimately come to nothing; Aldus marries Maria Torresani, daughter of his partner Andrea
December 1505	Aldus in Carpi, ostensibly waiting for Maximilian's summons; the activity of the press stops
28 October 1507	Erasmus of Rotterdam, in Bologna, writes to Aldus, back in Venice, offering him his translations of Euripides to publish; printing activity resumes; at the start of the next year Erasmus is living in Andrea d'Asola's house and working on a vastly expanded edition of the *Adagia*
11 August 1508	Luca Pacioli in Venice to lecture on Euclid, with Aldus in attendance
September 1508	Erasmus' *Adagia* (including 'Festina lente') published by Aldus
December 1508	League of Cambrai, an anti-Venetian military alliance, agreed between Louis XII of France, Maximilian I and Ferdinand II of Aragon, later joined by Pope Julius II; Alberto Pio a negotiator for the French king
14 May 1509	Battle of Agnadello: Venice defeated by the League
1509–12	Shop closes and Aldus leaves Venice, taking his family to Ferrara; final meeting with Erasmus in Siena; meeting with Jean Grolier in Milan; Venetian position recovers
1512–15	Aldus back in Venice; printing activity resumes
September 1513	First edition of the works of Plato, dedicated to Pope Leo X

6 February 1515	Death of Aldus Manutius in Venice; funeral follows two days later
December 1516	Aldine books in Utopia (according to Thomas More)
September 1527	Alberto Pio, exiled from Carpi, to France, where he spends his last years feuding with Erasmus
1597	Death of Aldo the Younger brings an end to roughly a century of printing under the dolphin and anchor

REFERENCES

Abbreviations

Abbreviations for ancient authors and works follow the *Oxford Classical Dictionary*, 4th edition (2012).

Allen   *Opus epistolarum Des. Erasmi Roterodami*, ed. P. S. Allen et al., 12 vols (Oxford, 1906–58)

AMGC   Aldus Manutius, *The Greek Classics*, ed. and trans. N. G. Wilson (Cambridge, MA, 2016)

AMHLC   Aldus Manutius, *Humanism and the Latin Classics*, ed. and trans. John N. Grant (Cambridge, MA, 2017)

ASD   *Opera omnia Desiderii Erasmi Roterodami* (Amsterdam and Leiden, 1969–)

BAV   Vatican City, Biblioteca Apostolica Vaticana

BNCF   Biblioteca Nazionale Centrale di Firenze

BnF   Paris, Bibliothèque nationale de France

BSB   Munich, Bayerische Staatsbibliothek

BWKC   Hans Rupprich, ed., *Der Briefwechsel des Konrad Celtis* (Munich, 1934)

DBI   *Dizionario Biografico degli Italiani* (1960–2020)

Fletcher   Harry George Fletcher III, *New Aldine Studies: Documentary Essays on the Life and Work of Aldus Manutius*, with documents (San Francisco, CA, 1988)

HP   Francesco Colonna, *Hypnerotomachia Poliphili*, ed. Marco Ariani and Mino Gabriele, Tomo primo: riproduzione dell'edizione aldina del 1499 (Milan, 1998)

Infelise   Mario Infelise, ed., *Aldo Manuzio. La costruzione del mito* (Venice, 2016)

ISTC   Incunabula Short Title Catalogue

JRBW   Johannes Reuchlin, *Briefwechsel*, vol. I, ed. Matthias dall'Asta and Gerald Dörner (Stuttgart, 1999)

Lowry   Martin Lowry, *The World of Aldus Manutius: Business and Scholarship*
             in Renaissance Venice (Oxford, 1979)
Nolhac   Pierre de Nolhac, ed., *Les Correspondants d'Alde Manuce: Matériaux*
             nouveaux d'histoire littéraire (1483–1514) (Rome, 1888)
ÖNB   Vienna, Österreichische Nationalbibliothek
Orlandi   Giovanni Orlandi, ed., *Aldo Manuzio editore. Dediche, prefazioni,*
             note ai testi (Milan, 1975)
RBME   Real Biblioteca del Monasterio de El Escorial
Renouard   Antoine-Augustin Renouard, ed., *Lettere di Paolo Manuzio*
             copiate sugli autografi esistenti nella Biblioteca Ambrosiana (Paris,
             1834)
Sanudo   *I Diarii di Marin Sanuto*, ed. Rinaldo Fulin et al., 58 vols
             (Venice, 1879–1903)
Schück   Julius Schück, *Aldus Manutius und seine Zeitgenossen in Italien und*
             Deutschland (Berlin, 1862)
WPBW   *Willibald Pirckheimers Briefwechsel*, ed. Emil Reicke, vol. 1
             (Munich, 1940)

Introduction

1 Leon Battista Alberti, *De componendis cyfris*, ed. Augusto Buonafalce
   (Turin, 1998), p. 4: 'Germanum inventorem qui per haec tempora
   pressionibus quibusdam characterum efficeret ut diebus centum plus
   CCta volumina librorum opera hominum non plus trium exscripta
   redderentur dato ab exemplari.'

2 François Rabelais, *Gargantua*, ed. Pierre Michel (Paris, 1972), p. 391
   (ch. 51): 'Aultre mal ne leurs feist Gargantua, sinon qu'il les ordonna
   pour tirer les presses à son imprimerie, laquelle il avoit nouvellement
   instituée.'

3 For Bade generally, see Paul White, *Jodocus Badius Ascensius: Commentary,*
   Commerce and Print in the Renaissance (Oxford, 2013); for what follows,
   Isabelle Diu, '*Medium typographicum* et *respublica literaria*: Le Rôle de Josse
   Bade dans le monde de l'édition humaniste', in *Le Livre et l'historien:*
   Études offertes en l'honneur du professeur Henri-Jean Martin, ed. Frédéric
   Barbier et al. (Geneva, 1997), pp. 111–24; and, with a difference in
   emphasis, Katie Chenoweth, *The Prosthetic Tongue: Printing Technology and*
   the Rise of the French Language (Philadelphia, PA, 2019), pp. 82–4.

4 Erasmus, *Adagia*, II.v.34, 'Cassioticus nodus', in ASD, II.3, p. 428:
   'arctissimam atque indissolubilem amicitiam significamus . . . ab eo
   [nodo] supernae partes sic ad osculum coeunt'. More than 70 per

cent of Froben's titles in 1521–7 were by Erasmus. See Valentina
Sebastiani, *Johann Froben, Printer of Basel: A Biographical Profile and
Catalogue of His Editions* (Leiden, 2018), pp. 67–9.

5 Elizabeth Armstrong, *Robert Estienne, Royal Printer: An Historical Study of
the Elder Stephanus* (Cambridge, 1954), pp. 10, 221, 227.

6 Cic. *Off.* 1.150: 'Opificesque omnes in sordida arte versantur; nec
enim quicquam ingenuum habere potest officina.'

7 For example, Arist. *Pol.* 1.1252a, 1.1253b–1254a; see Catharina
Lis, 'Perceptions of Work in Classical Antiquity: A Polyphonic
Heritage', in *The Idea of Work in Europe from Antiquity to Modern Times*,
ed. Josef Ehmer and Catharina Lis (Aldershot, 2009), pp. 33–68;
and Catharina Lis and Hugo Soly, *Worthy Efforts: Attitudes to Work and
Workers in Pre-Industrial Europe* (Leiden, 2012).

8 For an introduction to the *paragone*, see Francis Ames-Lewis, *The
Intellectual Life of the Early Renaissance Artist* (New Haven, CT, and
London, 2002), pp. 141–61; for a thoroughgoing treatment of the
early stages of the debate, see Christiane Hessler, *Zum Paragone:
Malerei, Skulptur, und Dichtung in der Rangstreitkultur des Quattrocento*
(Berlin, 2014), with appendices of its sources; on the term, see
Claire Farago, *Leonardo da Vinci's Paragone: A Critical Interpretation with a
New Edition of the Text in the Codex Urbinas* (Leiden, 1992), pp. 8–14.

9 Baldesar Castiglione, *Il libro del Cortegiano* [1528], ed. Giulio Preti
(Turin, 1965), p. 80 (§49): 'la qual oggidì forsi par mecanica e poco
conveniente a gentilomo'.

10 Letter to Willibald Pirckheimer, 18 August 1506, in *Dürer schriftlicher
Nachlaß*, ed. Hans Rupprich, 2 vols (Berlin, 1956–69), I, pp. 52–4
(ep. 7): 'Jch pynn ein zentilam zw Fenedich worden.'

11 Text of the *Codex Urbinas* in Farago, *Leonardo da Vinci's Paragone*, p. 212
(§19): 'Se voi la chiamate mechanica perché è prima manuale, che
le mani figurano quella che trovano nella fantasia, voi scrittori,
disegnando con la penna manualmente quello che nello ingegno
vostro si trova'; p. 256 (§35): 'La scultura non è scientia ma è arte
meccanichissima'; (§36): 'lo scultore conduce le sue opere con
maggior faticha di corpo ch'el pittore, ed il pittore conduce l'opere
sue con maggior faticha di mente.'

12 Giorgio Vasari, *Le vite de' più eccellenti pittori, scultori ed architetti* [1550],
ed. Luciano Bellosi and Aldo Rossi (Turin, 1986), 'Proemio delle
Vite', p. 119: 'il disegno, che è il fondamento di quelle, anzi l'istessa
anima che concepe e nutrisce in se medesima tutti i parti degli
intelletti'. See also 'Proemio', pp. 5–18, pp. 15–16: 'la scultura e la

pittura per il vero sono sorelle, nate di un padre, che è il disegno, in un sol parto et ad un tempo'; a view held by Castiglione (*Cortegiano*, p. 81 (§49): 'l'una e l'altra da un medesimo fonte, che è il bon disegno'), who had privileged painting.

13 To Cardinal Juan de Carvajal, 12 March 1455, only in [Pius II], [*Epistolae saeculares et pontificales*] (Cologne: Arnold ther Hoernen, *c.* 1480: ISTC ip00726500), sig. p7v–q5v, q1v: 'De viro illo mirabili apud Francofordiam viso nihil falsi ad me scriptum est'; partially reproduced by Martin Davies, who addresses its ambiguities around whom and what Piccolomini saw and when, in 'Juan de Carvajal and Early Printing: The 42-Line Bible and the Sweynheym and Pannartz Aquinas', *The Library*, 6th ser., XVIII (1996), pp. 193–215.

14 In Cicero, *Epistolae ad familiares* (1469: ISTC ic00504000), sig. m11v: 'Primis in Adriaca formis impressit aenis/ Urbe libros Spira genitus de stirpe Iohannes./ In reliquis sit quanta vides spes lector habenda/ Quom labor hic primus calami superaverit artem.'

15 In Sallust, *Opera* (1470: ISTC is00051000), sig. f12r: 'Quadrigenta dedit formata volumina Crispi/ Nunc lector Venetis Spirea Vindelinus:/ Et calamo libros audes spectare notatos/ Aere magis quando littera ducta nitet.'

16 Colophon to Appian, *Historia Romana* (pt 2), trans. Pier Candido Decembrio (1472: ISTC ia00931000), sig. r7v: 'Hunc impressit et Vindelinus/ Quem Spira nobilis parens Dedalei/ Produxit ingeni faceti lepidique.'

17 A backhanded compliment disputed by Henri Estienne, *Nundinarum Francofordiensium encomium. Éloge de la foire de Francfort*, ed. Elsa Kammerer (Geneva, 2017), p. 43: 'Falso igitur dictitant Itali . . . Germanis ingenium in digitis dumtaxat esse collocatum.'

18 Colophon to Quintilian, *Institutiones oratoriae* (21 May 1471: ISTC iq00026000), sig. a1v: 'Magistri Nicolai Ienson Gallici alterius (ut vere dicam) Daedali'; to Cicero, *Epistulae ad Atticum, Brutum, et Quintum fratrem* (1470: ISTC ic00500000), sig. s5v: 'Gallicus hoc Ienson Nicolaus muneris orbi/ Attulit ingenio daedalicaque manu.' On Jenson's rhetoric of technical skill and ingenuity, see David R. Carlson, 'Nicholas Jenson and the Form of the Renaissance Printed Page', in *The Future of the Page*, ed. Peter Stoicheff and Andrew Taylor (Toronto, 2004), pp. 92–4; more broadly, see Martin Lowry, *Nicholas Jenson and the Rise of Venetian Publishing in Renaissance Europe* (Oxford, 1991).

19 Epigram of Jean Visagier, in *Ioannis Vulteii Remensis epigrammatum libri duo* (Lyon: Gryphius, 1536), vol. I, p. 54: 'Castigat Stephanus, sculpit

Colinaeus, utrunque/ Gryphius edocta manu menteque facit'; Simon de Colines (*c.* 1480–1546) was a Parisian printer. In some respects, the balance was shifting back towards *arte* and skill by the middle of the century: see Farago, *Leonardo da Vinci's Paragone*, pp. 129–37.

20 Theodor Mommsen, ed., 'Autobiographie des Venezianers Giovanni Bembo', *Sitzungsbericht der Bayerischen Akademie der Wissenschaften*, I (1861), pp. 605–6: 'Graecarum literarum reparator et latinorum librorum propagator'.

21 See Novella Macola, 'I ritratti col Petrarca', in *Le lingue del Petrarca*, ed. Antonio Daniele (Udine, 2005), pp. 135–57; and Giuseppe Patota, 'Petrarchino', *Bollettino di italianistica*, n.s., XIII.1 (2016), pp. 53–69.

22 See the Epilogue.

23 For example, AMGC, p. 8, AMHLC, p. 206; see also Oren Margolis, 'Hercules in Venice: Aldus Manutius and the Making of Erasmian Humanism', *Journal of the Warburg and Courtauld Institutes*, LXXXI (2018), pp. 116–18. On labour distinctions and overlaps within the printer's workshop, see Anthony Grafton, *Inky Fingers: The Making of Books in Early Modern Europe* (Cambridge, MA, 2020), pp. 29–55; on terminology more broadly, see David Shaw, '"Ars formularia": Neo-Latin Synonyms for Printing', *The Library*, 6th ser., XI (1989), pp. 220–30.

24 A good point of comparison, however: on whom, see William Kuskin, *Symbolic Caxton: Literary Culture and Print Capitalism* (Notre Dame, IN, 2008).

25 On some of these matters, see Ian Maclean, *Scholarship, Commerce, Religion: The Learned Book in the Age of Confessions, 1560–1630* (Cambridge, MA, 2012), pp. 97–133.

26 Margolis, 'Hercules in Venice'.

27 Erasmus, *Apologia adversus rhapsodias calumniosarum querimoniarum Alberti Pii*, in ASD, IX.6, p. 344: 'Quum rogarem quur hoc laboris caperet, "interim", inquit, "studeo".'

28 Lucien Febvre, *The Problem of Unbelief in the Sixteenth Century: The Religion of Rabelais*, trans. Beatrice Gottlieb (Cambridge, MA, 1982 [orig. 1942]), p. 16.

1 Carpi and Venice

1 See Romano Pelloni, 'S. Nicolò: Un felice compromesso', in *San Nicolò in Carpi. Un modello del classicismo Emiliano* (Modena, 1992), pp. 39–61.

2 On the figures, see Luisa Giordano, 'Alberto e i suoi maestri: I
   ritratti della cappella Pio', in *L'immagine del principe. I ritratti di Alberto III
   nel Palazzo dei Pio a Carpi*, exh. cat., Palazzo dei Pio (Carpi, 2008),
   pp. 59–87.
3 Valentina Gradellini, 'La caratterizzazione costruttiva dell'edilizia
   storica come base conoscitiva per la riduzione del rischio sismico.
   Il caso di studio del centro storico di Carpi' (Università di Bologna
   thesis, 2012), includes much useful information on the development
   of Carpi's urban fabric. See also Hans Semper, with Friedrich
   Otto Schulze and Wilhelm Barth, *Carpi. Ein Fürstensitz der Renaissance*
   (Dresden, 1882); and Manuela Rossi and Elena Svalduz, eds, *Il
   palazzo dei Pio a Carpi: Sette secoli di architettura e arte* (Venice, 2008).
4 Elena Svalduz, 'Bellissime investigazioni. Su alcuni progetti di
   Baldassarre Peruzzi per Alberto Pio da Carpi', in *Baldassare Peruzzi,
   1481–1536*, ed. Christoph L. Frommel et al. (Venice, 2005), pp.
   181–97. Archival references for the church of Carpi in the summary
   catalogue by Alessandro Giuseppe Spinelli, in *Memorie storiche e
   documenti sulla città e sull'antico principato di Carpi*, vol. VII (Carpi, 1897),
   pp. 7–8, 12–13.
5 Manfredo Tafuri, *Interpreting the Renaissance: Princes, Cities, Architects*,
   trans. Daniel Sherer (New Haven, CT, and London, 2006), p. 95.
   On style and on the Urbino model, see Elena Svalduz, '"Small Mice,
   Large Palaces": From Urbino to Carpi', in *A Renaissance Architecture
   of Power: Princely Palaces in the Italian Quattrocento*, ed. Silvia Beltramo,
   Flavia Cantatore and Marco Folin (Leiden, 2015), pp. 235–62.
6 AMGC, p. 38: 'Nam non modo assidue adiuvas provinciam nostram
   opibus tuis, sed agros quoque fertilissimos amplissimosque te mihi
   donaturum palam dicis; immo oppidum amoenum ex tuis ita meum
   futurum polliceris, ut in eo aeque ac tu iubere possim. Quod facis, ut
   bonorum librorum et Latine et Graece commodius faciliusque a me
   ibi fiat omnibus copia, constituatur etiam academia, in qua, relicta
   barbarie, bonis litteris bonisque artibus studeatur, ac tandem secentos
   annos et plus eo glandem depasti homines vescantur frugibus.'
7 On landholdings I am grateful for the advice of Robert Portass and
   Chris Wickham. On the distribution of land in Carpi, see Francesca
   Bocchi, 'I catasti quattrocenteschi a Carpi: Note per la loro
   utilizzazione storiografica', in *Società, politica, e cultura a Carpi ai tempi di
   Alberto III Pio*, 2 vols (Padua, 1981), pp. 427–67.
8 Leonello Pio to Aldus, Novi, 23 September 1498, in Renouard, pp.
   335–7 (ep. 2): 'perchè non è homo, che desidera più de mi, che Ms.

Aldo fusse, et stantiasse a Novi: de quello chio ho qui: che cognosco mio, al presente ghe ne consigneria cento biolche . . . et alhora ghe faro tale demonstratione chel cognoscerà chio lamo et forsi più chel non si crede.' On the lands, see Davide Ferretti, *Novi nel Medioevo e in età moderna* (Novi di Modena, 2013), pp. 49–51; Manuela Rossi, 'Aldo e Carpi', in *Per Aldo: 1515–2015. Scritti di bibliografia bibliofilia raccolti in occasione del quinto centinario*, ed. Alessandro Scarsella (Padua, 2015), pp. 28–9.

9 AMGC, p. 38: 'veniam equidem non invitus quocunque iusseris, ac tecum quem a teneris, ut aiunt, unguiculis educavi instituique, incumbam studio sapientiae, quam philosophian Graeco vocabulo appellamus.' Cf. Cic. *Fam.* 1.6.2: 'a teneris, ut Graeci dicunt, unguiculis'. See Semper, *Carpi*, pp. 20–21, 24.

10 Letter from Alberto Pio to Aldus, Carpi, 11 March 1505, in Nolhac, pp. 17–18 (ep. 8).

11 Leonello Pio to Aldus, Novi, 27 July 1508, in Renouard, pp. 344–5 (ep. 11): 'Del racolto delle vostre terre n'ho facto tenere conto a Jacomo Villano.' Cf. Luigi Balsamo, 'Alberto Pio e Aldo Manuzio. Editoria a Venezia e Carpi fra '400 e '500', in *Società, politica, e cultura a Carpi*, pp. 155–9.

12 Peter Humfrey, 'Cima da Conegliano and Alberto Pio', *Paragone*, XXIX, 341 (1978), pp. 86–97, and Peter Humfrey, *Cima da Conegliano* (Cambridge, 1983), pp. 33–4, 127–8 (cat. 95).

13 Nolhac, p. 17.

14 Cf. Lowry, p. 59. On his sisters, see Tiziana Plebani, '"Perché semo certi che chi nasce debbe morire": Aldo di fronte alla morte. I testamenti come fonte', in Infelise, p. 49; Annaclara Cataldi Palau, *Gian Francesco d'Asola e la tipografia aldina. La vita, le edizioni, la biblioteca dell'Asolano* (Genoa, 1998), pp. 31–3.

15 Renouard, pp. 344–5: 'Sopra tuto vorria chel fusse homo da bene, accostumato, et di bono aspecto, non altro me vi racomando.' The request for assistance in securing the *condotta* is in the same letter.

16 Sanudo, I, col. 681: 'un palazzo bellissimo, sopra il qual era dipente l'arme dil re di Franza con queste lettere: *Vivam, Vincam, et Regnabo*.'

17 Svalduz, 'Small Mice', p. 253.

18 Letter to Aldus, Novi, 12 March 1510, in Renouard, pp. 346–8 (ep. 14): 'altrove haveresti qualche obligatione, et qui seresti patron.'

19 Evident from letters of Alberto and Leonello Pio to Aldus, in Nolhac, pp. 17–18; and Renouard, p. 343 (ep. 9: Novi, December 1506).

20 Lowry, p. 58.

21 In Nolhac, p. 11 (ep. 1); Stefano Pagliaroli, *Per la biografia di Aldo Manuzio (1482–1496)* (Messina, 2021), pp. 121–5; see also Piero Scapecchi, 'Una lettera di Atramytteno a Manuzio e le prime testimonianze dell'attività di Aldo a Carpi', *La Bibliofilía*, XCVIII (1996), pp. 23–30.

22 For Poliziano, see below; for the letter of 'Candidus Romanus', 22 February 1502, see Stefano Pagliaroli, 'Gli anni bui di Aldo Manuzio', *Archivum mentis. Studi di filología e letteratura umanistica*, VI (2017), pp. 121–53, letter on pp. 143–5; and in Nolhac, pp. 28–32 (ep. 25).

23 Cic. *Sen.* 3. It has become more common to question the reality of Cato's Hellenophobia.

24 AMGC, p. 12: 'Nostris vero temporibus multos licet videre Catones, hoc est, senes in senectute Graece discere; nam [*sic*] adolescentulorum ac iuvenum Graecis incumbentium litteris iam tantus fere est numerus, quantus eorum qui Latinis.'

25 AMHLC, pp. 198–200.

26 Pagliaroli, 'Gli anni bui'.

27 AMGC, p. 24, AMHLC, p. 38.

28 AMHLC, p. 216.

29 In *Strozii poetae pater et filius* (Venice: Aldus, 1513/14), sig. o7r–p1v, o8v–p1r: 'cecropiae studiis celeberrima Divae,/ Musarumque'.

30 In preface (addressed to *literarii ludi magistris*, 'grammar-school teachers') to the second edition of his Latin grammar (1501), AMHLC, pp. 194–8.

31 For reference, see Franco Bacchelli, 'Pico, Giovanni, conte della Mirandola e Concordia', *DBI* (2015).

32 See Pagliaroli, *Per la biografia*.

33 Pagliaroli, 'Gli anni bui', pp. 129–31.

34 Manuscript and printed versions of both letters compared in Léon Dorez, 'Études Aldines III: Alde Manuce et Ange Politien', *Revue des bibliothèques*, VI (1896), pp. 319–23; see also Pagliaroli, *Per la biografia*, pp. 49–64; Schück, pp. 103–6 (epp. 1, 2).

35 BAV, MS Vat. lat. 3226, fol. 6r; BNCF, Banco Rari 97, fols 18v, 66v. See Carlo Vecce, 'Bembo e Poliziano', in *Agnolo Poliziano poeta scrittore filologo. Atti del Convegno internazionale di studi (Montepulciano, 3–6 novembre 1994)*, ed. Vincenzo Fera and Mario Martelli (Florence, 1998), pp. 477–503, esp. 482–3; and Gareth D. Williams, *Pietro Bembo on Etna: The Ascent of a Venetian Humanist* (Oxford, 2017), pp. 114–17; on

the collation, see Riccardo Ribuoli, *La collazione polizianea del codice bembino di Terenzio, con le postille inedite del Poliziano e note su Pietro Bembo* (Rome, 1981).

36   BSB, Clm 807, fol. 42v; Giovanni Pesenti, 'Diario odeporico-bibliografico inedito del Poliziano', *Memorie del Reale Istituto Lombardo di Scienze e Lettere. Classe di lettere e scienze morali e storiche*, 3rd series, XXIII (1916), p. 237.

37   This episode mentioned in Pico della Mirandola, *Oration on the Dignity of Man: A New Translation and Commentary*, ed. Francesco Borghesi, Michael Papio and Massimo Riva (Cambridge, 2012), p. 272 (§257).

38   Angelo Poliziano, *Opera omnia* (Venice: Aldus Manutius, 1498: ISTC ip00886000), sig. i2rv.

39   To Alberto Pio, in Aristotle, vol. I (1495): AMGC, p. 14; in Aristotle, vol. II (1497): AMGC, pp. 38–40; in Aristotle, vol. III (1497): AMGC, p. 48; in Gianfrancesco Pico, *De imaginatione* (1501): AMHLC, p. 202; to Gianfrancesco Pico, in Urbano Bolzanio da Belluno, *Institutiones graecae grammaticae* (1498 [or 1497]): AMGC, pp. 60–62.

40   Poliziano, *Opera omnia*, sig. l7r–m8r; cited among Poliziano examples in Erasmus, *De conscribendis epistolis*, in ASD, I.2, p. 579. On the exchange, see Martin L. McLaughlin, *Literary Imitation in the Italian Renaissance: The Theory and Practice of Literary Imitation in Italy from Dante to Bembo* (Oxford, 1995), pp. 228–48; and Jill Kraye, 'Pico on the Relationship of Rhetoric and Philosophy', in *Pico della Mirandola: New Essays*, ed. M. V. Dougherty (Cambridge, 2008), pp. 13–36.

41   Aldus, preface to Lascaris, *Erotemata*, in AMGC, p. 4 (colophon: 28 February); an alternative construction of how Aldus encountered the manuscript and used it in Lowry, pp. 224–5, and Williams, *Pietro Bembo*, pp. 130–34.

42   Martin Lowry, 'The "New Academy" of Aldus Manutius: A Renaissance Dream', *Bulletin of the John Rylands Library*, LVIII (1976), pp. 385–7.

43   See letter of Pico to Aldus, 11 February 1490, in Schück, pp. 115–16 (ep. 4).

44   In Schück, pp. 107–15 (ep. 3); with notes and translation: https://latlab.org/letter-4.

45   *Musarum panagyris* (Venice: Battista de Tortis, 1989: ISTC im00227000), poems at sig. a2r–a4r, a8rv. The whole is printed under this title in Orlandi, pp. 157–64. My edition of the poems with commentary and English translation will be available in *An*

Anthology of Neo-Latin Poetry by Classical Scholars, ed. Gesine Manuwald, Stephen Harrison, William Barton and Bobby Xinyue (London, forthcoming). Still see Curt F. Bühler, 'The First Aldine', *Papers of the Bibliographical Society of America*, XLII (1948), pp. 269–80.

46 *Theogony* (*editio princeps*: Aldus, 1496) would have been accessed in manuscript or otherwise mediated. *Works and Days*, printed *c*. 1480, is cited in a separate exhortation to Leonello.

47 Aus. *Epig.* 69; the *editio princeps*, ed. Bartolomeo Girardini (Venice: [Printer of Ausonius], 1472: ISTC ia01401000), follows the medieval fashion in rendering the name in the genitive without the diphthong: *pasiphae* (sig. c1r).

48 Jacopo Berengario da Carpi, *Isagoge breves perlucide ac uberime in Anatomiam humani corporis* (Bologna, 1522), sig. A2r: 'tecum in mansuetiorum musarum rudimentis sub foelici memoria Aldi Manutii Ro(mani) praeceptoris nostri conferebam . . . placuit autem ut porci Anotomia [*sic*] a nobis fieret'. See Charles B. Schmitt, 'Alberto Pio and the Aristotelian Studies of His Time', in *Società, politica, e cultura a Carpi*, pp. 45–6.

49 See AMGC, p. 80; Schmitt, 'Alberto Pio', pp. 47–57.

50 AMHLC, p. 182: 'cum infinitis prope rebus quibus alter orbis magis quam urbs mihi esse videtur'. The years spent by Aldus in Venice are datable from remarks in *Thesaurus, Cornu copiae, et Horti Adonidis* (August 1496), in AMGC, p. 26: 'Postquam suscepi hanc duram provinciam (annus enim agitur iam septimus)'.

51 Lowry, p. 75.

52 More information about the business and these documents: ibid., pp. 76–86.

53 *Dexteritas* or δεξιότης in Musaeus (sig. α10v), Aristotle, vol. I (sig. s6r), Theodore Gaza (sig. lΛ8r).

54 For Aldus and Griffo, see Giovanni Mardersteig, 'Aldo Manuzio e i caratteri di Francesco Griffo da Bologna', in *Studi di bibliografia e di storia in onore di Tammaro de Marinis*, ed. Giovanni Mardersteig, 3 vols (Verona, 1964), vol. III, pp. 105–47. On the italic and especially the Greek types (less praised by modern critics), see Nicholas Barker, *Aldus Manutius and the Development of Greek Script and Type in the Fifteenth Century*, 2nd edn (New York, 1992), with the influence of Aldus' own hand discussed on pp. 59–63, 111–13; also David Speranzi, 'La scrittura di Aldo e il suo ultimo carattere greco (con uno sconosciuto esemplare di tipografia)', in *Five Centuries Later. Aldus Manutius: Culture, Typography and Philology*, ed. Natale Vacalebre (Florence, 2018), pp. 29–60.

55 *AMGC*, p. 2: 'summis nostris laboribus et impendiis tantoque apparatui ad imprimenda Graeca volumina omnis generis'.

56 Sig. K6r: 'Excriptum Venetiis manu stamnea in domo Aldi Manutii Romani, & graecorum studiosi' (ISTC ia00959000, 11).

57 On this topic, see Deno J. Geanakoplos, *Greek Scholars in Venice: Studies in the Dissemination of Greek Learning from Byzantium to Western Europe* (Cambridge, MA, 1962), esp. pp. 53–70; and Nigel G. Wilson, *From Byzantium to Italy: Greek Studies in the Italian Renaissance*, 2nd edn (London, 2017), pp. 141–76. On the most important of these, see Luigi Ferreri, *Marco Musuro* (Turnhout, 2014). Some insight into this world in Erin Maglaque, *Venice's Intimate Empire: Family Life and Scholarship in the Renaissance Mediterranean* (Ithaca, NY, 2018), p. 33 ff.

58 A partial exception is the collection of astronomical texts published in 1499: see Chapter Three.

59 For example, criticism of Aristotle (vol. III) edition by Antonio Urceo Cordo, in letter to Battista Palmieri, Bologna, 15 April 1498, in *Orationes, seu Sermones, ut ipse appellabat. Epistolae. Silvae. Satyrae. Eglogae. Epigrammata* (Bologna, 1502), sig. S2r–S5r, esp. S3r; *AMGC*, pp. 40–42, 64. Cf. Vincenzo Fera, 'Aldo ai suoi lettori. Le "Prefazioni" tra progettualità e utopia', in *Aldo al lettore. Viaggio intorno al mondo del libro e della stampa in occasione del V Centinario della morte di Aldo Manuzio*, ed. Tiziana Plebani (Milan, 2016), pp. 125–6.

60 Preface to *Thesaurus*, et al.: *AMGC*, p. 26: 'Dura quidem provincia est . . . emendate imprimere Latinos libros, durior accurate Graecos, durissima non depravate vel hos vel illos duris temporibus. Quanam lingua curem ipse imprimendos libros et quo tempore, videtis.'

61 Preface to Lorenzo Maioli, *Epiphyllides in dialecticis*, et al., in *AMHLC*, p. 180: 'Undique enim vobis adsunt instrumenta ad liberales disciplinas comparandas. Habetis iam a nobis plurima Graeca volumina, tam in dialectice quam in philosophia.'

62 Codro, *Orationes*, sig. D1r: discussed in Chapter Two, and in detail in Oren Margolis, 'Printing as Architecture: Antonio Urceo Codro on Aldus Manutius', *Medioevo e Rinascimento*, XXXIII (2020), pp. 145–56, with a proposed date of late 1495 or early 1496.

63 *AMGC*, pp. 2: 'status et conditio horum temporum et bella ingentia, quae nunc totam Italiam infestant, irato Deo vitiis nostris, et mox totum orbem commotura ac potius concussura videntur, propter omnifariam hominum scelera multo plura maioraque iis, quae causa olim fuere ut totum humanum genus summergeret aquisque perderet iratus Deus.'

64 Oren Margolis, 'Hercules in Venice: Aldus Manutius and the
    Making of Erasmian Humanism', *Journal of the Warburg and Courtauld
    Institutes*, LXXXI (2018), p. 118; articulated in Patrick Baker, *Italian
    Renaissance Humanism in the Mirror* (Cambridge, 2015), p. 5.

65 AMGC, pp. 288–93 (trans. Wilson). The statutes do not propose
    a fine for mispronunciation but, alluding to the custom of this
    'sodalitas' in *De recta Latini Graecique sermonis pronuntiatione dialogus*
    (1528), Erasmus suggests that there was: ASD, I.4, p. 102; see also
    Judith Rice Henderson, 'Language, Race, and Church Reform:
    Erasmus' *De recta pronuntiatione* and *Ciceronianus*', *Renaissance and
    Reformation*, XXX (2006), pp. 12–14. For Gregoropoulos, see
    Stefanos Kaklamanis, 'Giovanni Gregoropulo, copista di libri greci e
    collaboratore di Aldo Manuzio a Venezia', in Infelise, pp. 105–25.

66 Blois, 24 December 1501, in Nolhac, pp. 26–8 (ep. 24): 'Et per che
    me scrivete volere dar fuori ἐγχειρίδιον de Homero come de Virgilio
    & Oratio, quanto ad me l'ho molto a charo & maxime andando
    vagabundo nel modo che facio . . . nihilominus ταῦτας πάντας
    προφάσεις ἡγοῦνται, & la vera causa de la vostra transmigratione dala
    Graecia alla Italia asseverano essere lo guadagno . . . tamen dicono
    che lo guadagno facto & che continuamente e per farsi da voi in
    Italia deve sublevare si quid est incommode nela Graecia, unde tuta
    la impresa hebe capo & principio.' See also Lowry, p. 86; and Stefano
    Pagliaroli, 'L'"Accademia Aldina"', *Incontri triestini di filologia classica*, IX
    (2009–10), pp. 178–9.

67 21 December 1505, in WPBW, pp. 280–82 (ep. 86): 'Alia vero in
    graecis isto toto anno non impressit . . . isto anno impressit opera
    Pontani in carmine, Aurelii cuiusdam elegias, opusculum de
    captivitate et liberacione regis Ro. apud Belgas per Italum quendam
    venuste compositum; quaedam insuper vulgaria de gradibus amoris.'
    On Cuno in Venice, see Henri-Dominique Saffrey, 'Un humaniste
    dominicaine, Jean Cuno de Nuremberg, précurseur d'Érasme à
    Bâle', *Bibliothèque d'humanisme et renaissance*, XXXIII (1971), pp. 25–33,
    and in Chapter Four.

68 WPBW, p. 281: 'Libros enim graecos a se impressos deinceps socer
    eius Andreas de Asula, bibliopola famosissimus, non accepturus erat,
    uti solebat.'

69 Letter to Aldus, 19 April 1505, in Nolhac, pp. 42–3 (ep. 35): 'La
    stampa greca havete in tutto intermessa, benche resumpturus,
    secondo che m'avisa ser Andrea.'

2 After Daedalus

1   *HP*, p. 69 ([Francesco Colonna,] *Hypnerotomachia Poliphili* (Venice: Aldus Manutius, 1499: ISTC ic00767000), sig. d7r): 'trovai uno marmoreo et vetustissimo ponte di uno assai grande et alto arco . . . Nel medio degli quali appodii alquanto supereminea allibella dil supremo dil cunto [*sic*: cuneo] dil subiecto arco, uno Porphyritico quadrato, cum uno egregio cimasio di polito liniamento, uno da uno lato, & uno pariforme da l'altro, ma di lapide Ophites. Nel dextro alla mia via, vidi nobilissimi hieraglyphi aegyptici di tale expresso. Una antiquaria galea cum uno capo di cane cristata. Uno nudo capo di bove cum dui rami arborei infasciati alle corna di minute fronde, & una vetusta lucerna. Gli quali hieraglyphi, exclusi gli rami, che io non sapea si d'abiete, o pino, o larice, o iunipero o di simiglianti si fusseron, cusi io li interpretai. PATIENTIA EST ORNAMENTVM CVSTODIA ET PROTECTIO VITAE. Da laltra parte tale elegante scalptura mirai. Uno circulo. Una ancora. Sopra la stangula dilla quale se rovolvea uno Delphino. Et questi optimamenti cusi io li interpretai. ΑΕΙ ΣΠΕΥΔΕ ΒΡΑΔΕΩΣ. Semper festina tarde.'

2   On the character of these hieroglyphs, see Christian Hülsen, 'Le illustrazioni della *Hypnerotomachia Polifili* e le antichità di Roma', *La Bibliofilia*, XII (1910), pp. 161–76, esp. 171–4; Karl Giehlow, *The Humanist Interpretation of Hieroglyphs in the Allegorical Studies of the Renaissance, with a Focus on the Triumphal Arch of Maximilian I*, trans. Robin Raybould (Leiden, 2015 [orig. 1915]), p. 143; Ludwig Volkmann, *Hieroglyph, Emblem, and Renaissance Pictography*, ed. and trans. Robin Raybould (Leiden, 2018 [orig. 1923]), p. 34; Giovanni Pozzi, 'Les Hieroglyphes de l'*Hyperotomachia Poliphili*', in *L'Embleme à la renaissance*, ed. Yves Giraud (Paris, 1980), pp. 15–27; and Brian Curran, *The Egyptian Renaissance: The Afterlife of Ancient Egypt in Early Modern Italy* (Chicago, IL, 2007), pp. 72–3, 147. No distinction between hieroglyph and *scalptura* would have been intended: see the frequent source, Plin. *HN* 36.14.64: 'scalpturae illae effigiesque quas videmus Aegyptiae sunt litterae.'

3   *HP*, p. 8 (sig. *4v): 'Sed rogo quis vero est nomine Poliphilus?/ Nolumus agnosci.'

4   Representative of these various views: Maria Teresa Casella and Giovanni Pozzi, *Francesco Colonna. Biografia e opere*, 2 vols (Padua, 1959); and Edoardo Fumagalli, 'Due esemplari dell'"Hypnerotomachia

Poliphili" di Francesco Colonna', *Aevum*, LXVI (1992), pp. 419–21;
Maurizio Calvesi, *Il Sogno di Polifilo prenestino*, 2nd edn (Rome, 1980);
and Maurizio Calvesi, 'Hypnerotomachia Poliphili: nuovi riscontri
e nuove evidenze documentarie per Francesco Colonna signore
di Preneste', *Storia dell'Arte*, LX (1987), pp. 85–136; Piero Scapecchi,
'L'"Hypnerotomachia Poliphili" e il suo autore', *Accademie e biblioteche
d'Italia*, LI (1983), pp. 286–98; Liane Lefaivre, *Leon Battista Alberti's
Hypnerotomachia Poliphili: Re-Configuring the Architectural Body in the Early
Italian Renaissance* (Cambridge, MA, 1997); Leonhard Schmeiser,
Das Werk des Druckers: Untersuchungen zum Buch Hypnerotomachia Poliphili
(Maria Enzersdorf, 2003). On the authorship question, see Patricia
Fortini Brown, *Venice and Antiquity: The Venetian Sense of the Past* (New
Haven, CT, and London, 1996), pp. 208–10, 287–90; Marco Ariani
and Mino Gabriele, 'L'autore del "Polifilo"', in Francesco Colonna,
Hypnerotomachia Poliphili, vol. II: *Traduzione e apparati* (Milan, 1998),
pp. lxiii–xc; and Paolo Veneziani, 'Alla ricerca del Polifilo',
Gutenberg-Jahrbuch, LXXVI (2001), pp. 123–42.

5 On the Arabic script in woodcut, see Anna Klimkiewicz, 'Cultura
sincretica dell'*Hypnerotomachia Poliphili* di Francesco Colonna',
Cuadernos de Filología Italiana, XXI (2014), pp. 181–94.

6 Inter alia, see Robert H. F. Carver, *The Protean Ass: The 'Metamorphoses'
of Apuleius from Antiquity to the Renaissance* (Oxford, 2007), pp. 183–235;
Edoardo Fumagalli, 'Francesco Colonna lettore di Apuleio e il
problema della datazione dell'*Hypnerotomachia Poliphili*', *Italia medioevale
e umanistica*, XXVII (1984), pp. 233–66; Peter Fane-Saunders, *Pliny the
Elder and the Emergence of Renaissance Architecture* (Cambridge, 2016),
pp. 128–44; and Kathryn Blair Moore, 'Ficino's Idea of Architecture:
The "Mind's-Eye View" in Quattrocento Architectural Drawings',
Renaissance Studies, XXIV (2010), pp. 332–52.

7 Brown, *Venice and Antiquity*, p. 212.

8 Curran, *Egyptian Renaissance*, pp. 22–3, 146–56; Giehlow, *The Humanist
Interpretation*; an understanding most significantly articulated by
Leon Battista Alberti, *L'Architettura* [*De re aedificatoria*], ed. Giovanni
Orlandi, 2 vols (Milan, 1966), vol. II, p. 697 (8.4); and by Erasmus,
'Festina lente', ASD, II.iii, pp. 11–12.

9 *HP*, p. 2 (sig. *IV): 'cum nostrati lingua loquatur, non minus ad eum
cognoscendum opus sit graeca & romana, quam tusca & vernacula.
Cogitavit enim vir sapientissimus, si ita loqueretur, unam esse viam,
& rationem, qua nullus quin aliquid disceret veniam negligentiae
suae praetendere posset, sed tamen ita se temperavit, ut nisi, qui

doctissimus foret in doctrinae suae sacrarium penetrare non posset,
qui vero non doctus accederet non desperaret tamen . . . Non hic res
sunt vulgo expositae & triviis decantandae, sed quae ex philosophiae
penu depromptae, & musarum fontibus haustae quadam dicendi
novitate perpolitae ingeniorum omnium gratiam mereantur.'

10 Tamara Griggs, 'Promoting the Past: The *Hypnerotomachia Poliphili* as
Antiquarian Enterprise', *Word and Image*, XIV (1998), pp. 17–39.

11 Baldesar Castiglione, *Il libro del Cortegiano* [1528], ed. Giulio Preti
(Turin, 1965), p. 297 (§70).

12 *HP*, p. 467 (sig. F4r): 'Venetiis Mense decembri. M.ID. in aedibus
Aldi Manutii, accuratissime.'

13 Discussed in Neil Harris, 'The Blind Impressions in the Aldine
Hypnerotomachia Poliphili (1499)', *Gutenberg-Jahrbuch*, LXXIX (2004),
pp. 93–146, esp. 111–17.

14 Carlo Dionisotti, *Gli umanisti e il volgare fra Quattro e Cinquecento*
(Florence, 1968), p. 10: 'un *pastiche* divertente'.

15 Giovanni Pozzi, *Francesco Colonna e Aldo Manuzio* (Bern, 1962), pp. 9,
14–15.

16 Giovanni Mardersteig, 'Osservazioni tipografiche sul *Polifilo* nelle
edizioni del 1499 e 1545', in *Contributi alla storia del libro italiano.
Miscellanea in onore di Lamberto Donati* (Florence, 1969), pp. 221–42,
222.

17 Lowry, pp. 119, 125.

18 *HP*, p. 3 (sig. β); Alessandro Scarsella, 'Giambattista Scita e l'autore
dell'*Hypnerotomachia*: lo status quaestionis', in *Bellunesi e Feltrini
tra umanesimo e rinascimento. Filologia, erudizione e biblioteche*, ed. Paolo
Pellegrini (Padua, 2008), pp. 107–19.

19 The history of Aldus' adoption of both motto and device is
discussed at length in Oren Margolis, 'The Coin of Titus and the
Hypnerotomachia Poliphili', in Infelise, pp. 58–68.

20 ASD, II.iii, pp. 7–28, 10.

21 Ibid., II.iii, p. 12: 'cuius ex libris excerpta suspicior ea, quae nos
nuper conspeximus, huius generis monimenta'.

22 AMHLC, p. 184: 'hortari non desinis . . . addito tamen Graeco adagio
σπεῦδε βραδέως.'

23 AMGC, p. 78: 'Etsi scio a plerisque me tarditatis crimine accusari,
Alberte, praesidium meum, quod plurimum differe videar, quae
toties pollicitus sum studiosis dare, tamen has literatorum querelas
aequo animo ferendas ducimus, tum quia possum vel graviora
perferre, dum prosim, tum etiam quod sum ipse mihi optimus

testis me semper habere comites, ut oportere aiunt, delphinum et ancoram. Nam et dedimus multa cunctando et damus assidue.'

24 Device at sig. π8v.

25 Anja Wolkenhauer, *Zu schwer für Apoll: Die Antike in humanistischen Druckerzeichen des 16. Jahrhunderts* (Wiesbaden, 2002), p. 40.

26 Harris, 'The Blind Impressions', pp. 113–19.

27 *HP*, p. 25 (sig. b1r): 'io di stupore insensato stave alla sua consideratione'; 'lo excesso dilla subtigliecia dil opulente & acutissimo ingiegnio, & dilla magna cura et exquisita diligentia dil Architecto'; p.28 (sig. b2v): 'Et el nome dell'architecto sopra lo Obelisco in graeco annotato. ΛΙΧΑΣ Ο ΛΙΒΥΚΟΣ ΛΙΘΟΔΟΜΟΣ. ΩΡΘΟΣΕΝ ΜΕ. LICHAS LIBYCVS ARCHITECTVS ME EREXIT.'

28 Ibid., p. 42 (sig. c1v): 'Pervenuto dunque ad questa veterrima porta di opera molto spectabile, & cum exquisite regulatione & arte, & praeclari ornati di scalptura, & di vario liniamento maravegliosamente constructa. Per le quale tutte cose essendo io studioso & di voluptate infiammato di intendere il fetoso intellecto, & la pervestigatione acre dil perspicace Architecto'.

29 Plin. *HN* 36.24.118: 'vesana dementia, quaesisse gloriam inpendio nulli profuturo, praeterea fatigasse regni vires, ut tamen laus maior artificis esset.'

30 Ibid., 36.24.118: 'quid enim miretur quisque in hoc primum, inventorem an inventum, artificem an auctorem, ausum aliquem hoc excogitare an suscipere an iubere?'

31 On Pliny's language and its impact, see Oren Margolis, 'Printing as Architecture: Antonio Urceo Codro on Aldus Manutius', *Medioevo e Rinascimento*, XXXIII (2020), esp. pp. 149, 151–2; also Fane-Saunders, *Pliny*, p. 20.

32 *HP*, p. 43 (sig. c2r): 'tamen il solerte Architecto, & industrioso, ad gratificare lo obiecto cum lo obtuto, Pole licentemente cum adiectione & detractione depolire l'opera sua. Sopra tutto il solido integro conservando, & cum l'universo conciliato . . . Indica . . . la praestantia dil suo ingiegnio, perche lo adornare poscia e cosa facile.'

33 Ibid.: 'Lo ordinare dunque, & la praecipua inventione e participata ad gli rari, & ad gli molti ancora vulgari, overo idiote commune ad lavore se praestano gli ornamenti.'

34 Ibid., p. 46 (sig. c3v): 'Questo e che optimamente primo ad isso s'appertene il solido disponere, & nell'animo definire . . . dila universale fabrica, cha gli ornate. Gli quali sono accessorii al principale. Dunque al primo, la foecunda peritia di uno solamente

si richiede. Ma al secundo molti manuali, overo operatori Idiote
(chiamati dagli Graeci Ergati) necessarii concorreno. I quali (come
dicto e) sono gl'instrumenti dillo Architecto.'

35   Alberti, *L'Architettura*, p. 2 (prologue): 'fabri enim manus architecto
pro instrumento est'; Arist. *Pol.* 1.1253b; Arist. *Met.* 1.981ab. The
diminishment of the status of ornament per se and its distinction
from architecture are not, however, Albertian: see Alina A. Payne,
*The Architectural Treatise in the Italian Renaissance: Architectural Invention,
Ornament, and Literary Culture* (Cambridge, 1999), pp. 75–6, and Alina
A. Payne, *L'Architecture parmi les arts: Matérialité, transferts et travail artistique
dans l'Italie de la Renaissance* (Paris, 2016), pp. 41–4.

36   Plat. *Stat.* 259e.

37   Alberti, *L'Architettura*, pp. 845–7 (9.8): 'complures mediocrum
artificum manus exerceantur'.

38   Ibid., p. 855 (9.10): 'Summo sit ingenio acerrimo studio, optima
doctrina maximoque usu praeditus necesse est, atque in primis gravi
sinceroque iudicio et consilio, qui se architectum audeat profiteri . . .
omnino ei fugienda est levitas pervicatia iactantia intemperantia, et
siqua sunt, quae bonam gratiam minuant in civibus odiumve augeant';
cf. Vitr. *De arch.* 1.1.1–13. See also Martin McLaughlin, *Leon Battista
Alberti. La vita, l'umanesimo, le opere letterarie* (Florence, 2016), p. 154.

39   *HP*, p. 43 (sig. c2r): 'Et oltra la doctrina sia bono, non loquace [*sic*:
loquace], benigno, benivolo, mansueto, patiente, faceto, copioso,
indagatore curioso, universale, & tardo. Tardo pertanto io dico, per
non essere poscia festino alla menda.'

40   Codro, *Orationes*, sig. D1r: 'Quosdam tamen . . . summopere
commendo, quibus plurimum lingua graeca debet; non artifices,
sed artificum auctores ac, ut ita dicam, architectos doctos et multae
probitatis viros: Lascarim Florentiae, Aldum Venetiis.'

41   Plat. *Stat.* 259e: 'Καὶ γὰρ ἀρχιτέκτων γε πᾶς οὐκ αὐτὸς ἐργατικὸς
ἀλλὰ ἐργατῶν ἄρχων.' Codro is emphatically not following Ficino's
translation: cf. Plato, *Opera*, trans. Marsilio Ficino (Venice: Bernardino
Cori and Simone da Lovere, for Andrea Torresani, 1491: ISTC
ip00772000), fol. 71r; see Margolis, 'Printing as Architecture', p. 153.

42   *AMHLC*, p. 188: 'miro hoc et quam laboriosissimo modo
scribendorum librorum'; 'Primum enim in quorum artificum manus
pervenerint sacra literarum monumenta videmus.'

43   Cf. Cic. *Nat. D.* 2.60.150: 'ad pingendum, fingendum, ad
scalpendum'; Poliziano, *Panepistemon* (1490), in *Opera omnia*, sig. z4r:
'Graphice pictoribus, statuariis, celatoribus, sculptoribus, fictoribus,

encaustisque communis est.' On 'relief', see Luba Freedman,
'"Rilievo" as an Artistic Term in Renaissance Art Theory',
Rinascimento, XXIX (1989), pp. 217–47; also Lorenzo G. Buonanno,
'Tullio Lombardo, Antonio Rizzo, and Sculptural Audacity in
Renaissance Venice', in *The Art of Sculpture in Fifteenth-Century Italy*, ed.
Amy R. Bloch and Daniel M. Zolli (Cambridge, 2020), pp. 259–80,
esp. 274. Note the usage of *sculptura/sculpo* in note 19 of this book's
Introduction.

44 *HP*, p. 54 (sig. c7v): 'sotto l'ordine dilla superiore coronice in esso nel
    pianato perfecte maiuscule Atthice appariano in scalptura queste
    due parole ΔΙΟΣ ΑΙΓΙΟΧΟΙΟ' ('[of] aegis-bearing Zeus'). In the
    woodcut, the text reads ΔΙΟΣ ΑΙΓΙΟΧΙΟΝ.

45 'In grammatoglyptae laudem', in *AMHLC*, p. 16: 'Qui Graiis dedit
    Aldus, en Latinis/ dat nunc grammata scalpta Daedaleis/ Francisci
    manibus Bononiensis.'

46 Cf. Aldus in Caesar (1513), *AMHLC*, p. 110: 'quaedam locorum
    nomina vix legi possunt . . . eius culpa qui incidit literas absente
    nobis'.

47 *HP*, p. 57 (sig. d1r): 'multiscio Architecto'; Nicolas Lévi, 'Multiscius:
    La Conception apuléienne de la polymathie au miroir de la notion
    grecque πολυμαθία', in *Les Savoirs d'Apulée*, ed. Emmanuel Plantade and
    Daniel Vallat, *Spudasmata*, CLXXV (Hildesheim, 2018), pp. 19–44.
    On Colonna's reliance on Apuleius and the incongruity between
    language and content, see Carver, *The Protean Ass*, pp. 187–90.

48 Apul. *Flor.* 9.24–5; *multiscius* also in *Apol.* 31, *Flor.* 3.9, *Met.* 9.13.
    Different attitudes to *artes sellulariae* were available: Romano Nanni,
    'La tecnica nel *Panepistemon* di Angelo Poliziano: *Mechanica e artes
    sellulariae*', *Physis*, XLIV (2007), pp. 349–76.

49 Preface to *Rudimenta grammatices latinae linguae* (1501), in *AMHLC*,
    p. 198: 'multa scientes . . . sunt quam pessimi'; Carver, *The Protean Ass*,
    p. 205.

50 Cic. *Acad. Pr.* 2, 7.22: 'qui distingues artificem ab inscio?'; a distinction
    explicitly cited by Benedetto Varchi, *Deux leçons sur l'art* [*Due lezioni*,
    1547], ed. Frédérique Dubard de Gaillarbois (Paris, 2020), p. 258.

51 For example, *HP*, p. 89 (sig. f1r): 'Opera daedalea & di admiratione
    conspicua'; p. 307 (sig. t6r): 'daedalice perplexa cancellatura'; p. 347
    (sig. y2r): 'di maximo & obstinato artificio faberrimamente daedale
    facti'.

52 For the name's possible semantic range, see Sarah P. Morris, *Daidalos
    and the Origins of Greek Art* (Princeton, NJ, 1992), esp. pp. 3–69, 215–37.

The scholiast of Euripides associated the arts of Daedalus (*Hecuba*, 838: 'Δαιδάλου τέχναισιν') with sculpture alone, also the implication of Pl. *Euthph.* 11c–e, *Meno* 97d, and Arist. *Pol.* 1.1253b.

53 The only surviving copy is BnF, MS gr. 3064, fol. 85r; text in AMHLC, pp. 244–52: 'gallicitatem quandam'.

54 Ibid., p. 246: 'In quibus omnibus nec est impressoris nomen nec locus in quo impressi nec tempus quo absoluti fuerint. In nostris vero omnibus sic est: "Venetiis in aedibus Aldi Romani illo vel illo tempore." Item nulla in illis visuntur insignia; in nostris est delphinus anchorae involutus, ut infra licet videre.'

55 Preface of Francesco Torresani, *Ex XIII T. Livii decadibus: Prima, tertia, quarta* . . ., 4 vols (Venice: in aedibus Aldi et Andreae soceri, 1518), I, sig. *2r–v: 'nam rostrum Delphini in partem sinistram vergit, cum tamen nostrum in dextram totum demittatur.' Cf. Wolkenhauer, *Zu schwer für Apoll*, pp. 167–8, 178.

56 For example, in the warning, AMHLC, p. 246: 'invicem connexas manumque mentientes'.

57 In *Opere volgari di Messer Francesco Petrarcha* (Fano: Soncino, 7 July 1503), sig. A6rv: 'el mio pensiero esser totalmente disposto, a fare in dicta cita el mio perpetuo domicilio et ivi condurre intagliatori de littere, et impressori non vulgari e vili, ma dei tucti gli altri li piu excellenti . . . E per mia exhortatione non solo sonno venuti quivi li compositori tanto notabili, et sufficienti, quanto sia possibile adire: ma anchora un nobilissimo sculptore de littere latine, graece, et hebraice, chiamato M. Francesco da Bologna, l'ingeno del quale certamente credo che in tale exercitio non trove unaltro equale. Perche non solo le usitate stampe perfectamente sa fare: ma etiam ha excogitato una nova forma de littera dicta cursiva, o vero cancellaresca, de la quale non Aldo Romano, ne altri che astutamente hanno tentato de le altrui penne adornarse, ma esso M. Francesco è stato primo inventore et designatore, el quale e tucte le forme di littere che mai habbia stampato dicto Aldo ha intagliato, e la praesente forma, con tanta gratia e venustate, quanta facilmente in essa se comprende.'

3 Divine Impressions

1 Petition to the Signoria, in Marie-Hyacinthe Laurent, 'Alde Manuzio l'ancien, éditeur de S. Catherine de Sienne (1500)', *Traditio*, VI (1948), p. 363 (Appendix I).

2 For example, in the colloquy *Naufragium*: ASD, I.3, pp. 325–32. For
   new responses to the saints and artistic implications, see Stephen
   J. Campbell, *Andrea Mantegna: Humanist Aesthetics, Faith, and the Force of
   Images* (London and Turnhout, 2020), pp. 108–21 ff.

3 In Oren Margolis, 'Hercules in Venice: Aldus Manutius and the
   Making of Erasmian Humanism', *Journal of the Warburg and Courtauld
   Institutes*, LXXXI (2018), pp. 97–126.

4 Anticipation evident in letters of William Grocyn to Aldus (27
   August 1499: AMGC, p. 286), Aldus to Conrad Celtis and Vincenz
   Lang (7 July 1501: BWKC, p. 452 (ep. 262)), Willibald Pirckheimer to
   Anton Kreß (19 July 1501: WPBW, pp. 121–3 (ep. 40)), and Erasmus
   to Aldus (28 October 1507: Allen, I, pp. 347–88 (ep. 207)); trial
   sheet date surmised from reference in letter of Aldus to Celtis,
   3 September 1504, in BWKC, pp. 568–9 (ep. 315).

5 See Alexander Marx, 'Aldus and the First Use of Hebrew Type in
   Venice', *Papers of the Bibliographic Society of America*, XIII (1919), pp. 64–7;
   Moses Marx, 'Gershom (Hieronymus) Soncino's Wanderyears in
   Italy, 1498–1527: *Exemplar Judaicae vitae*', *Hebrew Union College Annual*, XI
   (1936), pp. 427–501, esp. 441–2, 445–56. I am grateful to Theodor
   Dunkelgrün for sharing his insights on Hebrew printing and
   Soncino with me.

6 Preface to *Poetae christiani veteres*, vol. II (1502), to Daniele Clario of
   Parma, teacher at Ragusa, AMHLC, pp. 30–32, 32: 'ut e spinis rosas
   . . . accipient'; see also prefaces to vol. I (1501), ibid., pp. 10–14,
   to the Aldine Latin grammar (1501), ibid., pp. 194–200, and to
   Gregory Nazianzen (1504), AMGC, pp. 158–60.

7 'Statuta Paulinae scholae', in Joseph Hirst Lupton, *A Life of John Colet,
   D.D., with an Appendix of Some of His English Writings* (London, 1887),
   p. 279.

8 Ep. 273 (ep. 103 in *Epistole devotissime de Sancta Catharina da Siena* (Venice:
   Aldus, 1500: ISTC ic00281000), fols 126v–27v, sigs q5v–q6v).
   The letters are available at www.centrostudicateriniani.it/it/santa-
   caterina-da-siena/scritti, in text-only version (2002) and critical
   edition with commentary (2016–), both by Antonio Volpato.

9 Lowry, p. 125.

10 The only other exception is Proba, composer of a Virgilian cento
   published in the second volume of *Poetae christiani veteres*.

11 AMGC, p. 52 (Aristotle, vol. IV (1497), dedication to Alberto Pio):
   'an potiores Herculis erumnas credam saevosque labores et
   Venere et coenis et plumis Sardanapalli'; AMHLC, p. 116; ASD, II.6,

pp. 439–40 (*Adages* III.viii.25: 'Sardanapalus'): 'Huius cognomen
ob insignem hominis molliciem abiit in proverbium . . . Fuit . . .
caeterum delitiis usque adeo effoeminatus'.

12 ASD, II.3, p. 18: 'Herculanum mehercule facinus ac regio quodam
animo dignum, rem tam divinam quasi funditus collapsam orbi
restituere, latentia pervestigare, eruere retrusa, revocare extincta,
sarcire mutila, emendare tot modis depravata.'

13 Lisa Jardine, *Erasmus, Man of Letters: The Construction of Charisma in
Print* (Princeton, NJ, 1993); Lisa Jardine, 'Isotta Nogarola: Women
Humanists – Education for What?', *History of Education*, XII (1983),
pp. 231–44; Lisa Jardine, '"O decus Italiae virgo", or the Myth of the
Learned Lady in the Renaissance', *Historical Journal*, XXVIII (1985),
pp. 799–819; and Anthony Grafton and Lisa Jardine, *From Humanism
to the Humanities: Education and the Liberal Arts in Fifteenth- and Sixteenth-
Century Europe* (London, 1986); cf. Anna Clark, 'Repurposing
Rhetoric: Lady Jane Lumley and Early Modern Female Latinity',
Eranos, CXII (2021), pp. 99–119, revising some of these notions.

14 David Wallace, 'General Introduction', in *Europe: A Literary History,
1348–1418*, ed. David Wallace (Oxford, 2016), pp. xxiii–xxiv; see
also the chapter by F. Thomas Luongo, 'Siena', pp. 708–19; and
F. Thomas Luongo, 'Catherine of Siena, *Auctor*', in *Women Intellectuals
and Leaders in the Middle Ages*, ed. Katherine Kerby-Fulton, Katie Ann-
Marie Bugyis and John van Engen (Cambridge, 2020), pp. 97–111.

15 Orazio Lombardelli, *De' fonti della lingua toscana* (Florence: Giorgio
Marescotti, 1598), p. 33. I am grateful to Eloise Davies for bringing
this text to my attention. Modern scholarship recognizes 352
discrete letters published by Aldus.

16 F. Thomas Luongo, 'Saintly Authorship in the Italian Renaissance:
The Quattrocento Reception of Catherine of Siena's Letters', in
Catherine of Siena: The Creation of a Cult, ed. Jeffrey F. Hamburger and
Gabriela Signori (Turnhout, 2013), pp. 136–7; Karen Scott, '*Io
Caterina*: Ecclesiastical Politics and Oral Culture in the Letters of
Catherine of Siena', in *Dear Sister: Medieval Women and the Epistolary
Genre*, ed. Karen Cherewatuk and Ulrike Wiethaus (Philadelphia,
PA, 1993), pp. 88–9.

17 Luongo, 'Saintly Authorship', pp. 153–62.

18 Jane Tylus, 'Caterina da Siena and the Legacy of Humanism', in
Perspectives on Early Modern and Modern Intellectual History, ed. Joseph
Marino and Melinda Schlitt (Rochester, NY, 2001), pp. 119–20;
Jane Tylus, *Reclaiming Catherine of Siena: Literacy, Literature, and the Signs of*

Others (Chicago, IL, 2009), p. 273; and Luongo, 'Saintly Authorship',
p. 138; cf. Massimo Zaggia, 'Varia fortuna editoriale delle Lettere di
Caterina da Siena', in *Dire l'ineffabile. Caterina da Siena e il linguaggio della
mistica*, ed. Lino Leonardi and Pietro Trifone (Florence, 2006),
pp. 143–4; and Dionisotti, *Gli umanisti e il volgare fra Quattro e Cinquecento*
(Florence, 1968), pp. 3–5.

19 Luongo, 'Saintly Authorship', pp. 135, 162–3; see also Tylus,
'Caterina', p. 118.

20 Though appreciated by Carlo Dionisotti, in 'Introduzione' to
Orlandi, pp. xxxv–xxxvi. Aldus had published the Latin astronomical
works of Firmicus Maternus and Manilius as well as Aratus in
the translations of Germanicus and Cicero in 1499; Lucretius is
also a didactic work, but its literary value is different (as implicitly
acknowledged by its stand-alone publication in quarto). Other Latin
works previously published had been by contemporaries.

21 *AMHLC*, pp. 6–8; ibid., pp. 164–8, though still dedicated to Alberto Pio.

22 On the editorial responsibility, see Cecil H. Clough, 'Pietro Bembo's
Edition of Petrarch and His Association with the Aldine Press',
in *Aldus Manutius and Renaissance Culture: Essays in Memory of Franklin
D. Murphy*, ed. David S. Zeidberg and Fiorella Gioffredi Superbi
(Florence, 1998), pp. 70–77.

23 *AMGC*, pp. 28–30 (in preface to *Thesaurus, Cornucopiae, Horti Adonidis*
(1496)): 'Imitamur tamen hanc linguarum varietatem et copiam
lingua vulgari . . . Utinam tantam copiam Latine haberemus.' See
also Dionisotti, *Gli umanisti*, pp. 1 ff.

24 Angelo Poliziano, *Miscellanies*, ed. Andrew R. Dyck and Alan Cottrell,
2 vols (Cambridge, MA, 2020), I, p. 176 (1.26); printed by Aldus in
Poliziano, *Opera omnia*, sig. D5r.

25 In Valla's *praefatio* to the *Elegantiae*, in *Prosatori latini del Quattrocento*, ed.
Eugenio Garin (Milan, 1952), pp. 596–8; cf. Cic. *Arch.* 10.23.

26 'Aldo agli lettori', in Petrarch (1501), in Orlandi, p. 53: 'ogni semplice
Thosco sa che in questa lingua non si segue così il latino in ogni nota';
on 'la regola del loro parlare' for feminine words ending with -e in
the singular, -i in the plural: 'se a me non credono, credanlo al meno
al Poeta, di mano del quale ho veduto io scritto in questi luoghi così'.

27 Recalled in dedication to Desiderio Curzio of Petrarch (1514), in
Orlandi, pp. 147–8; see also dedication to Jacopo Sannazaro of his
Arcadia (September 1514), in *AMHLC*, pp. 226–8.

28 Laurent, 'Alde Manuzio', pp. 361–3; Henri D. Saffrey, 'Les Images
populaires de saints dominicains à Venise au XVe siècle et l'édition

par Alde Manuce des "Epistole" de Sainte Catherine de Sienne',
Italia medioevale e umanistica, XXV (1982), pp. 299–300; Tylus, *Reclaiming
Catherine*, pp. 15–16, 282.

29   Jennifer McFarland, 'Relics, Reinvention, and Reform in Renaissance
Venice: Catherine of Siena's Stigmata at the Basilica dei Santi
Giovanni e Paolo', *Renaissance Studies*, XXXIV (2020), pp. 278–302, esp.
297–9; Maria H. Oen, 'Ambivalent Images of Authorship', in *Sanctity
and Female Authorship: Birgitta of Sweden and Catherine of Siena*, ed. Maria H.
Oen and Unn Falkeid (New York and Abingdon, 2020), pp. 122–7.

30   *Epistole utile e divote de la beata e seraphicha vergine, Sancta Chaterina da
Siena* (Bologna: Giovanni Giacomo Fontanesi, 18 April 1492: ISTC
ic00280000), sig. f7v: 'Vero e che la dicta gloriosa vergine Caterina
multe altre Epistole scrisse a diverse persone, prelati, religiosi, e
seculari homini e donne de diverse conditione: ma queste sole al
presente son recolette.'

31   Tobias Daniels, 'Margarete Ugelheimer – eine Geschäftsfrau
im Venedig der Renaissance', in *Hinter dem Pergament: die Welt. Der
Frankfurter Kaufmann Peter Ugelheimer und die Kunst der Buchmalerei im
Venedig der Renaissance*, ed. Christoph Winterer (Munich, 2018),
pp. 42–53; Angela Nuovo, *The Book Trade in the Italian Renaissance*
(Leiden, 2013), pp. 31–4; Laurent, 'Alde Manuzio'.

32   In Laurent, 'Alde Manuzio', p. 363 (Appendix II).

33   Sig. *1r: 'queste Epistole, che essendo state adunate insemi con
grandissima diligentia & faticha per spatio di circa vinti anni'.

34   See Peter Humfrey, 'Fra Bartolommeo, Venice and St Catherine of
Siena', *Burlington Magazine*, CXXXII (1990), pp. 476–83.

35   The addresses to readers (both sig. B1r–B3v) differ between the 1501
and 1514 Petrarch editions; the dedication of the 1514 edition to
Curzio is in Latin.

36   In Orlandi, pp. 31–3 (sig. *1v), 32–3: 'perché ho stimato farli cosa
grata, donandoli uno tale fructo esciuto da una fructifera pianta de
la vostra inclyta cità de Siena; item perché, havendo la dicta vergine
scripto de molte epistole a summi Pontifici e Cardinali circa la
reformatione de la sancta Chiesia, e che se despiegasse il Confalone
de la Croce contra li pagani, et essendo state dicte epistole fino a
questi tempi, credo per volontà di Dio, quodammodo incognite et
ascose, e se publichino hora che l'infideli sono in arme con stupendo
exercito et apparato per mare e per terra con animo de destrure la
fede di Christo, e già habino comenciato a mandare ad executione
il desiderio suo con grandissimo danno e strage di Christiani, si pò

ALDUS MANUTIUS   *182*

pensare che siano scripte più presto alli Pontifici de li tempi nostri
che a quelli de allhora; ancora, per esser stata canonizata la decta
sancta per la bona memoria de papa Pio secondo, tio de v.s.r., et
ordinato per sua Sanctitate l'officio in honore di essa vergine, e più
essendo Sua Sanctità tanto desiderosa se andasse contra li pagani,
che scripse una grande e degna epistola al gran Turco per convertilo
alla fede di Christo, e tandem commosse tuta la Christianità ad
opprimere la superbia e forze soe: qual cosa harebbe facta felici
successu s'el non fosse mancato in ipso apparatu.' Though it was
likely never sent, the 1461 letter to the sultan circulated widely in
manuscript and incunable editions.

37 Ibid., pp. 31–2: 'È già venuto così ogne vitio al summo che per tuto
    sarebbe abondante materia da fare Satyre e Tragedie'.
38 Ibid., p. 32: 'non è remaso in l'homo altro che la forma et il nome,
    non si stima più né honore né fama, come se li altri homini fossero
    tante picture o statue. Però è da temere grandemente che, sì come
    publice se commette ogne grande ribaldaria, così publice l'ira di Dio
    ne mande le discipline e li flagelli.'
39 Ibid.: 'E veramente ardisco dire che chi legerà con devotione queste
    sancte epistole non potrà fare che non se reforme tuto e non li
    entre nel core il nome di Iesù Christo crocifixo e non si infiamme
    de l'amore di Dio . . . non solo exhortano al ben fare, ma anco
    constrengono per modo maraviglioso.'
40 Saffrey, 'Les Images populaires', pp. 248–50, 274–8, 297–8;
    McFarland, 'Relics'; Oen, 'Ambivalent Images'.
41 'Transiit ad sponsum tribus exornata coronis'; *Libro della divina
    providentia* (Venice: Matteo Capcasa di Codeca, for Lucantonio
    Giunta, 17 May 1494: ISTC ic00284000), sig. x7r.
42 'Dulce signum charitatis/ Dum amator castitatis,/ Cor mutat in
    Virgine.' See Guido Maria Dreves, ed., *Analecta hymnica medii aevi*,
    vol. x (Leipzig, 1891), pp. 224–5.
43 Raimondo da Capua, *Legenda maior*, ed. Silvia Nocentini (Florence,
    2013), pp. 120–21 (I. prol., 20–21): 'non cognovit literaturam'.
44 Tylus, *Reclaiming Catherine*, p. 276.
45 A *capriccio* to Dionisotti, in Orlandi, p. xxxix.
46 As shown by Heather Webb, 'Catherine of Siena's Heart', *Speculum*,
    LXIII (2005), pp. 804–8 and, for what follows, esp. 812–17 (though
    note that the recipient of the letter discussed is Raymond); Heather
    Webb, *The Medieval Heart* (New Haven, CT, and London, 2010),
    pp. 135–8.

47 The translations are abridged but both include the heart episode:
    Legenda dell'amirabile vergine, Beata Chaterina da Siena (Florence: Convent
    of San Jacopo di Ripoli, March 1477: ISTC ivoo295800), sigs
    i8v–k1r; *La vita de la virgine admirabile Sancta Catherina da Siena* (Milan:
    Giovanni Antonio Onate, March 1489: ISTC ivoo296000), sig.
    i7rv. On the manuscripts of Raymond's text: Silvia Nocentini, 'The
    Legenda maior of Catherine of Siena', in *A Companion to Catherine of
    Siena*, ed. George P. Ferzoco, Carolyn A. Muessig and Beverly Mayne
    Kienzle (Leiden, 2012), pp. 339–57. On this flexible iconography,
    inspired in part by Tommaso Caffarini's supplement: Emily A.
    Moerer, 'The Visual Hagiography of a Stigmatic Saint: Drawings of
    Catherine of Siena in the *Libellus de Supplemento*', *Gesta*, XXIV (2005),
    pp. 89–102; Keith Christiansen, Laurence B. Kanter and Carl
    Brandon Strehlke, *Painting in Renaissance Siena: 1420–1500*, exh. cat.,
    Metropolitan Museum of Art, New York (1988), pp. 218–42, esp.
    cat. no. 38d.
48 Raimondo, *Legenda maior*, pp. 249–51 (11.6, 1–9).
49 Ibid., p. 250 (11.6, 7): 'Ecce carissima filia, sicut pridie abstuli tibi cor
    tuum, sic in presentarum trado tibi cor meum quo semper vivas.'
50 Ep. 371 (ep. 107, fols 132r–133v, sigs r3r–r4v), dated Ash Wednesday
    (15 February 1380). Text follows the Aldine edition.
51 Ibid., fol. 132v, sig. r3v: 'la sua benignita respondeva che tu di novo
    offeri la vita tua, & mai non dare riposo ad te medesima.'
52 Ibid., fol. 133rv, sig. r4rv: 'Dio poseme dinanci ad se . . . con tanto
    lume si speculava questa verita che in quello abysso allhora si
    rinfrescavano i mysterii dela sancta Chiesia, & tute le gratie ricevute
    nela vita mia passate & presenti, & il di che in fe [*sic*: se] fu sposata
    l'anima mia . . . Allhora le demonia con exterminio cridavano sopra
    di me vedendo impedire & allentare col terrore loro el libero &
    affocato desiderio. Unde questi percotevano sopra la corteccia del
    corpo, ma el desiderio piu s'accendeva cridando, O dio eterno,
    riceve el sacrificio della vita mia in questo corpo mystico dela sancta
    Chiesia. Io non ho che dare altro, se non quello che tu hai dato a
    me. Tolle el core dunque & priemelo sopra la faccia di questa sposa.
    Allhora Dio eterno volgendo l'occhio dela clementia sua divelleva el
    core & premevalo nela sancta Chiesia . . . Allhora le demonia molto
    magiormente cridavano come se essi havessero sentito intolerabile
    dolore, & sforzavansi di lassarmi terrore minacciandomi di tenere
    modo che questo cosi facto exercitio non potessi fare. Ma per che ala
    virtu del'humilitade col lume della sanctissima fede l'inferno non po

resistere, piu s'univa & lavorava con ferri di foco, udendo parole nel conspecto dela divina maiesta tante attractive & promesse per dare alegrezza; & per che in verita era cosi in tanto mysterio, la lingua hoggimai non e piu sufficiente a poterne parlare. Hora dico gratia gratia sia ad l'altissimo Dio eterno che ci ha posti nel campo della battaglia come cavalieri a combattere per la sposa sua con lo scudo della sanctissima fede.' With thanks to Martin McLaughlin for discussion and advice on this passage.

53 Raimondo, *Legenda maior*, pp. 371–3 (III.2, 3–7).

54 See Karen Scott, 'Mystical Death, Bodily Death: Catherine of Siena and Raymond of Capua on the Mystic's Encounter with God', in *Gendered Voices: Medieval Saints and Their Interpreters*, ed. Caroline M. Mooney (Philadelphia, PA, 1999), pp. 136–67; John W. Coakley, *Women, Men, and Spiritual Power: Female Saints and Their Male Collaborators* (New York, 2006), pp. 170–92; Beverly Mayne Kienzle and Travis Allen Stevens, 'Words, Deeds, and the Hagiography of Italian Women Penitents', in *Mendicant Cultures in the Medieval and Early Modern World: Word, Deed, and Image*, ed. Sally J. Cornelison, Nirit Ben-Aryeh Debby and Peter Howard (Turnhout, 2016), pp. 129–35.

55 Raimondo, *Legenda maior*, pp. 120–21 (I. prol., 20–21).

56 From Bologna, 28 October 1507, in Allen, I, pp. 437–8 (ep. 207); Margolis, 'Hercules in Venice', pp. 103, 110–11, 119.

4 The Printer as Prince

1 *AMHLC*, p. 16: 'Est animus dare posthac iisdem formulis optimos quosque authores.'

2 Ibid.: 'Caetera quae poeta exercendi sui gratia composuit et obscoena quae eidem adscribuntur non censuimus digna enchiridio.'

3 First published in *Lucubratiunculae aliquot* (Antwerp: Dirk Martens, 1503); as a stand-alone by Froben in Basel. On the *Enchiridion*, see the discussion in William Barker, *Erasmus of Rotterdam: The Spirit of a Scholar* (London, 2021), pp. 68–73.

4 In dedication of 1514 Virgil edition to Pietro Bembo: *AMHLC*, p. 162.

5 *AMHLC*, p. 10: 'ut loco fabularium et librorum gentilium infirma puerorum aetas illis imbueretur'.

6 Craig Kallendorf, *Virgil and the Myth of Venice: Books and Readers in the Italian Renaissance* (Oxford, 1999), pp. 46–7.

7 Discussed in Oren Margolis, 'The Book Half Open: Humanist Friendship in Holbein's Portrait of Hermann von Wedigh III',

in *Openness in Medieval Culture*, ed. Manuele Gragnolati and Almut Suerbaum (Berlin, 2022), pp. 289–310.

8 Including whole and partial editions, in Latin and in translation, with and without commentary: see Martin Davies and John Goldfinch, eds, *Vergil: A Census of Printed Editions, 1469–1500* (London, 1992).

9 In William J. Connell, 'La lettera di Machiavelli a Vettori del 10 dicembre 1513', *Archivio Storico Italiano*, CLXXI (2013), pp. 665–724, Appendix I, pp. 717–18: 'Partitomi del bosco, io me ne vo a una fonte, e di quivi in un mio uccellare. Ho un libro sotto, o Dante o Petrarca, o un di questi poeti minori, come Tibullo, Ovvidio, et simili: leggo quelle loro amorose passioni, et quelli loro amori, ricordomi de' mia, godomi un pezzo in questo pensiero. Transferiscomi poi in sulla strada, nell'hosteria'.

10 William A. Pettas, *The Giunti of Florence: A Renaissance Printing and Publishing Family. A History of the Florentine Firm and a Catalogue of the Editions* (New Castle, DE, 2013), pp. 15–19, 30, 225–6, 230, 232–3.

11 In Connell, 'La lettera', p. 718: 'mi metto panni reali e curiali . . . entro nelle antique corti delli antique huomini . . . mi pasco di quel cibo che *solum* è mio et che io nacqui per lui'.

12 *AMHLC*, p. 20: 'Eum igitur ad te dono mittimus, Marine Sannute, vir omnium humanissime, ut libris quorum plenam tibi esse bibliothecam vidimus et Flaccus brevissima hac forma excusus addatur quo te sua parvitate ad se legendum, cum vel a muneribus publicis vel a Venetarum rerum componenda historia cessare potes, invitet.'

13 Sanudo, XIX, col. 425.

14 In Cicero, *Familiares* (April 1502), in *AMHLC*, p. 26 (to Thurzó, referring also to György Szathmári, Bishop of Várad/Oradea): 'ut, cum et propriis et regiis negotiis occupatissimi non queatis domi in bibliothecis vacare politioribus studiis, habeatis hosce libellos a nobis quos commode foris legatis'.

15 Correspondence on these matters, from July 1501 to June 1503, in Clifford M. Brown, *Isabella d'Este and Lorenzo da Pavia: Documents for the History of Art and Culture in Renaissance Mantua* (Geneva, 1982), pp. 55–9, 72, 74–5 (epp. 39–41, 43–4, 71–5); see Brian Richardson, *Women and the Circulation of Texts in Renaissance Italy* (Cambridge, 2020), pp. 204–5.

16 Published with the *Prodigiorum liber* of the rather less significant Julius Obsequens.

17 *AMHLC*, p. 206: 'excusa typis nostris'.

18 'Aldo Manutio Romano horum librorum commendatio', sig.
     c4v–c5r; for Augurello, see Matteo Soranzo, *Giovanni Aurelio Augurello*
     (1441–1524) and Renaissance Alchemy (Leiden, 2020), pp. 1–77.

19 As implied in his dedication to Lucrezia Borgia, explaining why
     he had delayed in publishing Tito and Ercole Strozzi, AMHLC, pp.
     216–18: 'tum quia nondum videretur commodum antiquis me
     includere curis.' Cf. Dionisotti, *Gli umanisti e il volgare fra Quattro e*
     Cinquecento (Florence, 1968), p. 11.

20 AMHLC, p. 244: 'tantae molis erat Romanam condere linguam';
     Verg. *Aen.* 1.33: 'Romanam condere gentem'.

21 See letter of Alberto Pio to Aldus, Carpi, 18 February 1505, in
     Renouard, p. 342 (ep. 7), on his Ovid; on the Chamber of the
     Muses, see Alessandra Sarchi, 'The *Studiolo* of Alberto Pio da Carpi',
     in *Drawing Relationships in Northern Italian Renaissance Art: Patronage and*
     Theories of Invention, ed. Giancarla Periti (Aldershot, 2004), pp.
     129–45.

22 In Aristotle, vol. VI, AMGC, p. 50: 'Optime enim gubernarentur
     respublicae, si aut philosophi regnarent aut principes
     philosopharentur'; citing and then paraphrasing Plato, *Republic*,
     473cd. See also the dedication of Xenophon et al. (1503) to
     Guidobaldo da Montefeltro, Duke of Urbino, in AMGC, pp. 118–24.

23 Compare the letter of Mario Equicola to Aldus, Mantua, 10 March
     1510, in Nolhac, p. 91 (ep. 81), with AMHLC, p. 216, where the
     request is presented as coming from Ercole's surviving brothers
     alone.

24 Dated at Venice, 27 March 1506: in Fletcher, pp. 160–62, 160;
     see Tiziana Plebani, '"Perché semo certi che chi nasce debbe morire":
     Aldo di fronte alla morte. I testamenti come fonte', in Infelise,
     p. 49.

25 ASD, II.iii, pp. 10–11; cf. Suet. *Aug.* 25.4 and Gell. *NA* 10.2.5.

26 ASD, II.iii, p. 16: 'Itaque dictum hoc, σπεῦδε βραδέως, ex ipsis vsque
     priscae philosophiae mysteriis profectum apparet, unde ascitum
     est a duobus omnium laudatissimis imperatoribus, ita ut alteri
     adagionis esset loco, alteri insignium vice, utriusque moribus
     ingenioque mire quadrans. Nunc vero in Aldum Manutium
     Romanum ceu tertium haeredem devenit . . . Neque vero symbolum
     hoc tum illustrius fuisse crediderim, cum inscalptum imperatorio
     nomismati negociatorum manibus terendum circumferretur, quam
     nunc, cum ubique gentium, vel ultra Christiani imperii terminos,
     una cum omnigenis utriusque linguae voluminibus propagatur,

agnoscitur, tenetur, celebratur ab omnibus, qui liberalium studiorum
colunt sacra.'
27 Ibid.: 'pulcherrimis planeque regiis Aldi nostri votis'.
28 Ibid., p. 18: 'quod quantumlibet exaggeres eorum laudem, qui
respublicas sua virtute vel tuentur, vel etiam augent, in re certe
prophana, tum angustis circumscripta spatiis versantur. At qui
literas collapsas vindicat, nam id pene difficilius quam genuisse,
primum rem sacram molitur et immortalem, tum non unius alicuius
provinciae, sed omnium ubique gentium, omnium seculorum
negocium agit. Postremo quondam principum hoc munus erat,
inter quos praecipua Ptolemaei gloria; quanquam huius bibliotheca
domesticis et angustis parietibus continebatur, Aldus bibliothecam
molitur, cuius non alia septa sint, quam ipsius orbis.'
29 Ibid.: 'praecipue vulgarium istorum excusorum vitio, quibus unius
etiam aureoli lucellum antiquius est quam vel universa res literaria'.
30 On this use of *excusor* in Erasmus and Poliziano, see Oren Margolis,
'Hercules in Venice: Aldus Manutius and the Making of Erasmian
Humanism', *Journal of the Warburg and Courtauld Institutes*, LXXXI (2018),
pp. 114–16.
31 See specifically Oren Margolis, 'The Coin of Titus and the
Hypnerotomachia Poliphili', in Infelise, p. 63.
32 Margolis, 'Hercules in Venice'; see also Alexandre Vanautgaerden,
Érasme typographe: Humanisme et imprimerie au début du XVIe siècle (Geneva,
2012), pp. 89–169; and Thomas M. Greene, 'Erasmus' "Festina
lente": Vulnerabilities of the Humanist Text', in *The Vulnerable Text:
Essays on Renaissance Literature* (New York, 1986), pp. 1–17.
33 Tours, Bibliothèque universitaire, Rés. 3744, fol. 112v (sig. t4v).
On the differences between Grolier's sketch and the original coin,
see Margolis, 'The Coin of Titus', p. 64; also Anthony Hobson,
*Renaissance Book Collecting: Jean Grolier and Diego Hurtado de Mendoza, Their
Books and Bindings* (Cambridge, 1999), pp. 44–5.
34 George Hill, *A Corpus of Italian Medals before Cellini*, 2 vols (London,
1930), I, p. 138.
35 AMGC, p. 116: 'simulque ut nos abhinc triennium non parvis donatos
a te opibus familiaeque tuae gentilitio perornatos nomine hisce
ad te literis publice fateamur, quo sciant omnes, qui haec legerint,
quantum tibi debemus; tum ne mirentur, si me cognomento Pium
posthac appellatum vel legerint vel audierint.'
36 On these plans: Hans Ankwicz von Kleehoven, 'Aldus Manutius
und der Plan einer deutschen Ritterakademie', *La Bibliofilia*, LII

(1950), pp. 169–77; Lamberto Donati, 'La seconda Accademia Aldina ed una lettera ad Aldo Manuzio trascurata da bibliografi', *La Bibliofilía*, LIII (1951), pp. 54–9; Lowry, pp. 199–201; Stefano di Brazzano, 'Pietro Bonomo, Aldo Manuzio e Jakob Spiegel tra Venezia, Trieste e la corte imperiale (dicembre 1505–marzo 1506)', in *Tu felix Europa: Der Humanismus bei den Slowenen und seine Ausstrahlung in den mitteleuropäischen Raum*, ed. Vincenc Rajšp, Feliks J. Bister and Miroslav Polzer (Vienna and Ljubljana, 2011), pp. 209–57.

37 *WPBW*, pp. 280–81.

38 11 October 1504, in Nolhac, pp. 39–40 (ep. 32): 'et quid cogitas? quid nuptiae tuae? quid imperator? quid caetera?'

39 Aldus to Celtis, Venice, 13 October 1497, in *BWKC*, pp. 287–8 (ep. 175): 'Quod si videndae etiam Italiae desiderio teneris, non modo cupio ut venias, sed te etiam id quantum possum rogare, rogo.'

40 Pirckheimer to Anton Kreß at Padua, Nuremberg, 19 July 1501, in *WPBW*, pp. 121–3 (ep. 40); to Celtis, Nuremberg, 17 November 1503, ibid., pp. 197–8 (ep. 60); and *BWKC*, pp. 541–2 (ep. 302).

41 As discussed in the correspondence between Aldus and Johannes Reuchlin: in *JRBW*, pp. 374–5 (ep. 118: to Aldus, Denkendorf, 10 November 1502) and pp. 376–7 (ep. 119: to Reuchlin, Venice, 24 December 1502).

42 Émile Offenbacher, 'La Bibliothèque de Wilibald Pirckheimer', *La Bibliofilía*, XL (1938), pp. 241–63.

43 From Rome, November/December 1500, in *BWKC*, pp. 435–43 (ep. 256), 436–7: 'Felicem portum tandem nacti Venetiis clarissimum virum, Graecanicae antiquitatis restauratorem, Aldum Manutium accessimus. Quem cum tuo nomine salutassem, me liberalissima fronte excepit moxque duos mihi nuper impressos libellos Musaei poetae antiquissimi obtulit cum interpretatione Latina; unum, quem tuae humanitati afferem; alio vero libello me donavit.' The great antiquity of the early Byzantine poet was only subsequently disproven. This is the 1497 second edition of the Greek Musaeus of 1495, with Latin translation by Marcus Musurus for interleaving.

44 Letter of Cuspinianus to Aldus, Vienna, 28 December 1502, in *Johann Cuspinians Briefwechsel*, ed. Hans Ankwicz von Kleehoven (Munich, 1933), pp. 2–8 (ep. 2), 6; *AMHLC*, pp. 44–6.

45 To Celtis and Lang, 7 July 1501, *BWKC*, pp. 451–2; to Celtis, 3 June 1503, ibid., p. 532 (ep. 296): 'alterae Athenae fient hominibus nostris'.

46 To Celtis, 3 September 1504, ibid., pp. 568–9 (ep. 315).

47 Offenbacher, 'La Bibliothèque'; Andrew Robison, 'The Drawings
    of Albrecht Dürer', in *Albrecht Dürer: Master Drawings, Watercolors,
    and Prints from the Albertina*, exh. cat., National Gallery of Art,
    Washington, DC (2013), pp. 17–43, 26; David Hotchkiss Price,
    Albrecht Dürer's Renaissance: Humanism, Reformation, and the Art of Faith
    (Ann Arbor, MI, 2003), pp. 13–16, 78–82. Summarizing the
    debate on Dürer's visits to Venice, see Susan Foister, 'Dürer's
    Early Journeys: Fact and Fiction', in *Dürer's Journeys: Travels of a
    Renaissance Artist*, exh. cat., National Gallery, London (2021),
    pp. 61–75. Regardless of whether he made a 'first visit' (1494–5),
    he could not then have purchased Theocritus; all the illuminations
    in Pirckheimer's Aldines are datable to the period before his 'second
    visit' (1505–7), during much of which the press had effectively
    ceased to operate: the library was surely at least the initial point
    of contact.

48 BSB, Rar. 515, purchase note 'ex bibliotheca Alberti Dÿreri' on
    sig. *1r (reordered, now fol. 231r). Pirckheimer also owned a copy.
    See Georg Leidinger, *Albrecht Dürer und die 'Hypnerotomachia Poliphili'*
    (Munich, 1929); and Giovanni Maria Fara, 'AD 1506: Disegni di
    architetture veneziane', in *Albrecht Dürer e Venezia* (Florence, 2018),
    pp. 7–8; cf. Lowry, pp. 274–5.

49 *BWKC*, p. 569. Celtis' exemplar: ÖNB, cod. Suppl. gr. 43, with contents
    and notes for Aldus, fol. 1r: 'Et accentus addantur . . .'; 'Vocabularium
    . . . nuper a Conrado Celte in hercinia silva apud druidas inventum'.
    See Christian Gastgeber, 'Greek Studies at the University of
    Vienna', in *A Companion to Medieval Vienna*, ed. Susana Zapke and
    Elisabeth Gruber (Leiden, 2021), pp. 453–4; on the contents, see
    A. C. Dionisotti, 'From Ausonius' Schooldays? A Schoolbook and
    Its Relatives', *Journal of Roman Studies*, LXXII (1982), pp. 83–125.

50 *Oratio ad Alexandrum VI pro Philippo Bavariae duce* (1 September 1498:
    ISTC ir00153500). Cf. Alessandro Benedetti, *Diaria de bello Carolino*
    (after 27 August 1496: ISTC ib00320400), a contract job in which
    Aldus' name did not appear at all; and Girolamo Amaseo, *Vaticinium*
    (20 September 1499: ISTC ia00550000), addressed by the author
    to the French ambassador but published anonymously.

51 From Heidelberg, 23 April 1499, in *JRBW*, pp. 314–15 (ep. 97): 'Dixi
    quidem causam tuam, uti Venetiis coram egimus'.

52 27 March 1504, in *AMGC*, pp. 126–8. Alberto had a copy, though:
    Renouard, p. 341 (ep. 6).

53 May 1505 (dedication date), in AMHLC, pp. 206–8; letter of Aldus
    to Collaurius, 6 December 1505, in 'Lettere inedite dei Manuzii', ed.
    Antonio Ceruti, *Archivio Veneto*, XXI (1881), p. 269.

54 Laura Casarsa, 'Emiliano Giovanni Stefano', *Dizionario
    biografico dei friulani*, Nuovo Liruti II: L'età veneta, ed. Cesare
    Scalon, Claudio Griffio and Ugo Rozzo (Udine, 2009), www.
    dizionariobiograficodeifriulani.it; Maurizio Moschella, 'Emiliano,
    Giovanni Stefano, detto il Cimbriaco', DBI, XLII (1993). On the
    Encomiastica, see Dennis Pulina, *Kaiser Maximilian I. als Held im lateinischen
    Epos: Ein Beitrag zur Methodik epischer Heroisierungen und zur Aktualisierung
    antiker Heldennarrative* (Berlin and Boston, MA, 2022), pp. 73–110.

55 *Cimbriaci poetae encomiastica ad divos Caesares Foedericum imperatorem et
    Maximilianum regem Romanorum* (Venice: Aldus, August 1504), sig. aIv:
    'facturus copiam, me in Aldi Romani Academiam contuli, ut accurate
    inibi, atque emendatissime imprimerentur, id quod est ex sententia
    factum; nam nihil gratius, nihil accidere iucundius Aldo ipsi potuit,
    quam ut divi Caesaris acta, sua cura excusa ob ipsius incredibilem in
    tuam maiestatem observantiam[,] emitteret in manus hominum.'

56 Dedication copy: New Haven, Yale University, Beinecke Rare Book
    and Manuscript Library, Marston MS 161; tomb in the duomo of
    Cividale del Friuli.

57 Cuspinianus' manuscript: ÖNB, cod. 3506, fols 1r–16v; see Florian
    Schaffenrath, 'Das erste Großepos über Kaiser Maximilian I: Ein
    Vergleich der beiden Fassungen der *Encomiastica* des Helius
    Quinctius Cimbriacus', *Bibliothèque d'humanisme et renaissance*, LXXXI
    (2019), pp. 103–39.

58 In BWKC, p. 569: 'Equidem tam libenter tibi morem gererem quam
    cuivis alii, sed timendi sunt reges; non enim immemor sum Ovidiani
    illius: "An nescis longas regibus esse manus?"' [Ov. (attr.) *Her.* 17,
    166].

59 *Divo Maximiliano Augusto Chunradi Celtis ραφωδια laudes et victoria de
    Boemannis* . . . (Augsburg: Johannes Otmar, 1505); commendation on
    sig. B1r, and in BWKC, pp. 552–4 (ep. 306).

60 In Ceruti, 'Lettere inedite', p. 269; Lowry, p. 200.

61 JRBW, p. 314: 'Sed tum quid de literis in medio armorum? de Phoebo
    in ventre Martis? de Helicone in castris? . . . sed nosti Germaniam:
    numquam desiit esse rudis.'

62 Letter of Cuno to Pirckheimer, Padua, 26 December 1506, in WPBW,
    pp. 456–8 (ep. 139), 457: 'Vestra igitur, ut memini, divinatio in hac
    re non fuit inanis.'

63 Ibid.: 'Aldum . . . se accingere rursus ad excudendum litteras graecas';
    'Id mihi facile creditu est, cum videam, Aldum longa expectacione a
    rege Ro(manorum) frustratum.'

64 *Ioannis Reuchlin Phorcensis scaenica progymnasmata . . . cum explanatione Iacobi
    Spiegel Selestani* (Tübingen: Thomas Anshelm, 1512), fol. 52r (sig.
    κ8r): 'erat enim Aldus ipse Caesaris cum primis Germanorumque
    observantissimus'; Spiegel to Aldus, Trieste, 27 February 1506, in
    Nolhac, pp. 69–70 (ep. 58). See Di Brazzano, 'Pietro Bonomo',
    pp. 233–57.

65 Allen, I, pp. 437–9 (ep. 207); pp. 440–42 (ep. 209).

66 ASD, II.3, p. 22.

67 List in *Euclidis megarensis [sic] . . . opera*, ed. Luca Pacioli (Venice:
    Paganino Paganini, 1509), fol. 31rv (sig. d7rv).

68 On the overlap between the Aldine and D'Alviano circles, see John
    Gagné, 'Dinner with the Greatest Man on Earth, or Erasmus's Sword
    and d'Alviano's Pen', *Sixteenth Century Journal*, LI (2020), pp. 989–94.

69 For most dates, see Ester Pastorello, 'Di Aldo Pio Manuzio:
    Testimonianze e Documenti', *La Bibliofilía*, LXVII (1965), pp. 177–81,
    though the visit to Bologna/Siena was in 1509 (not 1511). See also
    letters of Alberto and Leonello Pio, 1 June 1509 and 12 March 1510,
    in Renouard, pp. 345–8 (epp. 13, 14); Giovanni Fantuzzi, *Notizie degli
    scrittori bolognesi*, vol. II (Bologna, 1782), p. 281; Maximilian to Isabella
    d'Este, Augsburg, 26 May 1510, in Armand Baschet, ed., *Aldo Manuzio:
    Lettres et documents* (Venice, 1867), pp. 37–8 (doc. 18); AMHLC, p. 218;
    Fletcher, pp. 166–9, for the will. On the correct dates of Aldus and
    Erasmus in Siena, see Martin Lowry, 'The "New Academy" of Aldus
    Manutius: A Renaissance Dream', *Bulletin of the John Rylands Library*,
    LVIII (1976), pp. 415–16.

70 AMHLC, p. 168.

71 To Antonio Trivulzio in Lactantius, sig. aa1v–aa3r: 'ut nemo fere in
    omni Europa sit vel mediocriter eruditus, qui non singulari aliquo
    Manutii beneficio sit affectus.'

72 Sanudo, XIX, col. 425; final will of 16 January 1515 in Fletcher,
    pp. 170–72.

Epilogue: Utopia

1 In Lactantius (1515), sig. aa2r: 'Neque enim ulla tam barbara, tam
   remota gens hodie Europae finibus includitur, cui non notissimum
   Aldi nomen, ac celeberrimum fuerit.'

-

2 Thomas More, *Utopia*, ed. Edward Surtz and J. H. Hexter, Yale Edition of the Complete Works of St Thomas More, vol. IV (New Haven, CT, 1965), p. 182: 'Ex poetis habent Aristophanem, Homerum, atque Euripidem: tum Sophoclem minusculis Aldi formulis.'

3 See Annaclara Cataldi Palau, *Gian Francesco d'Asola e la tipografia aldina. La vita, le edizioni, la biblioteca dell'Asolano* (Genoa, 1998).

4 'Epitaphium Aldi', in *V. illustris Bilibaldi Pirckheimeri . . . opera*, ed. Melchior Goldast (Frankfurt, 1610), p. 27 (sig. C2r): 'Posset ubi tandem concepta Academia condi,/ Nullus in hoc Aldo cum locus orbe foret,/ Seclum, ait, insipiens, tellusque indigna valete,/ Atque opus ad campos transtulit Elysios.'

5 See Peter Humfrey, 'Cima da Conegliano and Alberto Pio', *Paragone*, XXIX/341 (1978), p. 88; Romano Pelloni, 'S. Nicolò: Un felice compromesso', in *San Nicolò in Carpi. Un modello del classicismo Emiliano* (Modena, 1992); and Manuela Rossi, 'Aldo e Carpi', in *Per Aldo: 1515–2015: Per Aldo: 1515-2015. Scritti di bibliografia e bibliofilia raccolti in occasione del quinto centenario*, ed. Alessandro Scarsella (Padua, 2015), pp. 30–31.

6 Maurice Roy, *Artistes et monuments de la Renaissance en France: Recherches nouvelles et documents inédits*, 2 vols (Paris, 1929–34), I, pp. 140–42. The convent was at the time subject to Observant reform: see Laure Beaumont-Maillet, *Le Grand Couvent des Cordeliers de Paris: Étude historique et archéologique du XIIIe siècle à nos jours* (Paris, 1975), pp. 71–81.

7 Maria Minning, *Giovan Francesco Rustici (1475–1554): Forschungen zu Leben und Werk des Florentiner Bildhauers* (Münster, 2010), pp. 211–32; Tommaso Mozzati, *Giovanfrancesco Rustici, le compagnie del Paucolo e della Cazzuola: Arte, letteratura, festa nell'età della Maniera* (Florence, 2008), pp. 165–72; Philippe Sénéchal, 'Il monumento funebre del Louvre', in *L'immagine del principe. I ritratti di Alberto III nel Palazzo dei Pio a Carpi*, exh. cat., Palazzo dei Pio, Carpi (2008), pp. 117–23; Philippe Sénéchal, *Giovan Francesco Rustici, 1475–1554: Un sculpteur de la Renaissance entre Florence et Paris* (Paris, 2007), pp. 164–74, 206–7.

8 RBME, 54-IV-3, arms on sig. A3r. See Anthony Hobson, *Humanists and Bookbinders: The Origins and Diffusion of Humanistic Bookbinding, with a Census of Historiated Plaquette and Medallion Bindings of the Renaissance* (Cambridge, 1989), pp. 104–5 (fig. 84), p. 221 (cen. 15b); and Anthony Hobson, *Renaissance Book Collecting: Jean Grolier and Diego Hurtado de Mendoza, Their Books and Bindings* (Cambridge, 1999), p. 83 (fig. 36), p. 147 (cat. 89), though *pace* Hobson there is no 'special printed dedication' beyond the letter found in all copies.

9   In Émile Raunié, ed., *Épitaphier du vieux Paris*, vol. III (Paris, 1901),
    pp. 284–5 (no. 1154): 'CARPENSIVM PRINCIPI./ FRANCISCI REGIS
    FORTVNAM SECVTO..'

10 1st edn: *Epistolae obscurorum virorum* ([Haguenau: Heinrich Gran],
    [October] 1515), colophon on fol. 17v (sig. c5v).

11 ASD, II.3, pp. 18–19.

12 Alberto Pio, *Tres et viginti libri* (Paris: Josse Bade, March 1531), fol.
    74r (sig. k4r): 'velis nolis quodam tempore tuum herum'. On the
    controversy generally, see Myron P. Gilmore, 'Erasmus and Alberto
    Pio, Prince of Carpi', in *Action and Conviction in Early Modern Europe:
    Essays in Memory of E. H. Harbison*, ed. Theodore K. Rabb and Jerrold E.
    Seigel (Princeton, NJ, 1969), pp. 299–318.

13 Both 1531: in ASD, I.3, pp. 676–85 (*Opulentia sordida*) and 686–99
    (*Exequiae seraphicae*).

14 *Index librorum prohibitorum* (Rome: Paolo Manuzio, for Stamperia del
    Popolo Romano, 1564), p. 34.

15 Verg. *Aen.* 6.847–53.

SELECT BIBLIOGRAPHY

For a catalogue of editions by Aldus Manutius, see *The Aldine Press: Catalogue of the Ahmanson–Murphy Collection of Books by or Relating to the Press in the Library of the University of California, Los Angeles, Incorporating Works Recorded Elsewhere* (Berkeley and Los Angeles, CA, 2001).

Barker, Nicholas, *Aldus Manutius and the Development of Greek Script and Type in the Fifteenth Century*, 2nd edn (New York, 1992)

Barker, William, *Erasmus of Rotterdam: The Spirit of a Scholar* (London, 2021)

Beltramini, Guido, Davide Gasparotto and Giulio Manieri Elia, eds, *Aldo Manuzio. Il Rinascimento di Venezia* , exh. cat., Gallerie dell'Accademia, Venice (Venice, 2016)

Brown, Patricia Fortini, *Venice and Antiquity: The Venetian Sense of the Past* (New Haven, CT, and London, 1996)

Carver, Robert H. F., *The Protean Ass: The 'Metamorphoses' of Apuleius from Antiquity to the Renaissance* (Oxford, 2007)

Casella, Maria Teresa, and Giovanni Pozzi, eds, *Francesco Colonna. Biografia e opere*, 2 vols (Padua, 1959)

Cataldi Palau, Annaclara, *Gian Francesco d'Asola e la tipografia aldina. La vita, le edizioni, la biblioteca dell'Asolano* (Genoa, 1998)

Curran, Brian, *The Egyptian Renaissance: The Afterlife of Ancient Egypt in Early Modern Italy* (Chicago, IL, 2007)

Davies, Martin, *Aldus Manutius: Printer and Publisher of Renaissance Venice* (London, 1995)

Dionisotti, Carlo, *Aldo Manuzio: Umanista e editore* (Milan, 1995)

—, *Gli umanisti e il volgare fra Quattro e Cinquecento* (Florence, 1968)

Fane-Saunders, Peter, *Pliny the Elder and the Emergence of Renaissance Architecture* (Cambridge, 2016)

Fletcher, Harry George, III, *New Aldine Studies: Documentary Essays on the Life and Work of Aldus Manutius* (San Francisco, CA, 1988)

Forner, Fabio, 'Pio, Alberto', in DBI, LXXXIV (2015)

Giehlow, Karl, *The Humanist Interpretation of Hieroglyphs in the Allegorical Studies of the Renaissance, with a Focus on the Triumphal Arch of Maximilian I* [1915], trans. Robin Raybould (Leiden, 2015)

Grafton, Anthony, *Inky Fingers: The Making of Books in Early Modern Europe* (Cambridge, MA, 2020)

Greene, Thomas M., 'Erasmus' "Festina lente": Vulnerabilites of the Humanist Text', in *The Vulnerable Text: Essays on Renaissance Literature* (New York, 1986), pp. 1–17

Hobson, Anthony, *Renaissance Book Collecting: Jean Grolier and Diego Hurtado de Mendoza, Their Books and Bindings* (Cambridge, 1999)

Infelise, Mario, 'Manuzio, Aldo, il Vecchio', in DBI, LXI (2007)

—, ed., *Aldo Manuzio. La costruzione del mito* (Venice, 2016)

Lis, Catharina, and Hugo Soly, *Worthy Efforts: Attitudes to Work and Workers in Pre-Industrial Europe* (Leiden, 2012)

Lowry, Martin, *Nicholas Jenson and the Rise of Venetian Publishing in Renaissance Europe* (Oxford, 1991)

—, *The World of Aldus Manutius: Business and Scholarship in Renaissance Venice* (Oxford, 1979)

Mardersteig, Giovanni, 'Aldo Manuzio e i caratteri di Francesco Griffo da Bologna', in *Studi di bibliografia e di storia in onore di Tammaro de Marinis*, ed. Giovanni Mardersteig, 3 vols (Verona, 1964), III, pp. 105–47

Margolis, Oren, 'Hercules in Venice: Aldus Manutius and the Making of Erasmian Humanism', *Journal of the Warburg and Courtauld Institutes*, LXXXI (2018), pp. 97–126

—, 'Printing as Architecture: Antonio Urceo Codro on Aldus Manutius', *Medioevo e Rinascimento*, XXXIII (2020), pp. 145–56

Nuovo, Angela, *The Book Trade in the Italian Renaissance* (Leiden, 2013)

Orlandi, Giovanni, ed., *Aldo Manuzio editore. Dediche, prefazioni, note ai testi* (Milan, 1976)

Pagliaroli, Stefano, *Per la biografia di Aldo Manuzio (1482–1496)* (Messina, 2021)

Pastorello, Ester, 'Di Aldo Pio Manuzio: Testimonianze e Documenti', *La Bibliofilia*, LXVII (1965), pp. 163–220

Payne, Alina A., *L'Architecture parmi les arts: Matérialité, transferts et travail artistique dans l'Italie de la Renaissance* (Paris, 2016)

Semper, Hans, with Friedrich Otto Schulze and Wilhelm Barth, *Carpi: Ein Fürstensitz der Renaissance* (Dresden, 1882)

Società, politica, e cultura a Carpi ai tempi di Alberto III Pio, 2 vols (Padua, 1981)

Vanautgaerden, Alexandre, *Érasme typographe: Humanisme et imprimerie au début du XVIe siècle* (Geneva, 2012)

Williams, Gareth D., *Pietro Bembo on Etna: The Ascent of a Venetian Humanist* (Oxford, 2017)

Wilson, Nigel G., *From Byzantium to Italy: Greek Studies in the Italian Renaissance*, 2nd edn (London, 2017)

Wolkenhauer, Anja, *Zu schwer für Apoll: Die Antike in humanistischen Druckerzeichen des 16. Jahrhunderts* (Wiesbaden, 2002)

Zeidberg, David S., and Fiorella Superbi Gioffredi, eds, *Aldus Manutius and Renaissance Culture: Essays in Memory of Franklin D. Murphy* (Florence, 1998)

ACKNOWLEDGEMENTS

The origins of this book are in a conversation I had in 2014 with Clare Hills-Nova at the Taylor Institution Library in Oxford. She suggested it would be a good idea for someone (that is, me) to put on an exhibition at the Bodleian for the upcoming five-hundredth anniversary of the death of Aldus Manutius. The resulting display involved the contributions of three of my then-undergraduate students from Somerville College (Jennifer Allan, Anna Clark and Qaleeda Talib), a collaboration of which I am most proud. Ian Maclean helped to get things off the ground, as did Chris Wickham, whose belief and generosity have been constants in my career.

I have truly been a beneficiary of the learning and culture of colleagues from across the disciplines that make up the humanities. I have profited from invitations to present my work at the Institute of Historical Research in London, the peripatetic Venetian Seminar, the universities of Cambridge, Florence, Kent, L'Aquila and Venice, Villa Vigoni, and my own institutional homes. These include the Ludwig Boltzmann Institute for Neo-Latin Studies (Innsbruck), where I was a researcher in the early days (theirs and mine), and whose director, Florian Schaffenrath, offered real backing for me and this project. I was fortunate in having a year in Florence at Villa I Tatti alongside an exceptional bunch of *borsisti*: of these, for their impact on the book, I would like to name in particular Alexandra Bamji, Daniele Conti, Janna Israel, Pablo Maurette, Kathryn Blair Moore and Michael Waters. Martin McLaughlin was there as well, and so for another time (but not the last) I received the gift of his friendship, support and expertise. For the same gift I owe thanks to Stephen J. Campbell, and to Stephen Harrison for his interest and erudition. The ideas and enthusiasm of Micha Lazarus have regularly been a source of inspiration: he read the full manuscript, but long before that he helped me believe in my approach. More recently, Jack Hartnell became for me both an incisive reader and a valued colleague and friend. Michael Leaman's faith in this book allowed me to realize it as a

Renaissance Life. I am thankful to him, to Alex Ciobanu, Phoebe Colley and Martha Jay, to François Quiviger and the anonymous readers, and also to the designer, who collectively through their guidance, advice and efforts have surely improved what has resulted and made this book a very fine object indeed.

This research and its researcher were generously and gratefully supported by a Deborah Loeb Brice Fellowship from Villa I Tatti: The Harvard University Center for Italian Renaissance Studies. The University of East Anglia gave me the space and encouragement to write, and an award from the UEA Faculty of Arts and Humanities Publication Fund covered the costs of image licensing and new photography.

One of the most rewarding aspects of being a university academic is the opportunity to think about research alongside people who are coming at the texts, artworks and societies in which one is so invested almost entirely fresh. Aldus Manutius often addressed his publications *studiosis omnibus*, but this book is dedicated to my students.

PHOTO ACKNOWLEDGEMENTS

The author and publishers wish to express their thanks to the sources listed below for illustrative material and/or permission to reproduce it:

From Augustine of Hippo, *Opera*, vol. 11 (Antwerp, 1576), photo Bibliothèque nationale de France (BnF), Paris: 4; Bayerische Staatsbibliothek, Munich: 10 (Clm 807, fol. 42v), 40 (Rar. 1631); BnF, Paris: 17, 21 (MS grec 3064, fol. 85r), 24 (MS grec 3064, fol. 86r); © The British Library Board, London (C.20.b.29, sig. a1v–a2r): 28; from John Calvin, *Institutio Christianae religionis* (Geneva, 1553), photo Universitätsbibliothek Basel: 3; from Catherine of Siena, *Epistole* (Venice, 1500), photo Simon Fraser University Library, Burnaby, BC: 26; from Francesco Colonna, *Hypnerotomachia Poliphili* (Venice, 1499), photo BnF: 16; from Francesco Colonna, *Hypnerotomachia Poliphili* (Venice, 1499), photos McGill University Library, Montreal, QC: 13, 15, 18, 19, 20; from Francesco Colonna, *Hypnerotomachia Poliphili* (Venice, 1499), photo Metropolitan Museum of Art, New York: 14; from Erasmus of Rotterdam, *Adagia* (Venice, 1508), photo Universitätsbibliothek Basel: 5; from Euclid, *Opera* (Venice, 1509), photo BnF, Paris: 35; from Euripides, Εὐριπίδου τραγῳδίαι ἑπτακαίδεκα (Venice, 1503), photo Biblioteca Nazionale Centrale di Firenze (BNCF): 33; from Euripides, trans. Erasmus of Rotterdam, *Hecuba, et Iphigenia in Aulide Euripidis tragoediae . . .* (Venice, 1503), photo BNCF: 34; Gallerie degli Uffizi, Florence, photo courtesy Ministero della cultura: 7; John Rylands Research Institute and Library, University of Manchester, photos © The University of Manchester (CC-BY-NC 4.0): 22 (20957, sig. a2r), 23 (16096, sig. a2r); Kunstmuseum Basel: 2; from Lucian of Samosata, trans. Erasmus of Rotterdam and Thomas More, *Dialogi et alia emuncta* (Paris, 1514), photo Universitätsbibliothek Basel: 1; photo Oren Margolis: 36; Minneapolis Institute of Art, MN: 12; photos © Musée du Louvre, Paris, Dist. RMN-Grand Palais/Pierre Philibert: 37, 38; Musei di Palazzo dei Pio, Carpi: 8, 9; The National Gallery,

INDEX

Illustration numbers are indicated by *italics*